THE MICROECONOMIC MODE

The Microeconomic Mode

POLITICAL SUBJECTIVITY IN CONTEMPORARY
POPULAR AESTHETICS

Jane Elliott

Columbia University Press
New York

Columbia University Press
Publishers Since 1893
New York   Chichester, West Sussex
cup.columbia.edu
Copyright © 2018 Columbia University Press
Paperback edition, 2021

Library of Congress Cataloging-in-Publication Data

Names: Elliott, Jane, 1969- author.
Title: The microeconomic mode : political subjectivity in contemporary
popular aesthetics / Jane Elliott.
Description: New York : Columbia University Press, [2018] | Includes
bibliographical references and index.
Identifiers: LCCN 2017045855 (print) | LCCN 2018040185 (ebook) |
ISBN 9780231174749 (cloth) | ISBN 9780231174756 (pbk.) |
ISBN 9780231547512 (electronic)
Subjects: LCSH: Mass media—Social aspects. | Storytelling in mass media. |
Choice (Psychology) in mass media.
Classification: LCC P95.54 (ebook) | LCC P95.54 .E45 2018 (print) | DDC
809/.04—dc23
LC record available at https://lccn.loc.gov/2017045855

Cover design: Mary Ann Smith

CONTENTS

ACKNOWLEDGMENTS

Most of this book was written in southeast London, within sight and sound of Deptford High Street. The noise and bustle of my neighborhood has been a constant companion during long days spent at my desk, and I'm grateful for the friends and strangers who make up its fabric. For their support, my thanks to my family and friends near and far, including my sister, Beth Elliott, and my sister-in-law, Shanna Cleveland; my parents, Bob Elliott and Fran Elliott; Adam Gutteridge; George Hallam; Liz Ho; Helen Mercer; Pat Palmer; Heather Patel; Cristina Rios; Gabe Sena; Lara Shalson; Jenny Worley; and David Wylot.

I have been very lucky to have such wonderful colleagues and students in the King's English department. Particular thanks to my heads of department, Jo McDonagh and Richard Kirkland, as well as my compatriots in contemporary studies, including Sita Balani, Amy De'Ath, Seb Franklin, and George Legg. Teaching on our MA in Contemporary Literature, Culture and Theory has been an ongoing source of delight and inspiration, and I thank all our students on the MA, both past and present. The very first seeds of this project were sown during an Anniversary Lectureship research leave at the University of York, and I also benefited there from lovely colleagues who encouraged my work in various ways, particularly Derek Attridge, Emily Morin, and Tom O'Donnell.

I am also grateful for invitations to present my work and for audience responses at the following events: the "What Is the Contemporary Novel?" symposium, Duke University; the PhD work-in-progress seminar, Duke University; the Contemporary Literature Seminar at the Institute for English Studies; "Neoliberalism as Theory, Policy, and Practice," at Manchester Metropolitan University; "Critical Temporalities," at the University of Manchester; "Is Inequality a Literary Value?" at the University of Uppsala; "Rethinking Economies," at the University of Tampere; "Freedom After Neoliberalism" and "Neoliberalism, Crisis, and the World System" at the University of York; and the 2015 and 2017 Post45 UK symposia. Thank you also to hosts and audiences at Cambridge University, Duke University, the National Autonomous University of Mexico, Oxford University, Umeå University, the University of Lincoln, Stony Brook University, the University of Washington, the University of Sussex, and Warwick University.

For intellectual engagement with and support of various kinds for this research, my thanks to Lisa Adkins, Nancy Armstrong, Derek Attridge, Timothy Bewes, Rey Chow, Maryanne Dever, Ziad Elmarsafy, Paul Gilroy, George Hallam, Mitchum Heuhls, Liz Ho, Cora Kaplan, Anna McCarthy, Helen Mercer, Diane Negra, Pat Palmer, John David Rhodes, Lara Shalson, Rachel Greenwald Smith, Sam Solomon, Mark Turner, and David Wylot. I am also grateful for the careful reading offered by the two anonymous readers at Columbia University Press. Particular thanks to Seb Franklin and Gillian Harkins, who each made this book immeasurably better through their indispensable comments and intellectual comradeship.

An earlier version of some of this material appeared in *Social Text* as "Suffering Agency: Imagining Neoliberal Personhood in North America and Britain." A portion of chapter 3 appears in *Novel: A Forum on Fiction* as "The Microeconomic Mode: Survival Games, Life-Interest and the Reimagination of Sovereignty." Thanks to Duke University Press for permission to republish this work here. At Columbia University Press, I am grateful to have had my book in the careful and talented hands of Philip Leventhal, Leslie Kriesel, and Brad Hebel.

Since the late 1990s in the United States in particular, the field of contemporary aesthetics has been marked by the appearance and growing prevalence of what I call the microeconomic mode.[1] This mode has proliferated across media and genres as well as the demarcations between high and low culture; it gives form to some of the most celebrated twenty-first-century literary novels as well as some of the most reviled products of popular culture—from the *Saw* horror-film series (2004–10) to Cormac McCarthy's *The Road* (2006), from the reality TV franchise *Survivor* (1997 to the present) to Steve McQueen's art-house film *Hunger* (2008). In this mode, abstraction results from a focus on delimited or capsule worlds in which option and decision, action and effect, have been extracted from everyday contexts and thus made unusually legible—for example, the life raft, the desert island, the medical experiment, the prison cell. Extremity registers in forms of painful, grotesque, or endangered embodiment, including deprivation, torture, mutilation, self-mutilation, and various threats to life itself. At the intersection of these two formal features, we find plots that produce what I call suffering agency: protagonists must make agonized binary choices between horrific options, each of which involves intense physical and potentially deadly consequences. In its fullest manifestations, the aesthetic effect of this mode is brutal in every sense of the word: crude, harsh, ruthless, unrelenting, and unpleasantly precise.

To get a sense of what this mode looks like in practice, consider the 2014 winner of the Carnegie Medal for Children's Literature, Kevin Brooks's young adult novel *The Bunker Diary* (2013). Critics decried the choice and described the novel as a "vile" and "uniquely sickening" read, and from one perspective, they weren't entirely wrong.[2] *The Bunker Diary* does indeed stand out as unusually grim even in a young adult literary field currently saturated with postapocalyptic dystopias. The novel begins with the kidnapping of the eponymous diarist, a teenage runaway named Linus, on the street in London. Linus awakens alone in a sealed bunker, where he is soon joined by other prisoners, including a nine-year-old girl named Jenny and a handful of adults. Their unseen captor torments the prisoners with cold, poison, starvation, and, most devastatingly, enforced mutual aggression: he promises that the first prisoner to kill one of the others will immediately be set free. One by one, the adults succumb to violence, illness, or dehydration until only Linus and Jenny are left. In the novel's final entry, which breaks off midsentence, Linus recounts that Jenny has died in his arms and welcomes his own imminent death. This ending is in part what incensed critics of the Carnegie selection and arguably what makes the novel such an unpleasant read. Because it also evokes young adult genre conventions, *The Bunker Diary* makes an implicit promise that something, if not someone, will be recuperated from this horror. As this promise dwindles to nothing along with Linus's own life, the novel denies its readers a reprieve they had some reason to expect.

From another perspective, however, what is striking about *The Bunker Diary* is how completely and relentlessly it enacts the aesthetic parameters that define the microeconomic mode. The setting of the novel produces an abstraction from the dense field of social complexity that makes up the surrounding world, materialized in the forcible relocation of the captives within the impermeable walls of the concrete bunker. Although the captives belong to different ages and social classes and bring with them different mores, they do not allegorize divergent types of personality or trajectories of historical determination. Rather, when the characters are plucked from the social field and located within the bunker, readers learn that none of those elements matter in the end, when it comes to decisions regarding life and death. As I argue in detail in chapter 1, the sparse, pared-down contexts of the microeconomic mode do not allegorize some more complex reality but instead press us to consider what transpires when the world itself shrinks to become a model. *The Bunker Diary* activates the overarching conventions of the microeconomic mode via tropes used to generate suffering agency across this mode, including the insertion of humans into a gamelike or faux-laboratory setting, the gruesome physicalization of individual choice as torture or self-torture, and the forced enactment of kill-or-be-killed, him-or-me decisions.[3] Brought together, these tropes produce extreme situations in which choice becomes quite literally a matter of life or death. When we consider *The Bunker Diary* in relation to the microeconomic mode, in other words, there is nothing uniquely "vile" or "sickening" about it—quite the opposite. Rather, the novel achieves its shock value by porting a particularly fulsome incarnation of the microeconomic mode into a genre in which these aesthetic conventions appear unusually unseemly.

In the chapters that follow, I trace the parameters of this mode and consider what specific dynamics and concepts it envisions and makes visible. By bringing abstraction and extremity to bear on individual choice, I argue, the microeconomic mode produces a specific and emergent fusion of human agency with living flesh.[4] In *The Bunker Diary*, for example, the few elements with causal significance in the bunker—the handful of inhabitants, the lack of food and water, the number of hours between supplies from or attacks by their captor—fixate the prisoners' attention on actions related to essential needs and capacities of the human body. Not only does choice within the bunker appear detached from any external processes that would render it something more than an expression of sheer individual choice, but also the extreme nature of the choices that result throws into relief each individual's intrinsic status as both an agential actor and a vulnerable unit of bodily being. For example, when Linus struggles to decide whether to kill one of his fellow prisoners so he might be freed and return with help to rescue Jenny, we witness precisely this sort of fusion—a version of human existence in which cost–benefit analysis becomes inseparable from a decision regarding the persistence of life. By activating individual attachment to life in circumstances variously stripped of ordinary evidence of social determination, works in the microeconomic mode reveal a form of human subjectivity I call life-interest, in which persistence as a life form and individual choice become so intertwined that each is measured in the coin of the other. Or, put from the opposite direction, we might say that the microeconomic mode emerges as an aesthetic technology through which the pressures and powers of life-interest can be imagined.

When the microeconomic mode insists that humans consider themselves subjects of life-interest, it indicates a shift in the imagination of political subjectivity that has thus far escaped cognition even if it has not escaped perception. In that sense, the microeconomic mode both registers and fills a gap in our understanding of the present, which is why I need recourse to an unfortunate number of neologisms to describe its central concerns. If apt terms were already in existence—if the transformation in question were either less radical or more established—then this mode would likely not exist in its same ubiquitous form. That my central terms—suffering agency, life-interest, the microeconomic mode—seem to embody or unfold across seeming contradictions indicates something of the stress this shift places on the forms of political experience associated with the liberal individual as a category. As I discuss throughout this volume, this shift has a crucial and complex effect on the vectors of differentiation that organize what Sylvia Wynter calls "genres of being human": when the microeconomic mode reworks the relationships between suffering and agency, body and will, and submission and sovereignty associated with the liberal individual as political subject, it both returns us to and seemingly undermines distinctions that have been central to distinguishing the exemplary liberal individual—the white man—from his constitutive others.[5] By reading the microeconomic mode as a form of condensed knowledge about this ongoing transformation, I aim to uncover what it is that this mode seems to think about our situation that has otherwise remained unthought. Although its forms of thinking resonate in certain ways with contemporary theory, especially those strands concerned with neoliberal governmentality, affective labor, and biopolitical decision, the microeconomic mode cannot be mapped against our existing assumptions about these categories, which may explain why it has unfolded in a critical blind spot. When we assume we will find the tide of the multitude, the dispersions of affect, or the inertia of bare life, it is difficult to know what to make of all these visions of a single individual subject's insistent, agential, agonized embodiment. As I track the microeconomic mode and its exploration of life-interest across its different subgenres, I document the way in which it requires a very different understanding of the politics of life itself in the present. In order to track this thinking, I approach this mode not as an object of existing theoretical discourse but rather as the theory that it is.

In suggesting that the microeconomic mode is concerned with a politics of life itself that has largely escaped critical attention, my point is not that this mode lacks conceptual antecedents, but rather that it does something to those antecedents that renders them difficult to register. The relevance of some of these antecedents will only become clear as my argument progresses, so I discuss them in the chapters that follow. Here, however, I want to offer necessary context for my description of this mode as microeconomic, terminology I have selected to signal the relevance of a particular way of modeling choice. I use the term "microeconomic imagination" to describe this model, which resonates across an array of postwar methodologies and theories, including microeconomics as a subdiscipline, rational choice theory, game theory, Chicago School economics, and some versions of libertarian political theory. I employ "microeconomic" as the umbrella term here in part because it emphasizes individual choice as taking place in a kind of microeconomy, where benefits necessarily incur costs, and in part because the model of choice that concerns me here is most visible in the microeconomic branch of this set of methodologies. Although it exists at a remove from the aggregate dynamics that are the focus of the bulk of economics as a discipline, this approach to choice echoes Lionel Robbins's now canonical definition of economics as "the science which studies human behavior as a relationship between ends and scarce means which have alternative uses."[6] Originally circulated in 1932, Robbins's definition only came to prominence as the field itself shifted toward the view it facilitated: an understanding of economics as the study of rational allocative choice made by individuals acting according to subjective preferences.[7]

As this analytic rubric coalesced in the postwar period, different ways of defining its component parts led to divergent approaches to the rubric itself.[8] Views of rationality have ranged from a "weak" version associated with transitive preferences—in which an individual's preferences are understood to be rational provided their ordering of them is consistent—to a "strong" version that conflates rationality with the capacity to optimize outcomes in relation to one's material welfare.[9] Some economists conceive of utility in ways that resemble the original utilitarians' narrow focus on pleasure or happiness, whereas others understand it as that which results from choosing whatever it is one prefers.[10] Choice has been conceived as leading to "utility maximization" or the creation of optimal outcomes but also as mere "satisficing," or achieving a baseline amount of satisfaction.[11] Privileging individual action in one's analysis—what is usually referred to as methodological individualism—can result in a focus either on the decisions of individual economic units or on the aggregate effects of those decisions. Rather than weakening this analytic rubric, these different definitions of its component terms have generated and characterized various forms of postwar choice theory within economics, mathematics, and political science. That is, the discourses that draw upon and contribute to this conception of choice share what Ludwig Wittgenstein calls a family resemblance, or a form of similitude based on a set of features that repeat in various selections and combinations.[12]

In orthodox economics, this model of behavior usually combines allocative choice, weak rationality, and optimal utility as the goal of individual choice. Because of its focus on the behavior of individuals and firms rather than aggregate dynamics, microeconomics in particular foregrounds this view of choice as the axiomatic foundation for its mathematical models and graphical representations. Yet even explanations of aggregate phenomena that exist at a far remove from individual choice are measured against this model, which guarantees the discipline as a whole.[13] In practice, this model most often presumes specific conceptions of utility maximization as a form of material self-interest in relation to explicit market phenomena such as price, wages, and so on. However, as economics has transformed from a study of material welfare to a methodology for the analysis of choice, this shift has been accompanied by an extension of the notion of rational allocative choice into areas ostensibly outside the conventional purview of economics as a discipline. Although such "economic imperialism" is often associated with the popularity of rational choice theory within political science, rational choice theory expressly avoids the focus on allocative choice that defines the economic presumption of scarcity as an inevitable condition of human existence.[14] As a methodological technology of public policymaking, rational choice theory seeks to locate best outcomes based on the aggregation of individual choices; it begins from the presumption of individual choice and ends with something like the identification of social utility as it relates to the matter in question.[15] There is no requirement that the decision at issue should involve the distribution of limited resources or aim to arrive at a predetermined form of utility, whatever that might be. There is significant historical and conceptual overlap between the two fields, but economic methods customarily entail and foreground the combined dynamics of allocative choice, based on an underlying presumption of scarcity, and utility maximization.

The expansion of this model into other domains is primarily associated not with rational choice theory but with the microeconomic research of Chicago School economist Gary Becker.[16] As he demonstrates, what makes the economic understanding of human behavior unique is precisely its universality: not only is there is no act of human choice to which the model cannot be said to apply, but also the model renders every choice by definition equally rational and allocative.[17] Becker's overarching methodology also requires aggregate presumptions of market efficiency and equilibrium, but his description of the behavior of what he calls "decision units" does not depend on those aggregate factors; instead, it emerges from the self-reinforcing concepts that make up the model alone.[18] For example, Becker argues that "When an apparently profitable opportunity . . . is not exploited, the economic approach does not take refuge in assertions about irrationality. . . . Rather it postulates the existence of costs, monetary or psychic, of taking advantage of these opportunities that eliminate their profitability—costs that may not be easily 'seen' by outsiders."[19] Because allocative choice takes place in conditions of scarcity, resources distributed in one area are necessarily not available for distribution in another. That is, within this closed system, every benefit comes with a cost, and vice versa; since there can be no purely costly choice, some benefit must exist, no matter how obscure or counterintuitive. Add to that closed system the definition of choice as the expression of individual preference, and any choice that at first glance appears irrationally costly can be understood to meet preferences that are not immediately apparent. If an individual choice does not yet appear to us to maximize utility, then that is because we have not yet identified the evaluation of cost and benefit, means and end, that determined the choice in question.

When combined with methodological individualism, this tautological view of maximizing behavior transforms every human action into an expression of unimpeded individual agency.[20] Not only does methodological individualism strip out contextual factors that might determine or mitigate individual choice, but also the factors that do remain in play become transposed into the closed system of costs and benefits. In this way, the very existence of constraints becomes the vehicle through which we enact our capacity to choose freely that which we most prefer. For instance, in his analysis of life expectancy, Becker argues,

A person may be a heavy smoker or so committed to work as to omit all exercise, not necessarily because he is ignorant of the consequences or "incapable" of using information he possesses, but because the span forfeited is not worth the cost to him of quitting something or working less intensively. These would be unwise decisions if long life were the only aim, but as long as other aims exist, they could be informed and in this sense "wise."[21]

Rather than taking into account contextual factors that for sociologists might play a role in the choice to smoke—which might range from the ideological manipulations of the advertising industry to the role of poverty in drug addiction—Becker reads the decision to smoke as the logical result of the pursuit of some end other than that of prolonging life. And once the existence of that end is proven by the choice to smoke itself, the choice can retroactively be determined to be "wise" since it leads to this end. By foreclosing the importance of any contextual factor that does not function as either a resource to be distributed or an end to be met, this model turns even the negotiation of profound constraints—for instance, the finitude of life itself—into the rational enactment of sheer individual will. Whereas sociological methods foreground the determining elements that produce, shape, and constrain human agency, the extension of the microeconomic model into the same areas leads to a conception of agency as a quality that inheres in the sheer fact of human choice.

This model of agency results in a particularly extreme version of the economic argument against interpersonal utility comparisons, as they are called within the discipline. Since the marginalist revolution, the notion that utility is by definition subjective has shifted attention from collective to individual conceptions of welfare.[22] Once utility is understood as a subjective property, the essential heterogeneity and opacity of individually held preferences make it increasingly difficult to argue that a predetermined collective outcome would be generally satisfying. In the twentieth century, this presumption took a more absolute form in the shift from "cardinal" to "ordinal" approaches to utility. Whereas cardinal approaches assume that utility can be quantified in absolute terms that allow it to be compared across individuals, ordinal approaches begin from the presumption that utility can only be measured in self-referential increments. From this perspective, for instance, it is possible to say that an individual gets more utility from a car than from a cat but not that he or she gets more utility from either than another individual might. Because utility is subjectively defined, it is impossible to measure different individuals' utility against a single, absolute mathematical scale.

Once we no longer have recourse to interpersonal utility comparisons, it becomes impossible to challenge the effects of choice on either the individual or collective level. If every act is by definition the rational result of subjective cost–benefit analysis, we must assume that each person acts in order to best meet his or her own self-defined ends given the options currently available. And we cannot question these self-defined ends because there is no way to judge one person's utility from the perspective of someone else. Such a judgment can immediately be rejected as paternalistic, since there is no reason to elevate someone else's rational assessment of a person's situation over that person's own evaluation—rather, the reverse. Because we cannot compare forms of utility across individuals, there is also no means to argue with anyone's choice from the perspective of some notion of collective or public good. Although it might appear obvious from one perspective that a homeless man would get more utility from having secure shelter than another man would get from upgrading his Porsche, this assumption cannot be supported from within the model of microeconomic choice, which provides no ground on which we might make such a comparison.[23] On the one hand, this model presents all human experience as an infinite series of choices that are fundamentally undetermined and agential. On the other hand, without a shared measure against which to evaluate utility, the motivations and results of these choices take on a quality of unchallengeable bedrock. The world that preference has wrought appears by nature indisputable.

When this model of choice becomes unmoored from the market focus of economics as a discipline, I refer to the result as "the microeconomic imagination." The discourses that I have examined here contribute to the development of this way of imagining choice, but often they do not elaborate this model so much as assume it. In foregrounding the work of the imagination, my terminology points toward both the visionary power of the discipline's way of modeling human action and the influence of this model outside the field of economics itself. What the microeconomic imagination refers to is not economic analysis as it is currently practiced but the axiomatic proposition that makes such analysis possible—the conceptual leap that designates agential allocative choice as an unquestioned and unquestionable foundation. In the microeconomic imagination, the key features of this foundation remain the same: methodological individualism, rational allocation, utility maximization, and the refusal of interpersonal utility comparisons. Crucially, however, this model no longer has any necessary relationship to market dynamics such as efficiency and equilibrium, which inform even Becker's avowedly imperialist approach. When the radically self-reinforcing model of microeconomic choice is detached from market-based methods and material concerns, it takes on a life of its own.

To outline the way this model of choice operates in the microeconomic mode, I augment the economic vocabulary of rational allocative choice with the political language of interest. If utility is a quality of the option that one most prefers, then interest is its subjective corollary: the option that represents maximal utility is that which the subject perceives to be in his or her own best interest.[24] Much as it is impossible to question the utility of any allocative choice an individual makes, it is not possible to force someone to have more interest in one existing option than another. Like preferences and the utility that results from them, interest is nonfalsifiable because it is defined unquestionably by each individual alone. Understood in this way, the word "interest" refers not to a type of preference—one that is self-interested rather than altruistic—but instead to any preference identified by a particular method. As Stephen Engelmann argues, this method requires approaching choice as an internal, speculative process in which every possibly relevant aspect of the internal and external environment is assessed and both means and ends are compared and evaluated. In effect, all subjective and objective factors must be conceived by the individual as constituting a kind of microeconomy, a system of existing and projective elements that must all be weighed against one another in order to locate the best option.[25] Only by imaginatively manifesting and surveying this microeconomy can the individual identify what is in his or her own best interest. Thus, we act out of interest not simply when we serve narrowly self-directed goals, such as improving our own material welfare or status, but rather whenever we approach choices as unfolding within this sort of microeconomy of costs and benefits, means and ends. As a form of imaginative interiority, interest is what propels the subject to experience the world as continually eliciting rational allocative choice. Or, to put it another way, we could say that "interest" is the word we give to the microeconomic imagination when it transpires inside subjects themselves.

As I argue in the following chapters, the microeconomic mode both activates and alters this model of choice, most significantly by infusing it with a fixation on choices made by and about individual living beings. We can understand this transformation, I suggest, if we locate the microeconomic imagination as part of a larger group of postwar choice discourses that have emerged alongside post-Fordism. When we extend the criteria of family resemblance a bit further than I have above, this family of discourses can be seen to include other methodologies concerned with individual units of binary decision—from the black boxes of cybernetics to the input/output theories of behaviorism to the moral value placed on individual choice in existentialism to, inevitably, the digital computer itself.[26] This larger conceptual nexus also includes neoliberal governmentality as famously theorized by Michel Foucault, which relies on something very like the microeconomic imagination to produce a form of rule that is itself based on the freedom to choose.[27] As various theorists have noted, this larger set of choice discourses accompanies and facilitates the forms of capital and governance associated with post-Fordism, or transformations variously addressed as affective labor, immaterial labor, "Empire," and so on.[28] By reading the subject of life-interest in relation to such arguments, I demonstrate that the microeconomic mode points to a very different capture of life itself than that dissected in Marxist arguments regarding the control society.[29] If theories of post-Fordism suggest an ongoing fusion of life with binary units of information, then the microeconomic mode indicates that there is another crucial result of this fusion that we have not yet noticed: the shift from the liberal individual to the subject of life-interest.

Although these theoretical investigations at times take me into more or less familiar terrain, my argument crosses this terrain from angles that often make it look rather different than it does in other accounts. For example, in order to situate and explore the properties of life-interest, I discuss Thomas Hobbes's *Leviathan*, natural law theory, and the importance of individual decision over life in chapter 2. However, for reasons that will become clear in the chapter, this investigation moves in directions nearly opposed to those that drive the sovereignty theory of Giorgio Agamben, perhaps the most prominent recent commentator on Hobbesian man in the state of nature.[30] Likewise, chapter 4 engages theorizations of becoming and affect in relation to forms of insistent, painful fixity and agential individuality that would appear at odds with the way the former set of terms have been theorized. Yet, as I try to indicate throughout, my intent here is not to launch a theoretical argument against any existing reading of the present but rather to try to track the different orientation toward life itself that the microeconomic mode insists we also inhabit. Glimpsed through the lens of the microeconomic mode, the guiding concerns of contemporary theory appear scrambled and reassembled, as if familiar positions on affect, control, sovereignty, and biopolitics are being viewed through a kaleidoscope. In mapping its theoretical work, I argue that the microeconomic mode offers a different incarnation of the contemporary subject than what we find in either biopolitical or post-Fordist theory.

In order to track the defining features of this subject, I focus here primarily on popular or widely known texts in the microeconomic mode. As a result, my archive indicates something of the remarkable ability of this mode to travel up and down the hierarchy of contemporary aesthetics—to retain its defining features within works possessed of vastly different levels of ambition and accomplishment. Texts I engage here range from acclaimed novels like Cormac McCarthy's *The Road*, which has generated a kind of critical industry in its wake, to the schlocky ticking-time-bomb film *Unthinkable* (2010), from the epic-fantasy novels on which the television series *Game of Thrones* is based to Jesmyn Ward's challenging, National Book Award–winning Hurricane Katrina novel, *Salvage the Bones* (2011). As my descriptions here suggest, I adopt this approach not because I believe there are no differences between the registers and rewards of these works. What I do believe is that in this context such differences are significant primarily for what they tell us about how the microeconomic mode works and what understanding of the human it generates. We learn something important from the way *The Road* turns the watertight, abstracted completeness of the microeconomic imagination into a narrative poetics of reduction, but we also learn something from the vile, unusually half-baked *House* episode focused on Hurricane Katrina, which in its very brokenness provides crucial evidence of the perceived racialized threat posed by the subject of life-interest. That is, quality is not insignificant here, but in this context it is not primarily significant of itself. Rather, varieties of aesthetic deftness and reach constitute some of the ways in which the microeconomic mode makes its meaning.

Because I largely stick to the path laid out by the microeconomic mode itself, my archive also tilts heavily toward certain perspectives and emphases, most notably as evidenced by the white male protagonists who take center stage in the majority of the texts in the microeconomic mode. As I suggest in chapter 2, they do so for all the customary, obvious reasons, but these reasons look a bit different to the subject of life-interest; that difference is part of the work and worry of depictions of suffering white male agents in the microeconomic mode. To counter this focus and consider its limitations, I relax my own criteria in chapter 5 to accommodate some quite different takes on the subject of life-interest. To do so, I incorporate works that are neither as popular as others I read here nor as complete in their evocation of the microeconomic mode. Thus, for example, I analyze both Dave Eggers's *What Is the What: The Autobiography of Valentino Achak Deng: A Novel* (2006), which relies on this mode for one strand of its narrative structure, and Kazuo Ishiguro's *Never Let Me Go* (2005), in which this mode appears in a kind of canceled form. Similarly, while *Never Let Me Go* became a Hollywood film, it would be a stretch to call the novels I examine in this chapter popular outside of certain literary-critical circles. I shift my approach in this way not only to resist the centrality of the white man in the microeconomic mode but also because it is essential to think about how the demise of the liberal individual looks from the perspective of those who never enjoyed the full benefits attached to the category.

My geographic and media choices arise from the same decision to follow primarily where the microeconomic mode leads. Although this mode can arguably be found to varying degrees across the global North, I have delimited my archive—selected from among an immense and ever-expanding array of examples—by focusing in the following chapters on works that either are products of American media or have achieved significant popularity within the American media landscape. For instance, Yann Martel, author of *Life of Pi* (2001), is a Spanish-born Canadian author. *Life of Pi* was a *New York Times* best-seller, is on Oprah's list of the "most addictive books of the last 25 years," and was adapted into a film that won an Oscar for best director in 2013.[31] The trajectory of *Never Let Me Go* begins in England but travels in similar ways. By focusing on texts either made or consumed in the United States, I am able to trace the microeconomic mode as it circulates in American media without excluding a work such as *Life of Pi* because its author is not from the United States—a distinction that for my purposes would be something of a misleading technicality. This approach does not, of course, mean that *Life of Pi* and *Never Let Me Go* are not concerned with Canadianness or Englishness respectively, nor that there are no national variations to be traced across the microeconomic mode. However, because my goal is to map the features of the microeconomic mode as they appear most consistently, interrogating these national variations remains outside the scope of my current project. Instead, I delimit my examples to those that have achieved notable prominence in the United States despite these variations and focus on what they suggest about the defining qualities of this aesthetic phenomenon as a whole. (Unfortunately, this rubric does prevent me from engaging with texts that might otherwise be productively read in this context, at least in this book—for example, Michael Haneke's film *Le temps du loup* [2003].) My choices among media are likewise guided by the versions that incarnate the microeconomic mode most completely, whether that be the original written text or its film or television adaptation. Some film adaptations leave behind the more difficult features of the novels and therefore mute key aspects of the microeconomic mode—*The Road* is a particularly good example—while others, such as Danny Boyle's film *127 Hours* (2010), push the source material much further into the microeconomic mode than the original. In some cases, notably the *Game of Thrones* television series (2011 to the present) and the novels on which it is based, both versions engage the microeconomic mode to an equal degree. In this particular case, I have chosen to focus primarily on the more manageable of the two—that is, the currently static set of novels rather than the still ongoing television series.

That I have been led to bring together works that differ so significantly in media, genre, and aesthetic ambition suggests something of the power and permeation of the microeconomic mode in the present. As I argue in chapter 6, we have now reached a point where this mode is coherent and consistent enough as an aesthetic formation that the subject of life-interest can be deployed in numerous contexts to support numerous (though not unlimited) political perspectives. In this way, if in few others, this subject is much like the liberal individual, its predecessor. Some of the works I examine in this book depict existence as a subject of life-interest in order to rail against it, to ask why we must see ourselves in this way and if there is anything to be done about it. Other novels and films in the microeconomic mode deploy this same subject to shore up faltering images of white male valor, validate settler-colonial hegemony, reauthorize forms of black subjection, and so on. Although I attend to such specific ideological valences, I am primarily concerned with the larger structure that houses them—with what makes this cultural formation potent and portable enough that at this point it can accommodate such different political stances. The very existence and circulation of this mode in its particular form represents an implicit argument regarding the emergence of the subject of life-interest, and that is the argument I aim to illuminate here.

As with the selection of my archive, the structure of this book reflects my concern with mapping the conceptual work that the microeconomic mode performs. Because the central concepts I explore in the process arise from the microeconomic mode itself, I must define these terms before I can situate them theoretically, and these definitions can only result from my engagement with the texts that provide the source of both concept and definition. To allow for this sequence, I postpone until later chapters much of the contextual framework that ordinarily forms the work of an introduction. Instead of addressing this contextual material here, I have divided the book into three sections, each of which contains its own theoretical chapter. In the first chapter in each of these three parts, I focus on a specific aesthetic strand of the microeconomic mode, as defined by genre, narrative form, and so on. In the second chapter in each section, I focus on the respective theoretical category that becomes visible within each of these particular strands. With the definition of these categories in hand, I am able step back in these theoretical chapters and read each concept in relation to current and historical modes of theorizing political subjectivity in relation to life itself as well as the specific operations these concepts enable or foreclose.

In chapter 1 I focus on what I call the live model, a genre that draws upon and revises the conventions of castaway, survival, and postapocalyptic narratives. I argue that, despite their many differences, these forms share a concern with social modeling: by ejecting protagonists from existing structures of human collectivity, they offer a means to depict existence in a minimal, schematic form. In classic versions of such tales, the stripped-down simplicity of the model serves to reveal truths of human behavior that are ordinarily submerged in the dense experiential texture of everyday experience, so that the world writ small enables us to understand the world writ large. In the microeconomic mode, however, this dialectic collapses, and the schematic version comes to appear as the totality of human experience. Rather than the model presenting a distilled version of human existence, existence itself is revealed to conform to the distilled shape of a model. Live models thus offer a vision of human life reduced to the dynamics of individual choice in extreme situations, but, through the transformation of generic conventions that they enact, they also register the occlusion of any forms of social organization beyond the model of choice that their protagonists inhabit. I focus here on three works in which the live model occupies center stage: Yann Martel's castaway novel, *Life of Pi*; Cormac McCarthy's postapocalyptic survival tale, *The Road*; and the survival film *127 Hours*. By analyzing the way in which these works both draw on and reconfigure existing generic conventions, I argue that live models serve to manifest life-interest as the defining feature of human existence. In the final section, I begin to suggest the challenges that the subject of life-interest makes to hierarchies of life that have historically depended on denying the agency of those classed as disposable, through a reading of an episode of *House* focused on the aftermath of Hurricane Katrina. As I demonstrate in my analysis of *House*'s treatment of its Katrina survivor, the definition and maintenance of genres of human being require different forms of cultural work when every being necessarily counts as a suffering agent and subject of life-interest.

Chapter 2 examines the category of life-interest in relation to its closest antecedent in political theory: the natural law theory that defines self-preservation as the first law of nature. Although most biopolitical critique has not been very attentive to the role of self-preservation, the definition and the rights of the liberal subject rest at bottom on the attachment to or duty regarding self-preservation. I return to foundational texts of natural law theory by John Locke and Hobbes to trace this contribution and to consider why and in what ways the microeconomic mode reactivates and revises tropes characteristic of this body of thought, including the state of nature, the slave, the cannibal, and the savage. Although the methodologies I associate with the microeconomic imagination also return to Hobbesian thinking in some respects—for example, in numerous rational choice readings of *Leviathan*—they eschew the focus on self-preservation that is prominent both in *Leviathan* and in the microeconomic mode. I argue that what we see in the subject of life-interest is a fusion of the tautological, totalizing account of interest offered in the microeconomic imagination with a renewed understanding of individual life as an inescapably propulsive and motile force, which is akin to that found in natural law theory. To describe how this fusion arises, I read the evolving status of self-preservation from natural law theory through liberal biopolitics and theorizations of immaterial labor. By evaluating the changing role of imaginative figures such as the cannibal in both natural law theory and the microeconomic mode, I document and define a shift from the liberal subject with a right to life to a microeconomic subject who chooses in the interest of life.

Part 2 advances from the self-understanding of the subject of life-interest to the forms of sociality and governance available to such subjects in the aggregate. In chapter 3 I examine one of the most prominent and recognizable forms within the microeconomic mode: the survival game. Unlike postmodern game narratives, which often express a concern with simulation overtaking reality, the survival game presents a different kind of nightmare: one in which the material world itself has been legislated into the form of a game and the consequences are life or death. I begin with Gillian Flynn's *Gone Girl* (2012), a novel that juxtaposes post-Fordist social realism with a potboiler, survival-game thriller. In its uneven invocation of these two generic registers, I argue, *Gone Girl* indicates something about the role of life-interest in the control society. Whereas the gamification process that accompanies immaterial labor disperses humans into streams of unspooling data, the survival game forcibly locates each person within the vulnerable container of his or her own living flesh. Players have no choice but to keep making choices with regard to their own lives and the lives around them, tethered to their mortal, mutually endangering vectors of existence. I argue that this forced segmentation of humans into living units of binary choice constitutes a form of sovereignty particular to the subject of life-interest. That is, the production of survival games attests to the capacity of sovereign power to produce humans as subjects of life-interest, even as those same subjects are also incorporated within aggregate flows of discretized data. I explore this operation by comparing a variety of survival game texts, including the first *Saw* (2004) film, the novels by George R. R. Martin on which the television series *Game of Thrones* is based, and the ticking-time-bomb torture scenario, as exemplified in the film *Unthinkable*. In the process, I suggest some of particular ways in which this form of sovereignty operates—including both the capacities it harnesses and the limitations it encounters.

In chapter 4, I draw on recent theoretical conversations regarding both sovereignty and the control society in order to further describe the form of sovereign power manifested in the survival game, which I define as sovereign capture. In digital theory, capture refers to the process of discretization and quantification that must transpire for digital logic to operate. In accounts of the control society, human life undergoes this form of capture when human behavior becomes segmented, valorized, and monetized. Sovereign capture, I argue, operates as a corollary to this process, but what is captured is the individual as a single unit of decision in relation to life— as a living binary toggle that moves between life and death, 1 and 0. If the theoretical perspective on capture takes the form of the network diagram, the map of information flows that we are increasingly asked to understand as the entire world, then the subject of life-interest offers the view from inside one of the nodes on this diagram: the vantage of a human switching point. As I suggest, this view is one from which capture appears sovereign, such that we cannot help but function as binary units of life. With this theoretical trajectory in place, I turn in my final section to consider the role of affect in the microeconomic mode. In Deleuzian readings of post-Fordism, the importance of affect lies in its capacity to traverse and challenge the boundaries of individual bodies via endless modulation and movement. For the subject of life-interest, in contrast, affect is expressly tied to horror; the essential liveness that is central to affect becomes activated through mortal threat, pain, and despair. In a fashion reminiscent of penal torture, sovereign capture manifests itself in its power to turn our existence as living bodies into unavoidable physical torment.

As I began to describe above, my final section moves outward from the core of the microeconomic mode in its most complete and mainstream manifestations in order to consider works that attempt to engage life-interest in relation to forms of social determination. In chapter 5, entitled "Partial Fictions," I turn to a set of texts that both draw on the microeconomic mode and insist that the costs of suffering agency are not universally borne. I refer to these works as partial fictions in order to signal several intertwined features: their selective use of the microeconomic mode, their insistence that only particular subjects must confront life-interest routinely, and their creation of a kind of pointedly partial view of their own represented worlds. In Eggers's *What Is the What*, Ishiguro's *Never Let Me Go*, and Ward's *Salvage the Bones*, the central characters perceive but cannot traverse a narrative and spatial horizon beyond which other lives flourish at their own expense. I read this partial view as a formal registration of the shift from persons, who must be treated as ends in themselves, to subjects of life-interest, who necessarily view all lives in terms of cost–benefit analysis. As these novels indicate, the irrelevance of personhood as a category within the microeconomic mode creates different consequences for liberal ameliorative and radical redistributive approaches to social transformation. Whereas liberal human rights narratives struggle to address situations in which agency functions as a problem rather than a solution, radical critiques of racial capital are mirrored in complicated and not always enabling ways by the depiction of life-interest, which can naturalize the use of some lives to benefit others even as it exposes the realities masked by myths of universal personhood. However, *Salvage the Bones* argues that there is also something important to be gained—or rather, salvaged—from the shift from the person possessed of rights to the subject defined by life-interest. Once the difference between life to be fostered and disposable life rests so obviously on individual human choice, the novel suggests, it is at least no longer possible to treat such disparities as the unavoidable, unintended consequences of an impartial or self-regulating system.

In chapter 6, I consider in more detail a feature that is especially evident in partial fictions: a logic I refer to as binary life. Across the microeconomic mode, we find situations in which life can only exist at the expense of other lives. Although these contexts can be plausibly related to material threats that circulate in twenty-first-century culture—for example, food scarcity arising from ecological crisis—the consistency of this logic is such that its importance seems to exceed the particular scenarios in which it circulates. The logic of binary life is particularly evident in partial fictions because they aim to denaturalize and consider the political consequences of this either/or choice between lives. Here, I consider why it is that the subject of life-interest seems condemned to make kill-or-be-killed, him-or-me choices between lives. Rather than reading this either/or logic as tied to the specific context in which it is envisioned, I argue that it functions as a reification of the status of the individual as a unit of binary choice. As I explore the way in which this reification functions, I indicate something of the range of arguments to which binary life can be put. Partial fictions draw on binary life to call into question the consignment of some lives to disposability while other works in the microeconomic mode engage it to insist on the inevitable consumption of some lives by others. Instead of understanding these narratives as emerging from a specific real-world distinction between lives that are and are not disposable, I suggest that binary life must be understood as the cultural formation through which such divisions are now being represented and interrogated.

To be clear, my fidelity in following in the path of the microeconomic mode does not mean that I like where it leads. But this book is driven by a desire to do interpretive justice to the unique account of contemporary subjectivity embodied in the specific formal parameters of this phenomenon. If the emergence of a new, increasingly ubiquitous aesthetic mode would seem to suggest an overarching transformation—that is, one significant enough to generate such a shift in cultural forms—then these aesthetic conventions can be understood as congealed information about that transformation and its significance. Like an alien transmission in a sci-fi film, the compressed data of the microeconomic mode flickers incessantly across our many screens and preempts what was once our regular programming; in this case, however, the transmission is both produced and received by the same society, sent from and to the twenty-first-century global North. Although I strive here to identify and elucidate the central conceptual figures propagated and embodied in this mode, there is no way at this moment to finish this analysis definitively given that the work of this mode remains unfinished; the transmission is ongoing. What it means to be a subject of life-interest—and what we might do about being told that that is what we are—is an issue still being thought through around us within the many forking paths that make up the microeconomic mode. To intervene in this imagination of human being, we must first come to understand what this mode comprehends about the present that, so far, we have not.

PART I
Political Subjectivity

Chapter One

LIVE MODELS

In their best-seller *SuperFreakonomics: Global Cooling, Patriotic Prostitutes, and Why Suicide Bombers Should Buy Life Insurance* (2009), Chicago School economist Stephen Levitt and journalist Stephen Dubner describe a study that analyzed the way in which young African American women in the poorest part of Chicago conducted the business of prostitution.[1] In their account, the very elements that constrain these women's choices become the means to indicate how cannily they manage to identify and act in their own best interests. We learn that for these young women, the choices for earning money are cutting hair, selling drugs, and selling sex, and we are offered an explanation of why they are right that prostitution is the best option among these—but why they only have these options and how that situation might be altered is a nonissue. The specific elements of their lives that do allow recoding in the register of interest become in the process stripped of their experiential and affective specificity. The question of whether to let men go without condoms in order to make a few more dollars per trick appears as a neutral, quantitative act of cost–benefit analysis—no different from the choice between taking the bus or the subway. Although Levitt and Dubner clearly expect the prostitutes' milieu to be unfamiliar and exotic to their readers, the point of the story is in fact how inconsequential the specifics of this world really are. What the study actually proves, it turns out, is that pricing structures work in the same predictable, logical way even when created by poor and uneducated prostitutes.

This is obviously a flawed account, ripe for any number of Left critiques, but I want instead to attend to its status as a particular type of representation—extracted from context, stripped down, and distilled. Only the elements that can be registered in the conceptual vocabulary of the microeconomic imagination are included, but this process of abstraction generates a sense that each anecdote reflects universal truths of human behavior. Precisely because the account deliberately excludes some data and reframes the rest in the language of individual interests and choices, it is presented as crystalline and complete, as producing no remainder and requiring no comparison to its denser and more opaque original. And while we might argue that the study ignores crucial processes of social determination, from the perspective of the microeconomic imagination that missing context is simply the product of other vectors of individual choice that happen not to be the subject of study in this instance. That is, the milieu in which the prostitutes encounter these choices appears not a register and effect of structural violence, but rather as the aggregate of an infinite number of individual decisions regarding housing, employment, child-rearing, and so on. From a single toothpaste purchase to large-scale events like presidential elections, the microeconomic imagination can render any event or system in the terms of individual choices based on prospective cost–benefit analysis; the only difference with complex events involving masses of people is the increased difficulty in tracing precisely how the cumulative effects of countless acts of individual choice create a given outcome. Redescribing dynamics large and small in the terms of individual interest in this way creates a peculiar and specific relationship between the description and what is being described. In the microeconomic imagination, representations offer expressly schematic, abstracted accounts of human experience, which always reduce to the same handful of principles but nevertheless purport to leave nothing of significance out.

In this chapter I begin to trace the relationship between this imagination and some of the dominant genres in the present. Each of the texts I examine—Cormac McCarthy's *The Road* (2006); Yann Martel's *Life of Pi* (2001); the film *127 Hours* (2010); and a 2006 episode of the television series *House* focused on a Hurricane Katrina survivor—center on a confrontation between the natural environment and the most basic human requirements for self-preservation.[2] In foregrounding interests that arise from the sheer fact of embodied consciousness, these works engage the imagination of interest as a facet of our basic existence as living human beings.[3] Because characters' experience of interest unfolds as a result of a direct struggle with the natural environment, these works envision human behavior extracted from the complexity of contemporaneous social existence. Choices unfold within tightly defined spheres of truncated causality that render both personal and collective history inconsequential and irrelevant. Underprovisioning is these texts' defining formal feature, as well as the primary threat faced by their protagonists. The same paucity of moving parts that activates the characters' vociferous interest in self-preservation—what I call life-interest—also distills interest, choice, and action into simple, self-evident vectors whose interactions unfold with schematic clarity. The result is a combination of abstraction and extremity on the level of both form and content—that is, the combination that I argue defines the microeconomic mode.

In producing this effect, the texts I analyze here rely on genres that combine an emphasis on threats to life with a focus on distilled, contracted worlds, most crucially the castaway, survival, and postapocalyptic genres. From *Survivor* (2000 to the present) to *Big Brother* (2000 to the present), from *Lost* (2004–2010) to *28 Days Later* (2002), revised and recombined versions of these genres have had a striking resurgence in the twenty-first century. I argue that the prominence and prevalence of such works must be understood in relation to an ongoing shift in their generic conventions. Customarily, these genres operate by offering a tellingly minimized model world in place of contemporaneous society as it would ordinarily be experienced; the model's reduction of complexity and shrinking of scale serves to shed light on the more complicated and variegated social landscape it has replaced. In what I call live models, this implicit comparison to a larger social field disappears, and we are instead asked to imagine that the contemporaneous world we inhabit possesses the reductive qualities of a model. I argue that this shift bestows on the models in question a strange quality of live-ness, a sense of intensified and exceptional immediacy that registers through the contravening of generic expectations. The result of this combination of intensity, immediacy, and relentless threat to life is an aesthetic form that borders on the assaultive. To be inside a live model is to confront the experience of interest in its starkest, most insistent, and least supportable form.

I read the creation and dissemination of the live model as an attempt to think on the level of form an emerging definition of human being, one in which the experience of action in one's own best interest is an element of life itself. This view of the subject of interest hinges on the conception of humans as inevitably self-preserving entities. Because of our compulsive interest in life, we can be presented as beings who are in essence interested; interest in life becomes indistinguishable from life as a being who acts from interest. In the works I analyze in the following, this conception of self-preservation serves as a means to document the transformation of the subject of interest from an analytic constant into an inescapable form of individual self-understanding. Rather than exposing interest as merely a convenient, discursive construction or as one ideological mystification among many—as one might expect from the previous history of Left aesthetics—these works explore and elaborate the concept of interest as an intrinsic quality of human being itself. They envision what transpires when interest is experienced, consciously and in real time, as the inevitable motivation that the microeconomic imagination understands it to be. I trace this aesthetic form in two directions. First, I map the live model as a genre and consider the account of the subject encoded in its conventions via readings of *127 Hours*, *The Road*, and *Life of Pi*. Second, I extend this thinking through the *House* episode to suggest the way in which the live model helps us understand the emergence of a version of political subjectivity in which human life and interest become forcibly fused. Ultimately, I suggest that life-interest requires us to expand our understanding of the contemporary politics of life itself.

Castaway, desert island, and other survival tales are customarily defined by subtraction. Whether characters wash up on a desert island, attempt to crawl down a mountain with a broken leg, or wake to the aftermath of a zombie apocalypse, they find themselves stripped of entrenched forms of human collectivity as they would ordinarily experience them.[4] In these works, the world is reduced to a subset or remainder of the full range of the behaviors, persons, and objects that would usually make up daily existence for characters or readers as selected by the logic of a realist plot.[5] Not only is the world that results bounded by geographic or temporal fissures from the everyday but it also appears as a self-contained stand-in for the full complexity of contemporaneous existence. In *Lord of the Flies* (1954), we read the events on the island in a particular way because the island has replaced the world as the protagonists would usually experience it. However, precisely because the castaway island constitutes a reduced and abstracted subset of the world at large, it begs comparison with the full-sized version for which it substitutes.[6] The island appears as a distilled version—a model— that refers us to that which it has replaced. This reduction process serves as an organizing principle of characters' experience in a fashion quite distinct from other forms of social allegory. Both *Oliver Twist* (1839) and *Gilligan's Island* (1964–67) feature characters that represent identifiable social types, but only in the latter is this reduction of the world to a minimal collection of people an acknowledged thematic and plot point. In that sense—and in contrast to realist social allegory in general—what these genres allegorize is the process of modeling itself. They dramatize the substitution of a tellingly and overtly simplified copy for an infinitely more complicated original.

When this process emphasizes a pleasingly miniaturized completeness— *Swiss Family Robinson* (1812) would be the quintessential example here—the model provides a concrete finitude necessarily lacking in the overwhelming complexity of the world at large. This dollhouse effect turns the model into a sort of fetish, a means of covering over any lack in the social reality being modeled. In other cases we find the reverse process, and the model reveals something hidden in and by the persistent facticity and plenitude of the original. In *The Road Warrior* (1981), for instance, a near-future war of scarcity sheds new light on the present-day oil economy, while in *Lord of the Flies* young boys' violent behavior exposes the false promises of civilization. In such models, what is revealed is something about contemporaneous social organization only visible when many of its elements are removed or repurposed; something about human nature masked by or unaccounted for within society as we know it; or, most commonly, some combination of the two. In each case, the distillation of the world illuminates fundamentals invisible in the elaborateness and pressing materiality of ordinary experience. The pedagogical power of the model arises from its difference from the original, but it is because of the immersive intricacy of the original that the model is instructive.

In texts in the microeconomic mode, this dialectic collapses and the model comes to appear complete on its own. We can see this transformation at work if we compare a recent survival tale, the film *127 Hours*, to the survival tales that circulated when the form last had its heyday as subgenre of American literary naturalism. Based on a memoir entitled *Between a Rock and a Hard Place* (2004), the film centers on the true tale of rock climber Aron Ralston (played by James Franco), who was trapped in a slot canyon when his arm became wedged between a falling boulder and the canyon wall.[7] The significant objects contained in the canyon include only Aron himself, the scanty and insufficient contents of his backpack, and the discrete number of hours that unfold as his body begins to expire. This radically minimal quality made the film appear a virtuoso effort to critics, who celebrated filmmaker Danny Boyle and actor James Franco for making a compelling story out of a man who interacts with no one, can hardly move, and battles an antagonist lodged in his own body.[8] What the film manages to do without, in effect, are all the typicalities of individual character and social circumstance that customarily function as the building blocks of mainstream cinema. Some of Aron's personal history appears in flashbacks, but it isn't presented as qualifying or shaping the choice that confronts him. The few elements with causal significance in the canyon— the trapped arm, the lack of food and water, the number of hours—concern Aron's sheer existence as a conscious mind that lives in a body with certain inborn needs and capacities. It is difficult to imagine any human being with this sort of body experiencing Aron's choice very differently, whatever the specifics of his or her personal psychology or place in the social order.

Yet this vision of pure human will pitched against unyielding natural forces reads very differently than in the survival tales that proliferated at the turn of the twentieth century. When naturalist texts stage a confrontation between human being and the forces of nature, they do so to interrogate the way in which the relationship between the natural and the social determines an individual's options and ultimate trajectory—either through a civilization process that has left the human animal unprepared for the extremities of nature or through the interaction of Darwinian social forces that have the force of natural law. Even in the "man versus nature" tales once so ubiquitous in high school English classes, the signal confrontation is triangulated through questions of civilization: what "man" has lost in the process of civilization and what he would need to know in order to correct for absent animal instinct. While we may read Aron's experience in *127 Hours* as revealing something essential about human being, this revelation doesn't in turn illuminate the key dynamics of any existing forms of social organization or the cost of the civilizing process; there is no sense that someone with better knowledge of the wild or more powerful animal instincts would fare better or differently than Aron. Instead, what is illuminated in the canyon is precisely the irrelevance of any such triangulation. Aron's action appears detached from any external processes that would render it something more than an expression of sheer individual choice. The knowledge the model provides is by definition inapplicable to any understanding of human behavior as it relates to social embeddedness; in a sense, this inapplicability is exactly what is being modeled.

This shift in the import of the model creates an aesthetic effect in its own right. As I have suggested, modeling genres usually represent a contracted world that in turn represents something submerged in or masked by the concrete totality of daily life.[9] In *127 Hours*, this second-order effect disappears. The perception of condensation that accompanies the modeling impulse persists, but its sense of standing in for something larger or more elaborate disappears. The canyon has all the bounded simplicity of a model, but it refers to nothing larger than itself. When the model lacks an external referent in this way, it makes the same claims to direct reference as the rest of the character's represented experience, despite still signifying as unusually restricted and condensed. As a result, the model becomes conspicuous as a realm of extraordinary subtraction and contraction, as a peculiarly compressed and minimal arena in which protagonists find themselves contained. The effect is something akin to witnessing a doll come to life. The model world is still in the shape of a miniature, toy-size version, but it lacks the simplified secondariness that usually defines modeling genres; instead, it hums with the same vitality and presence as everything around it. In fact, given the extremity of Aron's experiences, we might say the model—like the uncanny doll—conveys an excessive and unsettling degree of live-ness.[10] This live-ness makes an implicit argument regarding the triumph of the model, but it is an argument about the shape of reality rather than the power of representation. It's not that the map mimics the completeness of the territory, in dollhouse fashion, or that its simulated reality takes the place of the territory, in postmodern fashion; rather, we encounter a territory that is itself exactly map-shaped. The result is what I call a live model: a genre whose form encodes a claim about the comprehensive, undeniable reality of a profoundly abstracted world.

In this light, the gradual emergence of the live model since the late 1990s might be read as the formal register of the ongoing ascendancy of the microeconomic imagination of human behavior manifested at various stages of its evolution depending on the text in question. To the extent that modeling genres continue to allegorize social structures such as capitalism, race, patriarchy, and so on, they make an implicit statement regarding the ongoing importance of such concepts as a context for human agency. Although such works continue to appear, it is perhaps indicative that in recent years they often take on a parodic guise—for example, *Shaun of the Dead*'s account of the stalemate of heterosexual masculinity (2004) or *Cockneys vs. Zombies*' parable of London gentrification (2012)—as if such analyses could no longer be offered with a completely straight face. More commonly, the modeling of complex structures persists but intermingles with a consideration of model-like reduction as itself an aspect of contemporary existence—as in the television series *Lost* or *28 Days Later*—with the result that the more customary modeling operation becomes diluted or undermined. Even in works that concentrate entirely on live models, the question of social organization haunts the text in the form of generic expectation. When the customary allegorical interrogation of contemporary society fails to appear, this absence reads as a comment in its own right. In this way, live models enable a different kind of cultural work: they explore the ongoing transformation of the social field into a series of discrete, dehistoricized choices by individuals who take action in a contextual vacuum. By simultaneously intensifying and collapsing the conventions of modeling genres, these works dramatize the irrelevance of social complexity as they offer a vision of how life stripped of that complexity is experienced. When models in the microeconomic mode offer a world made of minimal moving parts, they both enact and comment upon this concept of a simplified and abstracted universe that nevertheless purports to be complete unto itself.

We can get a sense of how this double operation works by turning to Cormac McCarthy's novel *The Road*. Whereas *127 Hours* adapts a narrative form that by definition takes place in the geographical exterior of human civilization, *The Road* revises the conventions of the postapocalyptic, which ordinarily poses fundamental questions about contemporaneous social organization by imagining its demise. When they envision a future in which human collectivity is restructured by dramatically different relations to material goods, technology, and security, postapocalyptic models interrogate present-day conflicts regarding the distribution of wealth, the role of government, the inevitability of social antagonism, and so on. In *The Road*, these conventions are inverted, and the eradication of human collectivity takes center stage. The novel focuses on the aftermath of an unknown event that destroyed all life on the planet except that of human beings, who are themselves nearing extinction. The protagonists, a father and his young son, struggle to stay alive as they travel on foot, starving, freezing, and fleeing from roving bands of cannibals and rapists. The remaining humans' only defining characteristics are their proximity to death, their willingness to eat or do violence to one another, their size and strength, and—in the case of the father and the son—the blood tie of familial love. Except for the reproductive differences of male and female bodies, every aspect of social identity has become equally irrelevant and invisible, including race, state, nation, religion, monetary wealth, class, and education.

Obviously, the degradation of more elaborate and refined social structures into the crude behavior of violent gangs constitutes a familiar means by which the postapocalyptic comments on the present and its possible futures. However, *The Road* prevents this comparison through its termination of shared human temporality. Because their only collective experience of time will be a swift march to extinction, these gangs cannot evolve any behaviors that will structure experience beyond the immediate future. In that way, the amassed humans in *The Road* do not offer an alternate image of society so much as an image of the impossibility of society. Yet the dying world in *The Road* is also insulated from the type of social commentary that motivates and preoccupies postnuclear films such as *The Day After* (1983) or *On the Beach* (1959). Not only is the catastrophe in *The Road* given no political, historical, or meteorological specificity—that is, no chain of precipitating events we might avoid or prepare for—but also the novel fails to depict the process of social devolution in the fashion familiar from postnuclear films. Nuclear holocaust allegories underscore the importance of contemporaneous social mores precisely by asking us to imagine their death throes. When we witness a preacher's sermon fail to provide comfort in *The Day After* or a captain go down with his ship in *On the Beach*, the emotional charge depends upon the significance of religious belief and patriotic duty in contemporaneous society. In *The Road*, we join the protagonists after such social roles and mores have evaporated. If postnuclear films imagine the tragic demise of existing human society and the swift erosion of its attendant identities and customs, what *The Road* depicts is something different: a minimal world in which the social has already been utterly foreclosed as a staging ground for human action.

The novel underscores this foreclosure of social significance through its trope of eroded reference. The father perceives "the world shrinking down about a raw core of parsible entities. The names of things slowly following those things into oblivion. . . . The sacred idiom shorn of its referents and so of its reality."[11] Like the beautiful sextant the father finds—useless now that the stars are hidden by perpetual cloud—the remnants of human endeavor found in *The Road* serve only to mark that the civilization that made them has winked out. By dramatizing the end of reference, *The Road* calls attention to the way in which its own subtracted and contracted world signifies only *as itself*, as a world defined by reduction and scarcity. The model doesn't illuminate a more complex totality of lived experience but rather imagines what would transpire were the model to be the totality of lived experience. The implicit question *The Road* poses to its reader is not *What does this simplified model tell us about the more complex and complete world to which it refers?* but rather *What happens when the world itself shrinks to the shape of a model?* That is why readings that interpret the novel's nonspecificity as an invitation to fill in the gaps with the context of 9/11 or the importance of the human imagination miss the point. What the novel allegorizes is a world in which such contextual reference is by definition absent. In order to map this model onto contemporaneous society, we would need to seek out instances in which our daily existence has the same abstracted and pared-down quality of the model, in which the reduction of the model appears in ordinary life. By both evoking and foreclosing social allegory in its conventional form, *The Road* asks us to consider what the world looks like when we understand human behavior only in terms of the present-tense actions of atomized individuals completely detached from social and historical forces.

*   *   *

In live models, the conventions of castaway, survival, and postapocalyptic tales constitute a language for thinking about what is no longer there: social context as a staging ground for human behavior. The other, more obvious shared concern of these modeling genres—their emphasis on self-preservation—provides a means for thinking about what endures, in every sense of the word. Inside these model-shaped worlds, we encounter the same fundamental principles that underwrite the microeconomic imagination. In both discourses, to be alive as a human is to relate to the world through interest. In a fashion that both ratifies and extends its status as a methodological presumption, however, interest *animates* characters in live models. It is both the engine and the expression of their ceaseless becoming as life forms. By taking what is often called the "survival instinct" as their central example of individual interest, live models present interest as a facet of the subject's basic status simultaneously as a biological body with a need to persist and as a conscious agent with the capacity to choose whether and how to maintain life. When this focus on humans as self-preserving agents combines with the process of live modeling I have been describing, two mutually reinforcing forms of live-ness result: the perception of action in one's own best interest as a quality of human life itself and the conspicuously excessive claims to representational immediacy that accompany a model come to life. The aesthetic brutality of the live model arises from this conjoined perception of a transgressive immediacy on the level of form and embodied intensity on the level of content. Or, to put it from the opposite direction, the distinctive generic features of the live model serve to collapse interest and life.

For characters within these live models, endurance operates as the experiential register in which life-interest becomes manifest for subjects of life-interest. As an act of will that is also unwilling, endurance can be understood as a particular form of suffering agency.[12] Whether we are speaking of an athlete's endurance training or a person who has endured a tragedy, the attribution of endurance acknowledges both the draining or difficult nature of an experience and the persistence of the subject in the face of that experience. Even in the form developed by athletes, endurance implies that there is some part of the experience that is unwelcome or some part of the self that would prefer to desist. And even when the painful situation is externally imposed and enforced, endurance suggests some effort expended by the subject in order to be inside that situation. To say that someone endures solitary confinement, for example, is different from saying he or she merely experiences solitary confinement. Endurance indicates our persistence as vectors of conscious will in the face of what is exhausting and dispiriting. Although the second meaning of endurance—enduring as simply continuing to exist—lacks this sense of individual will, the two meanings become inextricably intertwined in the sort of survival situations that feature in live models. When life is threatened by hunger, thirst, and physical injury, we must withstand deprivation and deterioration if we are to survive. Endurance becomes our means and our end, merged in a kind of Möbius of will. When it operates in this self-reinforcing way, the simple fact of our existence comes to appear a register of interest. Interest and life become fused.

127 Hours provides a disturbingly clear account of this operation in its harrowing parable of endurance. In deciding to cut off his arm, Aron endures both the mental anguish of making a horrific choice and the physical agony of enacting that choice. As both enforcer and enforced in carrying through his decision, Aron's choice presents a nightmare version of the inevitable concessions that accompany action in one's own best interest, which always involves choosing one option over another. When the tremendous benefit of one option is only just greater than the huge cost of losing the other, the high stakes involved make clear that costs may still seem unbearable even when the benefit is freely chosen. Yet, as the film's title indicates, Aron's choice also emerges from another feat of endurance: the 127 hours that he spends trapped in the canyon without food and water while contemplating his own swiftly approaching demise. Immobilized and near helpless, Aron is reduced to the most rudimentary elements of bodily experience, which are likewise thrown into relief by the extreme privation of his situation. He not only endures his increasing debilitation but he also merely endures, in the sense of continuing to exist. As his death appears to approach, Aron's ongoing existence comes to seem itself a measure of his commitment to life. By continuing to draw breath, he demonstrates that he is clinging to life, with all the desperate fervor that the phrase suggests. Being alive transforms from a largely backgrounded and involuntary function to a profoundly important feat of individual tenacity.[13] Endurance-as-unwilling-will and endurance-as-existence collapse into each other, with the result that the unfolding of life appears both the content of Aron's interest and its moment-by-moment expression. Aron becomes a vector of life-interest: his interest is in life, and his continued being indexes that interest.

In *The Road*, we can see the full ramifications of this approach to life play out in the range of choices adopted by the postapocalyptic remains of humanity.[14] At one end of this spectrum, we find the conjunction of self-preservation and self-interest in the narrowest sense, in the form of the villainous gangs that threaten the father and son with rape, murder, and cannibalization. In embracing an otherwise unthinkable act in order to survive, the cannibal attests to the extreme hold of life-interest. Although all human nourishment requires consuming biological matter of some sort, cannibalism throws into sharp relief the process of maintaining one organism at the expense of another. When one human eats another human, what is eaten is self-evidently a *life*, a complete and equal being whose former existence now fuels someone else's survival.[15] By ingesting a life in order to stay alive, cannibals enact the Möbius quality of life-interest through consumption rather than endurance. They literalize their life-interest by feeding upon the lives of others. At the other end of the spectrum lies the boy's mother, who chose to end her own life several years before the present-day of the novel. Whereas the father argues that the three of them are survivors, the mother counters that they are merely "the walking dead in a horror film," a form of existence she does not want to continue inhabiting (57). Although she appears to escape from life-interest in choosing death, the mother must pay with her life in order to do so. That is, life is that which hangs in the balance of each choice, even when the choice is to end the life in question. There is no escaping this intersection of life and choice, whatever choice one makes.

The father instead chooses to endure. He makes staying alive his goal because of his commitment to keeping his son alive. As in Aron's situation, however, the father's commitment to life is registered in part through another commitment that it just barely overshadows: in this case, the desire to spare his son pain. The intolerable difficulty of this choice becomes clear when the father and his son are hiding from bandits who seem likely to find them. If they do, the boy will be tortured, enslaved, raped, and likely eaten in the end, and the father debates with himself the devil's choice between his desire to preserve his son's life and his desire to spare him extreme pain: "Can you do it? When the time comes? When the time comes, there will be no time. Now is the time. Curse God and die. What if [the rifle] doesnt [*sic*] fire? Could you crush that beloved skull with a rock? Is there such a being within you of which you know nothing? Can there be?" (120).[16] In contrast to an alien, imported "being within you," the father's drive to keep his son alive is inalienable and intrinsic—but so is his interest in protecting him from suffering. In this moment we are offered an excruciating portrayal of the way in which suffering agency is forged from the apparently unbreakable links between interest and choice and choice and agency. The father's overriding interest in his son's life renders the choice he faces here of riveting urgency and consequence, while the choice itself generates an overwhelming sense of personal responsibility since the outcome will determine the life or death of his son. At the same time, if the only escape from these choices would be for the father not to have an interest in his son's continued existence, then this is a solution that is difficult to imagine encouraging or endorsing. As a stranger that the man and boy meet on the road puts it, "Nobody wants to be here and nobody wants to leave" (180). The father's predicament thus suggests one of the most harrowing aspects of interest: it can serve abhorrent choices that we cannot even find it in ourselves to wish away.

By making the father's commitment to keep his son alive its primary measure of endurance, *The Road* suggests the way in which even otherdirected attachments can become expressed in and as life-interest. A father's inability to bear the sight of his child in pain or to take his child's life is the most natural thing in the world—but, as this extreme scenario makes clear, that doesn't mean it is also in the child's own best interest. Because the father's interest in protecting his son is set loose in a world so dangerous as to be almost uninhabitable, his interest becomes amplified at the same time and for exactly the same reason that its benefits become increasingly dubious. Just as it is clear that the father's interest in his son is inalienable, it is also clear that "if he is a good father, it might well be as [the mother said]," and death might be the better choice for them both (27). When we are confronted with a situation in which the parent's drive to protect the child no longer necessarily benefits the child, we see it for what it is: the *parent's* interest in the child's life. Because the protective impulses of parents are so celebrated and naturalized, this revelation reads less as an indictment of the father for selfishness than it does as an indication of the way in which even the most positive of actions inevitably emerges from the subject's negotiation of his or her own interests. In another self-reinforcing experience of life-interest, the father's commitment to his son's life arises from his own interest in escaping the pain of seeing his son die—a commitment that requires that the father preserve his own life as well. Not only is the father's commitment to his son an expression of his own interests but also that interest is expressed through an agonized attempt to survive. As this attachment propels the father down the titular road in the apparent absence of all hope of improvement in his lot, the forward momentum of the characters and the narrative itself appears as an expression of life-interest as a propulsive force.

The Road erects a bulwark against this overwhelming force through its characterization of the boy. Given the chance, we learn, the boy would seek out strangers and share his food with them, despite the fact that doing so seems likely lead to his own death either through starvation or through violent attack. The novel sanctifies this aspect of the boy's character through the father's recourse to hyperbolic religious imagery—for example, when the father describes the boy's blond head as a "golden chalice, good to house a god" (78, 183). Yet, read outside the father's narrow perspective, the boy's interest becomes legible as a commitment to another form of life—that is, the continuance of humans as a species. When the boy asks his father if there might be people alive on another planet somewhere and the answer is negative, the boy responds by saying, "I dont know what we're doing" (26, 1). For the boy, there is no point in surviving simply as an individual life if humanity itself is dying out. The boy's desire to trust and care for others is inseparable from his desire for people—rather than just his solitary loved one—to survive, and he is willing to risk his own life to advance that possibility.

Understood this way, the boy's choice is not at all uninterested in life; rather, it completes the set of logical permutations to which life-interest is subject in *The Road*. On the one hand, one can opt for violence against life to suit one's own narrowly selfish purposes. The cannibals take others' lives to save their own, and the mother takes her own life in order to die. Both of these choices involve direct destruction of life for reasons that are self-interested in the usual sense, but one results in prolonged life for the choosing agent and the other in death for that agent. On the other hand, one can opt to preserve the lives of others at cost to one's self. In this pairing, we have the father's agonized attempt to stay alive to save his son, and the son's willingness to sacrifice himself to preserve the lives of strangers. Both of these choices are focused on the survival of others, but the former requires prolonging the life of the choosing agent while the latter requires accepting the death of that agent. This conceptual symmetry demonstrates the way in which the boy's choice participates just as fully in the logic of life-interest as those of the adults around him. Like them, he can only attain his chosen benefit by putting his very existence as a living being in the service of that choice. Whether the subject chooses survival for himself or not, human life functions as the currency in which all costs are paid and benefits banked. In a fashion that exceeds the conflation of interest with self-preservation, human life itself—sheer continued existence or its lack—operates in *The Road* as the medium through which interest is identified and enacted.

Because the boy is not an adult, however, the nature of his choice remains effectively—rather than categorically—distinguished from the interested actions that surround him. For the vast majority of the narrative, the father hallows yet forestalls the boy's interest in fostering the lives of others by overruling almost all the boy's attempts to share food or other resources. When the boy thinks he sees another boy he wants to help, for instance, the father insists there is no other boy and drags his sobbing, protesting son away—an image of frustrated child will evident in any toy store. If the boy were instead allowed to enact his decision to care for the lives of others, this decision would become legible as yet another manifestation of life-interest. We would see the boy choose to bear the cost required to gain his intended benefit, just as everyone else around him does, and we could see that this cost is measured in the currency of life itself, just as it is for everyone else. Were the son to enact his own rational allocative decision in this way, in other words, we would recognize that he too chooses in his own best interest; his interest just happens to be in the preservation of strangers' lives. Until its final pages, *The Road* forecloses this recognition through the boy's status as a child whose will can easily be thwarted by his bigger and stronger father, who thereby forcibly prevents the boy from occupying the position of suffering agent. Because it remains mere potentiality, the boy's chosen option can thus be preserved as a seemingly sanctified escape from the dynamic of life-interest, an idealized moral high ground from which we are encouraged to judge the interested actions of the other characters.

Near the novel's conclusion, this cordon around the boy's interests abruptly dissolves, and he is forced to make a life-or-death choice based on his assessment of the available options. After the father succumbs to his long-endured illness, the boy is left alone with the body and his father's final, seemingly self-canceling instructions: "You need to find the good guys but you cant take any chances" (297–98). As the novel has proven repeatedly, not taking chances effectively means you can't get close enough to anyone to find out if they are good or not, and the number of people who are dangerous means that not taking chances is the wiser course. But precisely because of that very danger, the father's advice also makes sense. Given how predatory and merciless other people are in this world, the boy will not survive without some good guys to protect him. When a strange man approaches the boy and invites him to join the man's family, their conversation makes clear that, in this moment, the boy has no option but to make a choice from these seemingly impossible options since even not responding would be a consequential choice in itself:

You got two choices here. . . . You can stay here with your papa and die or you can go with me. If you stay you need to keep out of the road. I dont know how you made it this far. But you should go with me. You'll be all right.

How do I know you're one of the good guys?

You dont. You'll have to take a shot. (303)

In a reversal of all that's come before in the text, it turns out that we needn't fear that the boy's desire to trust will be the death of him because contextual clues have already suggested that the man is honorable. Described as a "veteran of old skirmishes" who carries "a shotgun upside down over his shoulder" and wears "a nylon bandolier filled with shells for the gun," this capable man clearly could have shot the boy from a distance or grabbed the boy's gun if he meant him harm (301). In fact, the most frightening possibility dangled over the reader seems to be that the boy won't trust the man and will therefore lose his one chance at gaining a new protector. Whereas until this moment *The Road* dramatizes life-interest as necessitating choices that are both appalling and freely enacted on one's own behalf, the boy's abrupt emergence as an agent seems to belie this necessity.

We might read this ending as suggesting that it would have been better to follow the boy's preferred path all along, a reading made easier to adopt now that the father's focalizing consciousness has been removed. Certainly the father's distrust is presented as so extreme—he even finds a blind, decrepit old man a potential threat—that the reader's sympathy is usually with the boy when the two struggle over who and how much to trust. But the convenient appearance of this kindly warrior does not so much prove the boy right as deny the logic of interest that the novel has assembled in such relentless detail. On page after page, *The Road* demonstrates with searing and even sadistic clarity that interest is a trap. Whether you opt for self-preservation out of self-interest (the cannibals), reject self-preservation out of self-interest (the mother), opt for self-preservation out of interest in another (the father), or reject self-preservation out of interest in others (the boy), the choices are suffering, death, or both in that order. Only by preventing the boy from achieving agency does the novel protect his choice from becoming hostage to this logic. If the point of this ending is to suggest the boy's chosen path through this dilemma was the right one all along, we would need to see him take exactly the risk to trust that is his forestalled choice throughout the novel, and we would be encouraged to view this choice as worth its potential price, whatever the outcome. Instead, because we as readers already know the boy should trust the man, there is no threat on the table and no potential cost to be borne. Rather than suggesting that trusting was worth its risk, as the boy consistently implied, the novel contravenes its own logic in order to insist there wasn't any risk in the first place; contrary to everything the novel insists about the inexorable trade-offs of life-interest, the boy's choice turns out to be all benefit and no cost. If the novel's denial of its own premises arguably represents a failure of nerve, it's also a remarkable instance of form following content: the novel seems unable to let go of its own interest in keeping the boy alive.

In this sudden and willed rejection of the logic it has otherwise made so watertight, *The Road* gestures toward its own status as a form of fictional hypothesis. That is, by abruptly setting aside its own rules, the novel reminds us that it can do so because it has put them into play in the form of one imagined future. This reminder of the novel's status as hypothetical conjecture pushes back against the sense of life-interest as an intrinsic and ineradicable feature of human existence. Although *The Road* brings life-interest to the fore as the defining feature of its world, it thus also demonstrates that it is only in a very specific possible world that its extreme zero-sum dynamics can be seen to prevail so completely. As I have argued, the gray, voided-out existence of *The Road* operates as a live model, with all details stripped away until only the bare dynamics of interest, choice, and action remain. But this model turns out to be profoundly unnatural, in the sense that it only comes into being after the destruction of plants, animals, and the larger environment.[17] It's as if the human characters in *The Road* have been imported into the sere register of mathematical formula itself, brought to play out their interests in a landscape whose defining feature is its extreme sterility. By conflating the exposure of life-interest with the destruction of life on the planet, *The Road* implies that there is something manufactured, aberrant, and abhorrent about a world in which human life is understood as a vector of interest, however intrinsic interest itself may be. When it puts life-interest into play in this deathly and pointedly hypothetical realm, *The Road* both acknowledges the living quality of interest and asks us to consider whether that live-ness is enough to justify the sort of revolting and lethal world that results when life-interest holds sway.

The novel suggests its own answer to this question by bookending its hypothetical world with two other models, both of which offer alternate ways of understanding the relationship between endurance and life itself. In the opening paragraph, the father wakes from a nightmare about a horrific life form, which provides the novel with its first images. The passage is worth quoting at length, as the cumulative effect of its details is notably unpleasant:

In the dream from which he'd wakened he had wandered in a cave where the child led him by the hand. Their light playing over the wet flowstone walls. Like pilgrims in a fable swallowed up and lost among the inward parts of some granitic beast. Deep stone flues where the water dripped and sang. Tolling in the silence the minutes of the earth and the hours and the days of it and the years without cease. Until they stood in a great stone room where lay a black and ancient lake. And on the far shore a creature that raised its dripping mouth from the rimstone pool and stared into the light with eyes dead white and sightless as the eggs of spiders. It swung its head low over the water as if to take the scent of what it could not see. Crouching there pale and naked and translucent, its alabaster bones cast up in shadow on the rocks behind it. Its bowels, its beating heart. The brain that pulsed in a dull glass bell. It swung its head from side to side and then gave out a low moan and turned and lurched away and loped soundlessly into the dark. (1–2)

Sightless fish are the classic example of evolutionary adaptation to deprivation and, given that humans are the only living creatures remaining in
The Road, this horrifying creature appears to suggest the monstrous quality of human adaptation to the world of utter deprivation they now inhabit.
The journey of the man and child within the cave invokes and amplifies
their wanderings through the austere, comfortless world outside, while the
glass bell in which the creature's brain pulses foreshadows the "cakebell"
they see later in a diner, which houses a decapitated human head (195). If
this cave and this sightless creature represents human nature laid bare by
a world of life-interest, then it is the result of a mutation of life that is literally nightmarish. Those who argue that acting in one's own best interest is
simply a fact of human life, in other words, are invited to consider that
there are many things that are technically part of the world of organic being
that we consider with distaste.

The novel's final sentences provide the counterweight to this vision.
Whereas the mutant animal appears in the father's dream and is an expression of his character's consciousness, this final passage is focalized instead
through an external narrator who seems to have stepped outside the live
model to remember and recount a previous reality. Instead of a sightless
"creature" in a dark, barren cave, we find a lush, verdant image of ordinary
brook trout and the infinitely complex and essentially mysterious natural
world they inhabit.

Once there were brook trout in the streams in the mountains. You could see them
standing in the amber current where the white edges of their fins wimpled softly
in the flow. They smelled of moss in your hand. Polished and muscular and torsional. On their backs were vermiculate patterns that were maps of the world in its
becoming. Maps and mazes. Of a thing which could not be put back. Not be made
right again. In the deep glens where they lived all things were older than man and
they hummed of mystery. (306–7)

The bleak, blank landscape of *The Road*'s possible future is replaced here
with vivid, shifting, kinetic forms whose relation to their habitat is rhizomatic rather than linear. The moving parts of this world resonate and relate
in a fashion that exceeds the basic cause-and-effect logic of human life-
interest as well as the time of human habitation on earth. Were we to imagine
human agency as an expression of living being as it is configured in this

image, human life-interest would appear as only one insignificant and fleeting element within the dazzling, incomprehensible intricacy that constitutes the interwoven strands of the biosphere. Here, maps refer not to a miniaturized completeness but rather to a world that is always changing and even unknowable: a map that attests to an essential unmappability. Given the past tense of this passage, humans' only notable form of agency in the context of this vital world would seem to be the danger that we will destroy it, thereby bringing about the gruesome rule of human interest that the novel hypothesizes. Yet, the alternative that *The Road* reinstates here is also a form of life itself; we might even say it is *the* form of life itself. Rather than returning us to the complexity of social forces, in other words, *The Road* displaces human life-interest in favor of a vision of life writ large, which endures without the benefit or blight of human agency. If life for humans can only be interested life, the novel suggests, then the only counter from interest may rest with life that is not human.

As this reading of *The Road* begins to suggest, nonhuman forms of life themselves appear to offer an alternative to life-interest as a defining feature of living being. However, in *The Road* the operation of human life-interest is replaced by a vision of life in which humans are not included. In the castaway novel *Life of Pi*, we see what transpires when a work attempts to imagine human life purged of the problem of life-interest. Unlike *The Road*, *Life of Pi* lodges its account of interest in a marginal section of the text and concentrates the bulk of its attention on alternative configurations of choice, embodiment, and survival. *Life of Pi* deploys and reconfigures the key terms of life-interest—consciousness and human life—in a series of contrasting live models whose relationship is best described as dialectical: two opposing models achieve synthesis in a third, which recombines the key terms of the first two in such a way that human choice is purged of its compulsive and unwelcome quality.[18] We can only circumnavigate suffering agency, *Life of Pi* suggests, if we can locate and harness expressions of embodied being considered as elemental, unmediated, and asocial as life-interest.[19]

Life of Pi performs this dialectical operation by creating three live models that focus on different forms of life: human, animal, and plant. Each of these models asks us to understand human life, as embodied in the eponymous hero, Pi, as a form with characteristics distinct from other species. That is, the novel is specifically concerned with the *life* of Pi, understood not as biographical narrative but as biological being. The animal-focused account, which occupies the vast majority of the novel, is a castaway story concerning the months Pi spends trapped on a twenty-foot raft with a Bengal tiger named Richard Parker. As Pi puts it, "to be a castaway is to be a point perpetually at the centre of a circle. However much things may appear to change—the sea may shift from whisper to rage, the sky might go from fresh blue to blinding white to darkest black—the geometry never changes. Your gaze is always a radius."[20] In this vastly simplified, geometric world, Pi recognizes in himself "a fierce will to live," and survival becomes his sole, overriding motivation (148). This minimalist stage is set, in other words, for an exploration of life-interest as a compulsion that sustains human existence against all odds and costs. As Pi puts it, "Life on a lifeboat ... [is] like an endless game in chess, a game with few pieces. The elements couldn't be more simple, nor the stakes higher" (217).

Pi finds himself in this situation through a turn of events that is simultaneously dire and fanciful—a combination that constitutes the signature style of the novel. Its founding conceit is that its author-narrator is merely recounting a tale he was told by Pi himself, after the author is told by someone in India that Pi's story "will make you believe in God" (xii). Once the author and Pi meet back in the author-narrator's native Canada, this frame narrative gives way to Pi's own tale, which in part 1 recounts his childhood before his family left India, where his father owned a zoo. When the family later immigrates to Canada, the steamship on which they are traveling sinks and fourteen-year-old Pi becomes trapped on a life raft. Several animals from the zoo are also on board the ship, and through various circumstances some of them come to share Pi's raft. These animals originally include a hyena, a zebra, an orangutan, and a Bengal tiger named Richard Parker, but within the first few days on the raft, the hyena dispatches the zebra and the orangutan, the tiger eats the hyena, and Pi is left alone with the tiger. In part 2—which occupies the vast majority of the novel—Pi recounts how, with luck, industry, and faith, he managed to survive for almost a year on a raft with little food, little water, and a ravenous tiger.

There is a twist, however. The novel recounts a second and very different version of these events in part 3, a very brief concluding section. Unlike the first-person narrative of the remainder of the novel, part 3 takes the form of a transcribed and translated interview with Pi conducted by two

Japanese representatives of the insurance firm that provided coverage for the sunken ship. After the businessmen refuse to accept the more whimsical tale of Pi and the tiger, Pi reluctantly offers an alternative account: a hair-raising, seven-page retelling of all of the events on the raft but with the animal characters replaced by humans, one of whom is Pi's mother. Although we may feel for the animals as they suffer their injuries and attack one another, the effect on the reader is much different when it is Pi's mother rather than a kindly female orangutan that is killed in front of him. This shift is particularly evident when it comes to the role of choice in the human version of the tale. In the first version, for example, the hyena consumes the dying zebra's leg, while in the second, the ship's cook cuts off the leg of a wounded sailor purportedly to save his life. Later he lets slip that he actually wanted the leg for fish bait, and, when the sailor finally dies, the cook skins, chops up, and partly consumes him.

By making the reader suddenly shift between these two competing models, one animal, the other human, *Life of Pi* directs our attention to that which makes them so different in their effects and affects. Although the hyena's actions are revolting—at one point it pushes its head into the belly of the still-living zebra to eat its organs—they are not perceived as the result of human will in the way that the cook's are. The disgusting nature of the cook's act and the sudden switch from animal to human actor throws into startling relief the distinction between an animal's survival instinct and a human's life-interest. We recoil from the cook in a way we do not from the hyena because the cook could have decided that his need for fish bait did not merit sawing off a living man's leg. At issue here is not simply the cook's choice, since choices may be made at random or enacted with indifference, but that his choice emerges specifically from a commitment to what he believes to be in his interest—a fact that is underlined when his true, selfish motivation is suddenly revealed. In the fashion of the microeconomic imagination as I have defined it, we read the cook's actions as emerging from a process of evaluating and ranking alternatives in order to decide which option he prefers. We project interest into the gap between option and action. When the cook saws at the sailor's leg as the sailor screams in agony, the intensity of the cook's interest is made manifest in the shocking extremity of the act it propels. The very quality that is presumed in the microeconomic imagination of interest, the ability to evaluate one's options for oneself, here produces something far more awful than fear and despair, hunger and thirst, which characterize the simple deprivation at work in the animal version. The distressing nature of this account is simultaneously underscored and displaced by the sheer bulk of pages the novel devotes to the animal version.

In offering readers the animal version, however, the novel ultimately does not undermine hierarchies of life that depend upon human agency. Rather, it seeks a way to preserve those hierarchies despite the destabilizing force of life-interest—to find a way to resurrect human agency as a prize rather than a punishment.[21] We can see this effort, for example, when Pi comes upon what he thinks is an island, a mass densely covered with algae-like plants, trees, and thousands of meerkats. The plants provide food and water for Pi, while the meerkats are devoured by the dozen by the tiger, Richard Parker. However, after inhabiting the island for some days, Pi comes to realize that what he thought was a tiny land mass with a "stripped down ecology" is in fact a single, carnivorous, floating plant. Pi makes this discovery when he finds a human molar in the fruit of one of the trees and realizes that the island has consumed a person who previously took shelter there. Rather than being an ecosystem made of parts with varying, inter-active degrees and forms of live-ness—animal, vegetable, and mineral—the island turns out to be itself a single living being that consumes other lives, even those of humans, to survive. Just as in *The Road* sightless fish were evoked as a classic form of adaptation to deprivation, the carnivorous plant here serves as a prototypical example of natural activity that nevertheless strikes us as unnaturally active. Pi's horror at this discovery arises in part from the uncanny nature of the island. Like a zombie or a Ouija board, the island displays a capacity for life and action where there should be none.[22] Crucially, unlike the examples most commonly associated with the uncanny, the island's creepy quality arises from its status as a natural rather than supernatural form of life. Pi flees from the island in terror and revulsion because it turns out to be a single biological entity, more alive and especially more actively engaged in self-preservation than it seems tolerable for it to be.[23] Although the revelation of this unsettling truth gestures toward Pi's horror at his own unavoidable drive for life, this resemblance rests on the presentation of the island as uncanny, which in turn requires and sustains the view that some entities should be agential and active while others should be inert and passive. Rather than life-interest prompting a positive recognition of the nonhuman living or animate world, the uncanny wrongness of the island as self-preserving entity is invoked to underline the wrongness of life-interest. In effect, the novel puts its energy toward redrawing the lines that distinguished the liberal individual from other lives, even as this very attempt cannot help but register the damage life-interest does to those lines in the first place.

Most of this energy manifests itself in the animal version of the tale, which attempts to cancel out both the unthinking attachment to life found in the plant version and the suffering agency that defines the human version. However, as with the island interlude, the animal tale functions not to undermine human distinctiveness but to reinstate agency as a measure of that distinctiveness—as the guarantor of humanity's place atop the hierarchy of life. In order to strip the animal version of the sense of dire threat that accompanies the other two models, the novel relies heavily on its characterization of Pi. Focalized through Pi's child perspective, subject to his supposedly non-Western interpretations and delivered in his correct but charmingly mannered English, the events in the animal version appear in the guise of the amusing exotic—unusual and offbeat despite their threat to Pi. When Pi lists everything he finds on the boat, his accounting demonstrates the way in which confinement with two predatory animals becomes a fanciful image of mismatched elements whose charm is more noticeable than its danger:

- 1 boy with a complete set of light clothing but for one lost shoe
- 1 spotted hyena
- 1 Bengal tiger
- 1 lifeboat
- 1 ocean
- 1 God (146; bullets in original)

The numbering of items usually encountered in the singular (1 ocean, 1 God), along with inclusion of Pi himself on the list, evokes the model's signature dynamic of miniaturization—as if Pi's raft were a toy-sized world viewed from above. Pi's list repurposes the modeling function of the castaway tale to convert the profound peril of his predicament and the sublime scale of his environment into something contained and even cute. As in the novel's signature image of a boy and a tiger sharing a lifeboat, such strategies replace the grim realism of the human model and the uncanny threat of the plant model with the promise of strange but ultimately benign wonders, delivered in a tone of Orientalist whimsy.

Within this little world of charming incongruity, the novel creates a potent synthesis of the conscious will that defines the human model and the unconscious attachment to life that defines the plant model. It does so by bringing together human consciousness and animal instinct in the pairing of Pi and Richard Parker. In the animal version, Richard Parker does the things that Pi most regrets doing in the human story, primarily killing the cook and eating his organs. But, unlike the other human characters, Pi appears in his human form in both versions of the tale, so Richard Parker doesn't function as his stand-in as much as his annex, into which Pi shunts all his own compulsive attachment to life. This distinction between animal instinct and human choice is reinforced by the training plot that occupies much of the animal tale. Trapped on a small boat with a soon-to-be-starving Bengal tiger, Pi decides his only hope of survival is to put in place the techniques he learned at his father's zoo to establish dominance over an animal. Richard Parker is seasick, hungry, and thirsty, so Pi uses these states to construct effective rewards and punishments that will keep Richard Parker's activities within certain bounds. In other words, Pi creates a rational system of incentives and disincentives that allow him to affect Richard Parker's behavior based on the tiger's already existing desires for stability, food, and water. In so doing, *Life of Pi* creates a seemingly universal and inevitable link between the possession of human consciousness and mastery through, rather than mastery by, an inborn drive for life. As Pi puts it, "when [Richard Parker] looked beyond the gunnel, he saw no jungle that he could hunt in and no river from which he could drink freely. Yet I brought him food and I brought him fresh water. My agency was pure and miraculous. It conferred power upon me. Proof: I remained alive day after day, week after week" (223). This vision of human survival as arising from "pure and miraculous" agency precisely counters the grim vision of humans driven by the life force of interest offered in the second, darker version of the tale.

While zoology assigns the compulsive element of interest to animals, religion takes care of the burden of autonomous action. As an adult, Pi double-majors in zoology and religious studies at a Canadian university and declares that, rather than finding them difficult to combine, he often mixes up his majors. Pi implies what is at stake in the connection in his defense of zoos: "I know zoos are no longer in people's good graces. Religion faces the same problem. Certain illusions about freedom plague them both" (19). In terms of zoos, these illusions arise because "misinformed people think animals in the wild are 'happy' because they are 'free'" (15). This is untrue, Pi argues, both because animals in the wild are not free—they are governed by territorial boundaries and other inflexible instincts—and because we fail to understand that freedom may simply be another word for dispossession:

If you went to a home, kicked down the front door, chased the people who lived there out onto the street and said, "Go! You are free! Free as a bird! Go! Go!"—do you think they would shout and dance for joy? They wouldn't. Birds are not free. The people you've just evicted would sputter, "With what right do you throw us out? This is our home. We own it. We have lived here for years. We're calling the police, you scoundrel." (17)

Just as birds are not free in the wild, they are not imprisoned in zoos—at least not any more than we humans are imprisoned in our homes. As Pi puts it, "Would you rather be put up at the Ritz with free room service and unlimited access to a doctor or be homeless without a soul to care for you? But animals are incapable of such discernment" (18). In other words, Pi suggests that human beings, who are capable of such discernment, will tend to use their capacity for choice to opt for comfort and care over dispossession and lack of protection. If the illusion regarding zoos is that they keep animals from freedom in the wild (when in fact this freedom is neither attainable nor preferable), then the parallel illusion regarding religion is that it robs humans of a freedom that is in reality both unavailable and unwelcome. In Pi's version of religion, the world is a human zoo we choose to inhabit, and God is the zookeeper who protects us from having a distressing and pointless amount of freedom.

Through its fanciful combination of zoology and religion, tigers and training, *Life of Pi* replaces life-interest with a model of survival that is at once miraculously agential and comfortingly constricted. Although this version is clearly an invention, the novel uses this very imaginary status to suggest that we should choose the animal version nevertheless. In the concluding pages of the novel, the Japanese insurance agents try to get Pi to confirm which of the stories, human or animal, is actually true. Given that neither version will affect the insurance claim that they have come to investigate, Pi insists that they must simply choose "which story [they] prefer" (317). When the interviewers choose the animal tale, Pi responds, "And so it goes with God" (317). Just as we should choose the animal version because it is "the better story," we should choose to believe in God because religion offers us a better account of the world (317). Pi's story will in fact "make you believe in God"—not because it provides evidence of his existence but because it makes clear how awful the alternative is. But choosing religion, as Pi describes the process, is a decision that aims to retroactively negate the very power that enabled it. Pi advocates that we use our freedom to choose in order to choose to be less free—more or less the definition of bad faith.

This bad faith plays out on the level of form in the novel's seeming enactment of postmodern narrative heterogeneity. By including two plausible and complete stories regarding Pi's survival as a life form, the novel appears to adopt a postmodern view of competing historical narratives.[24] *Life of Pi* declares its allegiance with this perspective when Pi gives his baffled interviewers what amounts to a brief lesson on the postmodern approach to language and story. "Isn't telling about something—using words, English or Japanese—already something of an invention? . . . The world isn't just the way it is. It is how we understand it, no? And in understanding something, we bring something to it, no? Doesn't that make life a story?" (302). When the businessmen insist that they "want words that reflect reality" instead, it is clear that the reader should prefer Pi's defense of imagination and invention to the shortsighted realism of the businessmen (302). Yet *Life of Pi* invokes this postmodern insight only to turn it inside out. Instead of presenting both of Pi's stories as making powerful and competing claims on the real, *Life of Pi* clearly designates the human version of Pi's life as the true account of events. In fact, it is only because Pi's preferred story does operate as a willed revision of the reality of his experience that it can be presented as such a profound and worthy act of imagination to the reader. And once we understand external reality to exist separately from narratives that either mask or tell the truth about that reality, the aesthetic question regarding which story one prefers is robbed of the world-shaping consequences assigned to narrative in postmodern aesthetics; instead, narrative becomes epiphenomenal, detached from the alternate plane on which actual events unfold. Rather than competing narratives producing competing realities, there is the truth and the feats of imagination through which we manage that truth—and once different stories have no effect on what actually took place, one is free to choose the "better story" as Pi invites the insurance men to do.

In creating this particular choice, *Life of Pi* attempts to foreclose the insight that the creative power of Pi's own imagination can be as interested as anything else. Once we are comparing Pi's whimsical tale to the narrowly self-serving, bottom-line concerns of the corporate world, the expressly motivated nature of the businessmen's insistence on truth makes Pi's act of imagination appear by contrast unmotivated. Consigning the choice to the businessmen redirects our attention from the revelation at the heart of this brief concluding section, which is that the story we have been reading is one that Pi made up in place of the truth. When we encounter the grisly human version at the same time that we realize that we have spent two hundred pages reading an invented animal tale, the suggestion is that Pi has preferred to use his imagination rather than engaging with the facts we have just learned. Just as the concept of the better story implies, Pi has chosen the story that best suits him. This motivation is never spoken in the text but rather—as interest does in the microeconomic imagination writ large—supplies the implicit reasoning that makes seemingly contradictory data cohere. Only by understanding why Pi would prefer the animal tale to the truth can we understand why both appear in the novel. Instead of imagination being outside of interest, it is the interested nature of Pi's storytelling that reconciles the two tales and makes the novel whole. As a means by which Pi endures what he has experienced, imagination becomes another expression of life-interest.

Because live models deliberately excise social context, they can appear detached even from more broadly conceived notions of the political. Yet the vision of the subject of life-interest that I have been tracing in these texts transgresses the boundaries that usually organize political subjectivity as incarnated in the liberal individual. In contrast to forms of rule that exploit the distinction between personhood and sheer existence, interest fuses the capacity for agential action with our status as mere living beings. And once our status as living humans guarantees that we are actors in our own interests whether we like it or not, it is no longer feasible to condemn as nonpersons those who fail to achieve agency nor to assume that those who are agents will necessarily also be recognized as full persons. As *Life of Pi* and *The Road* indicate, live models continue to rely on hierarchies of life— human/animal, male/female, adult/child, Western/non-Western—but they deploy these hierarchies differently. Rather than the capacity for agency being used to distinguish between valued and less valued life forms, the values assigned to different forms of life serve to foreground acceptable forms of agential action and to displace the experience of suffering agency. In *The Road*, for example, the relative powerlessness and perceived innocence of the child subject become a way to prevent benevolence from being read as yet another form of interest, while in *Life of Pi* the instinctive behavior of a starving animal covers over the torturous forms of responsibility that can accompany human acts of self-preservation.

In order to indicate in an initial way some of the consequences of this reorientation of the hierarchy of life, I want to conclude by considering it in relation to a distinction among life forms that has had particular critical and cultural prominence in the twenty-first century: that between those encouraged to live and those abandoned to death.[25] If, as *The Road* suggests, the native home of the subject of life-interest is a landscape as deathly as any to which devalued humans are assigned in the present, then how are we to conceive the relationship between these divisions and the perception of interest as an omnipresent force of life itself? What happens to the biopolitical distinction between the political subject and the mere life form if the most crucial aspect of our subjecthood emerges directly from our status as a living being—and appears most clearly when our lives are under threat? By answering this question, I begin to suggest some of the ways that the thinking contained in live models shifts our understanding of the relationships among agency, personhood, and living being.

Because Hurricane Katrina is the event that most forcefully brought the designation of lives left to die in the United States into mainstream consciousness and debate, I will consider these questions in relation to the cultural engagement with the aftermath of the storm in the hugely popular television series *House*. The episode in question, titled "Who's Your Daddy?" (2005), focuses on a sixteen-year-old African American girl who experiences bizarre medical symptoms after surviving Hurricane Katrina.[26] In general, *House* offers an extended paean to interest-based analyses in the form of its hero, the brilliant diagnostician Dr. Gregory House. House routinely argues that people always act in their own interests and that human behavior can be accurately predicted based on this fact—and his own reliably scandalous activities constitute a veritable personification of this maxim. A leg injury associates him with that most direct of interests, physical pain, while his shameless addiction to painkillers enacts the axiom that every individual has the right to pursue his or her own interests, provided no one else is harmed. House's other major interest, diagnosing unusual medical illnesses, gives this characterization a markedly utopian cast. Fortuitously, House's consuming and narrowly self-interested desire to solve puzzles just happens to save lives, such that his maniacal pursuit of individual interest results in benefits to all.[27]

In his tormented physicality and mastery of medical puzzles, House himself incarnates the combination of extreme embodiment and theoretical abstraction that characterizes the microeconomic mode. Although the medical case shares some formal features with modeling genres, particularly their paradoxical combination of the exemplary and the exceptional, the cases in *House* ordinarily do not share the live model's excision of social context. Instead, House's cases typically reorient our sense of contemporaneous social issues by highlighting the hidden importance of interest within them. "Who's Your Daddy?" continues this approach for part of its narrative by highlighting seemingly hidden dynamics of interest involved in the aftermath of Hurricane Katrina. The episode features an old friend of House's from college, Crandall, and Leona, a sixteen-year-old Katrina survivor who lost her mother in the storm and claims that Crandall is her father. Crandall, who is white, had an affair with Leona's African American mother while he was writing a book about Leona's grandfather, a famous jazz pianist. He accepts Leona's claim and brings her to House for treatment after she suffers from hallucinations and a heart attack on their flight out of New Orleans. House, knowing his friend for an easy mark, immediately decides that Leona is scamming Crandall and that he will prove she is not Crandall's daughter and diagnose her illness at the same time. On one level, this plot line offers a straightforward if revolting national allegory: Leona represents the destitute Hurricane Katrina survivors, desperate for assistance after the storm, while Crandall represents the decent if overly gullible American public, who allow themselves to be conned into thinking that it is somehow their responsibility to provide this help and are thereby positioned (as House puts it) as the "Katrina victim victim[s]."

In the transposition of the word "victim" from a poor African American woman to a middle-class white man who is providing assistance to her, we can hear echoes of the infamous "welfare queen" rhetoric of the 1980s, which positioned white, middle-class Americans as the victims of scheming African American women who bilked the system at the expense of hardworking white people; in both cases, the oppressed are transformed into the aggressors against the white middle class, who appropriate the mantle of innocent victim for themselves. Yet, as House's phrasing implies, Leona retains her own "victim" status to an extent that sharply distinguishes her from the imagined welfare queens of Reaganite lore. Rather than suggesting that she is overplaying her suffering, House's medical team describes Leona as having been "stuck in hell" because "New Orleans was a third world country." The hellish nature of her experiences is ratified for the viewer via Leona's harrowing hallucinations of the storm, and we ultimately learn that it was an infection related to the storm that has caused her illness. Unlike conservative news reportage of the period, the episode never blames Leona for her supposed decision to stay in the city in a fashion that would raise doubts about her status as a self-responsibilized subject, nor does it imply that she disdained other, more ethical or arduous means of self-support in favor of latching on to Crandall. Instead, "Who's Your Daddy?" takes a very different and ultimately more disturbing approach. The episode suggests that Leona was in fact "in hell," that Crandall was her only way out of hell, and that only an irrational individual would not find it in her own best interest to escape hell—but still argues that she is alien and repulsive. Rather than criticizing Leona as failing to function as a responsible citizen, the episode positions her bid for survival as a logical outcome of action in one's own best interest but then reviles her nonetheless.

Obviously, this is an oddly laborious and self-contradictory way to go about vilifying Hurricane Katrina survivors, particularly when the tools for painting them as inadequate citizens are so ready at hand. However, this approach makes sense if we view maligning survivors as a by-product or side benefit of a more overarching narrative project: differentiating the logic of interest from the desperate, chaotic struggle for survival in New

Orleans after the levees broke. While Leona's experiences are presented as unfolding in a space conceptually and materially distinct from those occupied by House and his team, these very circumstances mean that she is driven to take hugely significant action on her own behalf. When Crandall asks House how he can doubt Leona with "what she's been through," for example, House interrupts him to say that it is "because of what she's been through" that he doubts her, in particular "because she's still alive." As in the *SuperFreakonomics* analysis with which I began this chapter, House can interpret Leona's behavior by applying the assumption of interest to her situation. Given the deathly nature of post-Katrina New Orleans—"what she's been through"—the fact that she survived is evidence that she is profoundly committed to acting in her own best interest; if she hadn't been so determined to survive, she wouldn't have managed to do so. The very consignment to death that would seem to mark Leona as a nonsubject instead reveals her capacity for acting in the interest of life itself—that is, the form of interest that is equated with humanity in the microeconomic mode. Leona might not meet the standards of liberal personhood, but she meets those of the subject of life-interest perfectly. And that is the threat her survival poses: if the capacity for action in one's own best interest crosses the boundary between valued and devalued human life—if every conscious human is equally a subject of life-interest—then House's association with life-saving, rational action cannot be relied upon to elevate him or his ilk in distinction to those humans classed as disposable. Not only is he no better than Leona; in terms of life-interest, he is no different. He lives by the same principles according to which she saved her own life. Casting Leona as irresponsible would only disavow rather than refute the possibility she embodies: once humans are defined as subjects of life-interest, the distinction between the white man and his others is only a matter of context, not kind.

In order to refute this possibility, House cannot simply rely on Leona's racial difference as a means of vilifying her action since the ability of life-interest to cross such hierarchies of life is precisely the problem. Nor can the episode simply present Leona's actions as unethical, since House has proven in countless episodes that it can be supremely rational to set conventional morality aside in order to get what one wants, especially when life itself is at stake. Instead, the episode transforms Leona's life-interest from a disturbing incarnation of agency into a means by which she can be controlled. Initially, her most notable symptoms are gruesome hallucinations of post-Katrina New Orleans that erupt into her present surroundings. In the first scene, for example, a tidal wave of filthy water swamps her while she is sitting with Crandall on an airplane, but we quickly realize the flood has happened only in Leona's mind. By instantiating a single-occupant "reality" that is at once fiercely motivating and intensely individual, Leona's hallucinations of the storm both acknowledge the necessity of her life-interest and depict it as a chaotic force out of sync with the world around her. After both hallucination scenes, the episode cuts directly from her screams of horror to a shot of House struggling to withstand the chronic pain in his leg—that is, distracting himself from his own fiercely motivating and intensely individual experience via his other more socially beneficial interest in solving medical mysteries. The creation of this parallel explains an otherwise bizarre turn in Leona's diagnosis, in which House decides that Leona has a neurological condition in which physical pain is not perceived as such but instead results in hallucinations.

In producing this transformation, the episode relocates the struggle between Leona and House within the abstraction and extremity that characterize the microeconomic mode. First, House decides to prove his theory by systematically hurting Leona while her brain is being scanned. After feeble protests from his staff, we watch as House straps Leona down, mendaciously informs her, "This isn't going to hurt at all," and then begins to drive a needle into her body while demanding that she tell him the truth about her parentage. When this doesn't work, he bends back her finger until it breaks, and this more intense pain brings on a hallucination, thereby proving House's diagnosis right. Once House straps Leona into the MRI, the complexity of her case is abstracted into the reduction of variables that accompanies any laboratory experiment while the embedded nature of her horrific experiences post-Katrina is recoded into the bodily language of physical pain. In contrast to her hallucinations, which gestured toward her status as both a life left to die and a self-motivated survivor, her experience of bodily pain can be approached as a manageable interest that transcends individual circumstances.

With this translation in place, House can use against her the same interest in avoiding suffering that has led Leona to scam Crandall. In the process, the same feature that enables life-interest to cross the boundary between the liberal individual and his others—the universal location of human consciousness in living flesh—now serves as a means by which Leona can be subdued. It is because of this translation process, I think, that we are expected to look on, undisturbed, while a towering white man tortures a literally helpless, weeping teenage African American girl: every marker that would make them mismatched opponents has been cast as irrelevant to a clash of warring interests played out on the field of Leona's physical being. House completes the sense that they have entered into a discrete contest of wills when he suggests that the experiment was a sort of game in which he proved victorious: "Diagnostically, she needed to be hurt. I wanted to hurt her. Win, win."[28] Within the decontextualized realm of interest, House can present his own role in this process as innocent because, like his other interests, his desire to torture Leona just happens to result in benefits for others beside himself.

The completeness of this victory is indicated by the utter eradication of Leona as an active subject from the remainder of the episode. In a fashion that breaks with the series' own conventions, the episode presents no scenes in which House's underlings chat with Leona, and, in fact, after the torture scene, she never speaks another line. While many of House's patients enter comas or become otherwise unresponsive in the course of an episode, Leona's status is rendered rather more specific when her digestive system becomes blocked and feces ooze from her mouth—a notably abject and revolting mixing of consumption and excretion. If Leona's self-preserving behavior brought to mind the dangerous capacity of interest to dissolve boundaries between persons and nonpersons, this reduction of her to an inert abject body gone awry seems to suggest that this boundary confusion has now been confined to her insides, manifesting only enough to let us know that it is ensconced and raging within her. As she is immobilized, silenced, and rendered an object of disgust, the problems posed by Leona's experiences seem to be compressed into her physical being, safely cordoned off below the surface of a body that is then itself symbolically ejected from the social through the process of abjection. By replacing her agential statements in her own best interest with a mouth oozing excrement, the episode insists that, no matter what Leona says, she is full of shit; this cruel and repulsive literalization indicates the vitriolic vigor with which Leona is expelled from the narrative.

Having decisively dealt with her, the episode directs our attention to Crandall in order to promote its own version of action in one's own best interest. House at first attacks Crandall's desire to "manufactur[e] responsibility" for Leona but revises his opinion when Crandall argues that believing he is Leona's father "feels good" and "feels good is a good enough reason." This reasoning is endorsed by the episode's final shot, which shows House's morphine syringe next to test results that prove Crandall is not Leona's father, information House never shared with Crandall. If helping Katrina victims makes you "feel good," the juxtaposition implies, then it is reasonable, House seems to have decided, to be allowed to pursue this interest—just as the physical interest in avoiding pain makes it eminently reasonable to shoot morphine if you are in agony. In a fashion that unites the literal and figurative meaning of its title, the "Who's Your Daddy?" episode uses Leona's negotiation of her own best interests to turn her into an object to be mastered while designating its hero as a person who uses his understanding of interest to master those around him.

The intensely willed and deeply undesired choices produced in survival tales provide a harrowing picture of the problem of suffering agency, in which even benevolence and the power of the imagination offer no refuge from the inevitability of action in one's own best interest. Yet, as should now be clear, the relationship between interest and life in these texts isn't simply one of analogy. That is, situations of self-preservation do more than offer an imaginative vocabulary for describing the compulsive nature of interest. Rather, live models conceive of interest as emerging from and registering our existence as living beings. The microeconomic imagination assumes that interest is inherent in human action, but live models depict it as a form of life, with all the sense of inevitability and animation that the word entails. To put it another way, the microeconomic mode asks us to recognize life-interest as a biopolitical category in its own right. As my reading of *House* suggests, to define humans in relation to life-interest in this way is to call into question existing ways of differentiating among valued and devalued human lives. Although it is still clearly the case that, as Michel Foucault argues, race functions as a biopolitical technology for dividing lives that are fostered from lives that are not, the conflation of life-interest with human being in the microeconomic mode puts pressure on the racialized distinction between those who qualify as agential individuals and those designated as mere, disposable lives; it is precisely this threat that *House* scrambles to contain and ultimately expel.[29] This is not to say that identity makes no difference to the subject of life-interest. Rather, the difference that it makes has to do with when, why, and to what extent life-interest is activated. We can see this difference at work, for example, in the disparate causes that create abstraction and extremity for subjects of life-interest. Whereas the affliction faced by the African American teenage victim in the Katrina episode of *House* is fictionalized, the survival situation encountered by the white male hero of *The Road* is entirely science-fictional. When it depicts subjects who would otherwise be privileged confronting their status as suffering agents, the microeconomic mode stages the realization that life-interest is a given for any living human who can make a conscious choice. The obsessive rehearsal of this insight in relation to white men—the age-old standard bearers of liberal possessive individualism—serves as a measure of both the extent of this transformation and the anxiety it produces for those who have enjoyed the protections of that category.

Across works that form the core of the microeconomic mode, we find this oscillation between recognition that agency no longer signals a division between valued and devalued life and an attempt to mute or manage this recognition. This attempt emerges in the form of figures that themselves revalue the liberal concatenation of agency, freedom, and conscious will. Once human life is conflated with rational action in one's own best interest, for example, forms of being that depend on instinctive behavior or otherwise appear devoid of conscious agency—such as the animal in *Life of Pi* and the biosphere in *The Road*—take on a new meaning and new appeal. As the readings in this chapter suggest, displacing the human agent in this way may in fact serve as a nostalgic attempt to retain human agency as a unique and necessary good—a project precisely at odds with those customarily undertaken in radical critiques of the liberal individual. In other texts we find life-interest measured against the historic function of agential personhood in both manifesting and resisting injustice. As I argue in chapter 5, life-interest forecloses many of these functions even as it levels the hierarchies defined by liberal personhood, which enabled some lives and not others to be designated as full persons. In the microeconomic mode, there is no relying on the division between liberal individual and mere life, human and animal, agency and living being—but what is made of that remapping of oppositions is particular to the work in question. However, precisely because it scrambles these long-standing binaries, the microeconomic mode returns us to and reactivates many of the tropes, concepts, and narrative functions through which these binaries were initially theorized and instantiated. In the following chapter, I unpack this theoretical remapping by situating life-interest in relation to its closest antecedent, the political theorization of self-preservation found in natural law theory.

Chapter Two

LIFE-INTEREST

Desert island castaways, starving sailors adrift at sea, cannibals, savages, men who behave like lions or wolves: these are the central figures through which natural law theory attempts to locate the boundary beyond which positive law has no purchase. When it reanimates these tropes along with their related narrative arcs and propositions, the microeconomic mode evokes the conjoined aesthetic and conceptual signature of this strand of political theory. In a fashion echoed in the microeconomic mode, natural law theory not only insists that self-preservation is the first and primary rule of human existence but also attempts to document this law through hypothetical scenarios in which all the complexities of civilization are rolled back and Man—the name given to the political subject in natural law theory—is reencountered in what is seen as its original state.[1] In this chapter, I return to seventeenth-century natural law theory in order to consider both the rejuvenation of its aesthetic signature in the microeconomic mode and the relationship between the natural law of self-preservation and the embodied rationality of life-interest. Although it has not made much of an appearance in the explosion of biopolitical critique over the last fifteen years, self-preservation is crucial to the production of the Lockean liberal subject and the definition of this subject's relationship to sovereign power.[2] Life-interest both draws upon and significantly reworks this approach to self-preservation, I suggest, by revising the nexus between living being and rational action. To define the terms of this transformation, I track the function of self-preservation through preliberal and liberal natural law theory and liberal biopolitics. In the process, I describe a trajectory for the emergence of life-interest as a biopolitical category and the return of the imaginative tropes through which preliberal natural law theory advanced its arguments.

With the parameters of this movement from self-preservation to life-interest established, I turn in my final section to consider this trajectory in relation to the dynamics of exclusion and abjection that constitute the boundaries of the liberal subject. Just as self-preservation contributes to identifying possessive individuals who are granted certain rights, it also serves to justify the brutal usage of those who fall outside that category. As a result, the growing imaginative predominance of life-interest creates uneven conceptual and material effects depending on the position of human lives in relation to Man as he has been canonically conceived. In the previous chapter, I began to suggest some of these divergent effects in my consideration of the *House* Katrina episode. Here I consider the intellectual history of self-preservation as itself a racialized and racializing concept as exemplified in tropes that haunt both natural law theory and the microeconomic mode: the savage, the slave, and the cannibal. For the same reason that these figures embody a distinction between savagery and civilization so necessary to European colonization projects, they also operate as limit cases for the definitive link between self-preservation and liberty instantiated by John Locke. By exploring these conceptual antecedents, I begin to pinpoint the way in which life-interest draws upon and repurposes this hierarchy, even as it insists on purportedly universal facets of human life itself. Across the microeconomic mode, I suggest, we find both an insistence that certain forms of savagery are now universal and a wishful attachment to the hierarchies of life that separated the liberal individual from the savages consigned to the realm of natural law.

I want to start with the function of self-preservation in defining the political subject in the thinking of Locke because it is this liberal subject that is being dismantled and displaced within the microeconomic mode. In his account of the founding of the commonwealth, Locke designates self-preservation as the first law of nature and argues that it provides the foundation for individual liberty. For Locke, our duty to God to preserve our own lives and that of other humans requires our freedom; without freedom, we could not be sure we would be able to comply with this moral obligation. This duty links freedom to a kind of inalienable responsibility on the part of each human life for both self-preservation and the preservation of the species at large, even in the state of nature. In Locke's words, "though Man . . . have an uncontroleable Liberty, to dispose of his Person or Possessions, yet he has not Liberty to destroy himself."[3] Not only is he "*bound to preserve himself,* and not to quit his Station wilfully; so by the like reason when his own Preservation comes not in competition, ought he, as much as he can, *to preserve the rest of Mankind.*"[4] That is, we may theoretically have the capacity to consign the right to our lives to someone else via contract, but we nevertheless cannot contract away the moral responsibility to preserve ourselves, on which our very freedom rests. Because we cannot opt out of this responsibility, it remains present even once we have entered into a social contract and provides the ground to resist forms of sovereign power that transgress one's liberty: "To be free from such a force is the only security of my Preservation and reason bids me look on him, as an Enemy to my Preservation, who would take away that *Freedom* which is the fence to it."[5] The need and capacity to resist incursions upon individual liberty rests for Locke upon the God-given duty each Man has to preserve his own life and that of Mankind.

As C. B. Macpherson argues in his celebrated genealogy of possessive individualism, this approach to liberty links freedom to the individual capacity for action in one's own best interest. For Locke, Macpherson points out, "everyone, whether or not he has property in the ordinary sense, is included [in civil society], as having an interest in preserving his life and liberty."[6] Civil society arises to protect this property, and because Locke posits that "every Man has a *Property* in his own *Person,*" we each have an interest in civil society because we each have an interest in preserving that elemental property.[7] In Macpherson's words, Lockean "individuals are by nature equally free from the jurisdiction of others. The human essence is freedom from any relations other than those a man enters with a view to his own interest."[8] In addition to providing a ground to resist the abrogation of freedom by an unjust government, the individual right to life thus institutes boundary behind which the free pursuit of individual interest flourishes within a just government. On the one hand, then, self-preservation provides a limit for interference and a foundation for claims to liberty, but, on the other hand, it exemplifies the sort of interested action men invariably pursue provided they have the necessary freedom from interference to do so. The individual pursuit of survival both founds the claim to liberty in the contractual relationship between the subject and the state and typifies the inevitably interested actions pursued in freedom from the reach of that state.

Although he does not address the role of self-preservation in particular, Michel Foucault clarifies the distinction between these spheres in his comparison of the subject of interest and the subject of right. He argues that, for Locke and the other English empiricists, interest operates as "principle of . . . [a] non-transferable atomistic individual choice which is unconditionally referred to the subject himself" and as such it "constitutes something irreducible in relation to the juridical will."[9] For this reason, "the subject of interest constantly overflows the subject of right. . . . He overflows him, surrounds him, and is the permanent condition of his functioning."[10] The subject of right "accepts negativity, . . . agrees to a self-renunciation and splits himself, as it were, to be, at one level, the possessor of a number of natural and immediate rights, and, at another level, someone who agrees to the principle of relinquishing them and who is thereby constituted as a different subject of right superimposed on the first."[11] This is the subject who accepts limits on his liberty in order to preserve a negotiated, continued access within the state to what were once original, unmediated rights. In contrast, the subject of interest "is never called upon to relinquish his interest" but instead must be allowed and encouraged to pursue his interests to the utmost.[12] Rather than a negotiation or dialectic with the powers of the commonwealth, interest unfolds as a form of immediately and absolutely subjective will. Because of this "essentially different relationship with political power," the subject of right and the subject of interest "are absolutely heterogeneous and cannot be superimposed on each other."[13] For Foucault, "liberalism acquire[s] its modern shape precisely with the formulation of this essential incompatibility between the non-totalizable multiplicity of . . . subjects of interest and the totalizing unity of juridical sovereignty."[14]

As Foucault's account itself suggests, the role of self-preservation in creating and maintaining this "essential incompatibility" disappears from many theorizations of the liberal individual. However, as Hannah Arendt points out, self-preservation continues to play a role in "doctrines of self-interest" in the modern liberal political era. As she puts it,

Hidden behind . . . the sacredness of egoism and the all-pervasive power of self-interest, which were current to the point of being commonplace in the eighteenth and early nineteenth centuries, we find another point of reference which indeed forms a much more potent principle than any pain-pleasure calculus could ever offer, and that is the principle of life itself. What pain and pleasure, fear and desire, are actually supposed to achieve in all these systems is not happiness at all but the promotion of individual life or a guarantee of the survival of mankind. . . . In the last resort, it is always life itself which is the supreme standard to which everything else is referred, and the interests of the individual as well as the interests of mankind are always equated with individual life or the life of the species as though it were a matter of course that life is the highest good.[15]

For Arendt, governance through interest of the kind associated with utilitarianism rests upon and aims for the "reference point" of life itself. We can see the defining nature of this interest in the modern approach to suicide: "If modern egoism were the ruthless search for pleasure (called happiness) it pretends to be, it would not lack what in all truly hedonistic systems is an indispensable element of argumentation—a radical justification of suicide."[16] When we render suicide illegal in order to protect what we assume is any sane person's interest in life, we make clear the conviction that one's interest cannot truly be at odds with life.

With such life philosophy in place, Arendt argues, the protection and advance of the life of the species becomes the unifying and authorizing aim of good government. She blames the liberal adoption of life philosophy for what she sees as a catastrophic eclipse of the political by the social and economic sphere, which creates a fixation on material determination: "where life is at stake all action is by definition under the sway of necessity, and the proper realm to take care of life's necessities is . . . the sphere of social and economic life."[17] As a result, this sphere balloons and becomes "gigantic."[18] We can recognize in this account something akin to Foucault's description of modern biopolitics as that which governs in relation to the life of the species at large. Rather than the "individualizing mode" of disciplinarity, which produces forms of subjectivization and self-surveying interiority, biopolitics engages with the species-being of humans, understood as national populations, races, and so on.[19] As in Arendt's description of the social and economic spheres, biopolitical regimes divide human life into mass groupings to be actively either preserved or abandoned, as serves ends regarding the national population.

In the outpouring of biopolitical analyses that have drawn on these arguments, the preservation of life has largely been equated with this type of governmental action upon mass populations. Yet, as I have indicated, Arendt also ties individual self-interest to modern life philosophy in a fashion that resonates with the centrality of self-preservation in generating the Lockean commonwealth and defining possessive individualism.[20] For the subject of right, the state cannot abrogate the right to individual self-preservation, nor can the individual alienate it. For this reason, the biopolitical governance of mass populations can be understood to rely in part on this active commitment of individuals to their own welfare, which is ultimately based on the commitment to surviving as a life. Utilitarian philosophers approach individual interest in just this way when they try to increase the aggregate happiness of the population. Because we have certain inborn desires to experience pleasure and avoid pain, we can be expected to respond to set stimuli in predictably self-interested ways, which can then be activated in order to promote social welfare as a whole.[21] Although this function is difficult to glimpse if we center our analysis on the acts of biopolitical decision undertaken by sovereign power, individual self-preservation thus instantiates a specific intersection between governmental power and life itself. Self-preservation is both the hinge between general social welfare and individual interest and a limit to the direct application of juridical will. As the ultimate and most impervious form of interest, self-preservation unfolds in a radically unmediated relationship between individuals and their own, single, irreplaceable living bodies, but it does so at a remove from the rights and obligations of the liberal subject possessed of a right to life. As a category, the liberal individual embodies both these two vectors of self-preservation and their heterogeneous spheres of operation.

Given the significance of self-preservation in defining both the subject of interest and the subject of right, we can expect that its function and value will shift alongside the liberal balance between rights and interests. Just such a shift is indicated by Foucault's now well-known discussion of Ordo- and neoliberalism, in which he posits that in the postwar period economic reason becomes a "principle of intelligibility and a principle of decipherment of social relationships and individual behavior."[22] As a result, Foucault posits, "the economic grid [is applied] to a field which since . . . the end of the eighteenth century, was defined in opposition to the economy, or at any rate, as complementary to the economy."[23] When economic rationality is applied to fields that were formerly in opposition to it, these fields become populated with a subject of interest who formerly ensured that the economic sphere remained outside the reach of juridical will. Although this expansion rests on the conviction governmentality can encompass the subject of interest more thoroughly than the subject of right, the effect is a version of government that itself appears an instantiation of economic reason. Rights remain, but they register only within the comprehensive logic of interest, which treats every choice or action as an outcome of interest. Actions undertaken in the sphere of rights must be understood as contingent upon and activated by interests. In effect, the subject of interest engulfs and comes to contain the liberal subject of right.

From one widely circulated Marxist perspective, this transformation appears as an aspect of capital's increasing incorporation and valorization of all of human life, understood here as the totality of human behavior. Michael Hardt and Antonio Negri describe this process as one in which "capital has become a world. Use value and all the other references to values and processes of valorization that were conceived to be outside the capitalist mode of production have progressively vanished. Subjectivity is entirely immersed in exchange."[24] In this view, the spread of economic rationality to formerly opposed fields constitutes one vector of the transformation that makes capital a world. Yet, another facet of this process becomes visible when we attend to the link that I have been tracing between self-preservation and individual interest. The same expansion of capital that is seemingly poised to engulf all of human behavior enables and relies on the predominance of the subject of interest, and that subject, I have argued, is based on self-preservation—on a relationship of individual self to individual life that is essentially inaccessible to outside force. And once rights, normative strictures, and even vulnerability to juridical will become mere data to be fed into the calculus of interest, the politics of life in each of these realms will become recoded within the terms of individual interest in life. We see the results of this transformation in the microeconomic mode. Rather than a liberal individual with a right to life, we find a subject with an interest in life. Rather than awaiting sovereign decision over life and death, this subject actively pursues his or her self-preservation, such that even acts of juridical will become mere factors to be weighed in the course of this individual pursuit. Although this subject of life-interest does not appear recognizably political in the liberal sense of having rights and obligations as a citizen, it now occupies—with all the sense of forcible displacement that word can imply—the position formerly inhabited by the liberal individual. It is for this reason that I refer to the emergence of the subject of life-interest as a transformation of *political* subjectivity in particular: in its definition of the human, the liberal individual as a concept entails a specific relationship to rights, interests, and sovereign power, and it is this definition that comes under erasure in the microeconomic mode.

In order to map the antecedents to this emergent subject in political theory, we must return to a model of self-preservation conceived before the Lockean liberal individual becomes a template for the modern self: that found in Hobbes's vision of human behavior in the state of nature. Because Hobbes's model both renders self-preservation the primary impulse of human being and eschews the morality attached to that impulse for Locke, his account of Man in the state of nature provides a precursor to a subject for whom interest in life reigns supreme. For this reason, I want to consider in some detail both Hobbes's version of the state of nature and the perceived resonance of his account with what I refer to as the microeconomic imagination of choice, which undergirds but preexists the emergence of the microeconomic mode as a cultural formation. (As I have described, I use the term "the microeconomic imagination" to indicate the family resemblance visible across an array of methodologies and rhetorics that prioritize allocative choice in one's own best interest—an array that includes versions of microeconomics as a subdiscipline, rational choice theory, game theory, Chicago School economics, strands of libertarian political theory, and so on.)[25] References to Hobbes within this set of discourses range from vague descriptions of capitalist competition as authorized by a Hobbesian view of human nature to rigorous attempts to read the constitution of the Leviathan through rational choice theory and game theory.[26] By elucidating the areas and extent of overlap between the microeconomic imagination of choice and the Hobbesian state of nature, I identify the distinction between Hobbesian self-preservation and life-interest and draw on this distinction to pinpoint the revised significance given to natural law tropes and aesthetics in the microeconomic mode.

For Hobbes, passions set the object of our desires while reason only determines the means we use to pursue these ends. These passions include "Feare of Death; Desire of such things as are necessary to commodious living and Hope by their industry to obtain them," but the foremost passion is for self-preservation.[27] Within Hobbes's state of nature, this passion for survival paradoxically leads to an intolerable state of insecurity. Although not everyone desires ever more power and glory, everyone must fear that everyone else might act upon such desires, and thus everyone fears their life is under threat. For that reason, even those who merely want to be left alone must act as aggressors in a preemptive bid to preserve their own safety since to not do so would be to risk death from others who likewise fear for themselves. What results is a chaotic zone where, as Hobbes famously puts it in De Cive, "Man is a wolf to Man."[28] Institutions and the stability they imply are impossible because the insecurity of every life makes the future impossible to plan for or ensure. The same passion for life that leads to this intolerable state of nature also enables men to exit it by drawing on the "Liberty each Man hath, to use his own power, as he will himself, for the preservation of his own Nature; that is to say, of his own Life."[29] To do so, they contract to obey a sovereign "voluntarily, on confidence to be protected by him against all others."[30] Despite being motivated by passion rather than reason, self-preservation leads for Hobbes to the sort of trade-offs inherent in interest in the sense I have been using the term: like the "global maximizer" of contemporary choice theory, the Hobbesian individual embraces sovereign power because the passion for life is greater than other passions that can be satisfied in the state of nature, and so the ultimate benefit is seen as greater when a sovereign is constituted who can preserve life.[31]

Combined with the perception that every other person constitutes a threat to one's survival, the understanding of self-preservation as a passion renders the state of nature fundamentally outside the normative strictures of positive law. If survival is constantly at stake for everyone, then "nothing [in this state] can be Unjust. The notions of Right and Wrong, Justice and Injustice have no place."[32] Because Locke's state of nature is a more rational and, hence, peaceable place, this intrinsic opposition between survival and normativity is confined for him to situations of outright aggression or war, but the results are similar nonetheless: "And one may destroy a Man who makes War upon him, or has discovered an Enmity to his being, for the same Reason, that he may kill a *Wolf* or a *Lyon*."[33] In both cases, threat to survival necessarily releases Man from normative strictures regarding the treatment of one another and renders the aggressor no better than an animal; the central difference lies in the consistency of the threat. Whereas only overt aggression of enmity or war reveals men as "Beasts of Prey" for Locke, the universal mutual threat posed by others in Hobbes's state of nature makes every Man a wolf to Man and every action justified in the name of survival.[34]

When individuals' capacity for action in their own best interest unfolds in the absence of positive law, liberal rights, and sovereign control, we seem to be approaching something similar to the microeconomic imagination of individual choice in which such moral and juridical constraints become mere data to be factored into the single calculus of individual interest. But there are crucial distinctions to be made here as well, particularly regarding the notion of self-interest. Hobbes describes self-serving motivations in an inconsistent fashion to the extent that there has been sustained debate among political theorists regarding precisely what sort of "egoism" he attributes to Man and to what extent that egoism can be considered consistently maximizing in the technical sense.[35] Given that Hobbes lodges motivation in the passions rather than in reason, however, even the most nakedly egoistic actions for Hobbes cannot be considered interested in the specific way the term is deployed in the microeconomic imagination, which implies that reason is used to determine the ultimate object of choice. And, even among competing choice-theoretical accounts of *Leviathan*, there is little suggestion that Hobbes consistently subscribes to the view that all action can be traced to some form of self-interest since he also identifies actions undertaken in relation to passions that do not serve the individual's ends.[36] Most importantly, once men enter into the covenant to form the commonwealth, they almost entirely subject to the laws enacted by the sovereign—even should these laws contravene their best interests—rather than being governed through the activation of their interests.[37]

Despite these distinctions, however, Hobbes's political philosophy has apparently seemed particularly ripe for rational-choice analyses to his contemporary commentators. I think we can attribute both the emphasis placed on this resemblance and the seeming disregard for important discrepancies to the same source: the implicit yet constitutive link I have been tracking between self-preservation and interest in general. For Hobbes, the logic of the state of nature and the constitution of the commonwealth rest on the specifics of self-preservation as a passion rather than the power of interest at large. In the state of nature, for example, we distrust our neighbors because we expect that they will be as determined to preserve their own lives as we are, which means they may very well "invade" out of the same fear for their lives that we experience. We might well decide to trust them if actual death were not the risk at hand, since others would not have such an overwhelming fear for their own survival and our own risk would be less severe and compelling. In contrast, we cannot trust others in the microeconomic imagination because interest is constantly being redefined based on the latest information and circumstances, and we can expect others to shift their choices to whatever appears to their best advantage. In both cases—and this is what has made *Leviathan* appear so ripe for analyses via game theory's famous prisoner's dilemma model— decisions must be made in relation to one's own interest, and that requires considering what others will see as in *their* interest in a situation of fundamental untrustworthiness.[38] But in the prisoner's dilemma, this situation emerges from the presumption that interests change as one's context changes, whereas for Hobbes this inability to trust arises from the ultimate interest in life itself, which makes the risk of a poor choice overwhelming. For Hobbes, self-preservation is the overriding and inescapable interest; in the microeconomic imagination, interest is overriding and inescapable.[39]

This is a crucial distinction because it denotes the quite specific function of self-preservation in defining interest as an unavoidable, all-encompassing interpretive frame—a definition that I have suggested unites the various methodologies that contribute to the microeconomic imagination of choice. If all doctrines of self-interest rest at bottom on self-preservation, then we only find one particular element of this foundational connection preserved in the discourses that contribute to the microeconomic imagination: not the conflation of interest and life but rather the *force* that life bears as an interest, a force that is particularly evident in Hobbes's account. In Hobbes's description, self-preservation renders interest undeniably comprehensive, foundational, inextirpable, prevailing, and immune to interference by outside powers. In the microeconomic imagination, these same qualities decouple from self-preservation and attach instead to a methodological toolkit now seemingly capable of reducing every aspect of human behavior to an expression of interest. Rather than the primacy of interest in life guaranteeing submission to the sovereign, interest as an engulfing interpretive logic guarantees that every human action can be read as an act of allocative choice. No juridical power or liberal right can bring force to bear on the utterly subjective acts of evaluation that unfold according to this logic: whatever I decide is in my interest simply is so. Thus, instead of the utter absence of juridical will and positive law, the microeconomic imagination represents these same forces as mere data to be factored in the individual's calculation of interest. What was quite literally visceral in Hobbes's state of nature becomes in the microeconomic imagination the consequence and product of an analytic rubric.

Life-interest takes shape at the intersection of these two versions of the absolutism of interest: one that rests on the understanding of life as an interest that cannot be denied and one that rests on the microeconomic imagination of interest as a totalizing, tautological rubric that cannot be escaped. This convergence occurs because, as I have suggested, the pervasive explanatory reach of interest in post-Fordist capital necessarily transfigures the political significance attached to individual life. When the subject of interest absorbs the subject of right, our relationship to life becomes one of interest in self-preservation rather than individual right to or sovereign decision over life. Individual interest circulates as a ubiquitous and coercive rhetoric of government and self-government at the same time and for the same reason that individual self-preservation waxes as a biopolitical concern. The subject of life-interest embodies this convergence—the point at which the total reach of interest as a methodological instrument attaches to each individual's status as self-preserving living body. Interest becomes rational, calculating, and self-regarding even as it is desperate, propulsive, and compulsive. What the microeconomic imagination excluded in its genesis of interest as a universal explanatory frame—life as itself the ur-interest—returns with a vengeance for the subject of life-interest. The microeconomic mode reveals this confluence. It illuminates a world in which all action is parsed according to individual interest and all individual interest is tethered to interest in life.

Given the primacy of self-preservation for this subject, it is thus not surprising that works in the microeconomic mode so often appear to evoke the Hobbesian state of nature. When it explores life-interest, this mode reanimates key propositions regarding the compulsive power of self-preservation that the Hobbesian state of nature was designed to reveal in the first place. Crucially, as I have suggested, the state of nature, survival, and the absence of positive law arise together for Hobbes: when there is no positive law to enforce order, survival will be mutually threatened for everyone, and, because survival is a passion rather than a moral duty, there will be no bar to any action undertaken in pursuit of survival. Thrust out of civilization and onto desert islands, life rafts, and their more modern analogues—from postapocalyptic wastelands to the surface of alien planets—inhabitants of live models find themselves, like Hobbesian Man, in terrain defined by the absence of positive law, in which survival is everything and nothing can be unjust. When live models rework the aesthetic and conceptual lexicon of preliberal natural law theory, this repurposing measures the distance between the subject of life-interest and the liberal individual, who possessed both economic self-interest and a juridical right to life. That is, by evoking a version of self-preservation supposedly rendered obsolete by the institution of the commonwealth and the instantiation of the liberal individual, live models indicate that we are no longer in conceptual terrain defined in relation to that individual. Yet, as I have also suggested, the subject of life-interest cannot be collapsed with men in Hobbes's state of nature despite their significant resemblance. Life-interest combines existing elements, but the result is new: the totalizing, rational interpretive frame of interest animated by all the organic, motile unfolding that accompanies self-preservation as the first law of nature.

I want to turn now to the work that natural law theory performs in creating the intellectual foundations for the opposition between civilization and savagery, which served to justify the European imperial projects that also arose in this era. This opposition is foundational to what Alexander Weheliye describes as "a global color line . . . that clearly distinguishes the good/life/fully-human from the bad/death/not-quite-human."[40] Most obviously, Locke documented the existence of the state of nature by insisting that "in the beginning all the World was *America*," and even Hobbes—who did not claim that the state of nature was a universal historical circumstance—argued that "savage people in many places of *America* . . . have no government at all; and live at this day in that brutish manner" he ascribed to Man in the state of nature.[41] At the same time that natural law theory insists that every human reverts to natural law in the state of nature, the temporalization of that state as characteristic of prehistory enables the projection of its archaic nature onto contemporaneous cultures encountered outside of the European states.[42] Not only does this account of human nature lend itself to a defense of colonization and chattel slavery, but, as Orlando Patterson and others have argued, the converse is also true: the invention of freedom as the ideal state of Man in the West depends on the presence of slavery in various forms.[43] Rather than slavery persisting as an anomalous, atavistic feature of a civilization otherwise founded on individual freedom, freedom is identified and codified as a value in relation to slavery.[44]

When it draws on the tropes and narrative arcs of natural law theory, the microeconomic mode both reactivates and resituates these oppositions between civilization and savagery, freedom and slavery, man and beast. To begin to outline this process, I want to consider the function of self-preservation in defining and defending enslavement. As Patterson notes, the slave has consistently been understood to have given up freedom in order to escape death, a view Patterson links to the age-old practice of granting those captured in war the choice between slavery and execution. This "war slavery doctrine," as Mary Nyquist names it, was "formulated by Roman jurists and locates slavery's origins in warfare, specifically in the captor's decision to save—that is, enslave—rather than kill the vanquished."[45] On the one hand, this reasoning justifies what Patterson calls the "social death" of the slave.[46] As one who should have died, the slave maintains living existence while being erased from the cultural order and its systems of belonging. On the other hand, however, this origin story insists on an ongoing relationship between choice and self-preservation even for the slave. As Locke puts it,

This *Freedom* from Absolute, Arbitrary power, is so necessary to, and closely joyned with a Man's Preservation, that he cannot part with it, but by what forfeits his Preservation and Life together. For a man, not having the Power of his own Life, *cannot* by Compact, or his own Consent, *enslave himself* to any one, nor put himself under the Absolute, Arbitrary power of another, to take away his Life, when he pleases. No body can give more Power than he has himself; and he that cannot take away his own Life, cannot give another power over it. Indeed having, by his fault, forfeited his own Life, by some Act that deserves Death; he, to whom he has forfeited it, may (when he has him in his Power) delay to take it, and make use of him to his own Service, and he does him no injury by it. For, whenever he finds the hardship of his Slavery out-weigh the value of his Life, 'tis in his Power, by resisting the Will of his Master, to draw on himself the Death he desires.[47]

In Locke's view, we cannot enslave ourselves or enter into a compact equivalent to slavery because we cannot give someone else the power to take away our lives when we do not possess that power ourselves. Our lives ultimately belong to God, and we have a duty to preserve them for that reason. Thus, this form of slavery arises because the enslaved lives had been declared forfeited already. Yet even in this "perfect condition of slavery," a willed commitment to self-preservation persists.[48] The slave's life may be forfeited and preserved only for servitude, but that does not take away the evidence of his will. It is still "in his Power" to resist his master and choose death instead. In effect, the slave demonstrates his continued acceptance of and submission to his treatment by his survival.[49] For Locke, then, the opposition between the slave and the liberal subject rests in part on the different function of self-preservation for each of them. Whereas self-preservation requires and evidences an essential, necessary liberty for the liberal individual, self-preservation requires and evidences the surrender of autonomous will for the slave.

In contrast, Hobbes's lack of concern with preserving liberty as a value puts Man and slave on a continuum. As Hobbes puts it in his description of the captive-cum-slave, "It is not therefore the Victory, that giveth the right of Dominion over the Vanquished, but his own Covenant. Nor is he obliged because he is Conquered; that is to say, beaten, and taken, or put to flight; but because he commeth in, and Submitteth to the Victor."[50] Hobbes uses much the same logic and language to describe slavery as he does Man's decision to submit to sovereign power. Or, to put it from the opposite direction, we might say that he justifies submission to the sovereign in the Leviathan by drawing on the war slavery doctrine that had long justified the master's domination of the slave; what he added to the argument was the presumption that everyone's self-preservation is equally threatened in the state of nature.[51] For Hobbes, a slave is someone who had to forfeit more freedom to preserve his life than Man did to create the Leviathan.

In keeping with its Hobbesian elements, the microeconomic imagination of slavery resembles Hobbes's rather than Locke's account. As American libertarian arguments in favor of legalizing voluntary contractual slavery make clear, it is possible to interpret even enslavement as a choice in one's own best interest, provided one's commitment to reading every action according to individual cost–benefit reasoning is absolute enough.[52] Rather than violating the essential liberty required to preserve one's life, slavery becomes in such arguments simply a cost that might conceivably be worth the benefit it brings, depending on the context and one's own evaluation of what is in one's interests. Recoding slavery in terms of interest in this way obviously eradicates all of the specific and vile history of chattel slavery in the Americas—a dismissal of context universal in the microeconomic imagination but particularly revolting in this instance. However, this same shift to interest as a totalizing frame also eradicates the liberal distinction between the slave and the individual possessed of rights, along with the different versions of self-preservation on which this distinction rests. When recoded according to the calculus of interest, the choice between voluntary enslavement and some other identified action in one's own best interest can no longer index different "genres of being human," to use Sylvia Wynter's formulation.[53] Instead, all possible choices simply exist on a continuum between more and less optimal, depending on one's own assessment. Because it combines the totalizing frame of interest with the compulsive power of attachment to life, this shift is even more pronounced in the microeconomic mode. When we are all subjects of life-interest, the choice to put survival before freedom cannot divide those who deserve to be treated as slaves from those who qualify as liberal individuals. Instead, every human who can make conscious choices must be understood as both autonomous agent and hostage to interest in life. In the liberal regime of rights, self-preservation generates freedom for some and submission for others; in the microeconomic mode, life-interest eventuates suffering agency for all.

When self-preservation ceases to demarcate the boundary between the liberal individual and the slave, we are returned to the central paradox of seventeenth-century natural law theory: the same logic that enables the distinction between civilization and savagery also depends on a view of human nature as absolute and undifferentiated. This paradox is particularly clear in relation to cannibalism. As Cătălin Avramescu persuasively argues, the seventeenth-century genre of "speculative geography" included both accounts purporting to describe encounters with real-world cannibals and philosophical treatises that conjured cannibals in overtly hypothetical states of nature.[54] In both cases, the cannibal emerges as a figure for thinking through the content of natural law and the compulsions of necessity to which any human being can be returned given the right circumstances. At the same time that colonization narratives invoke the cannibal to justify and disavow the violent forms of human consumption inherent in chattel slavery and the colonization of the Americas, cannibalism simultaneously operates as a figure for thinking through what all humans essentially are, both inside Europe and out.[55] The cannibal of speculative geography is both savage Other meriting the most inhuman treatment and, in Avramescu's words, "an original subject of universal history."[56] By reactivating the conceptual and imaginative lexicon of natural law theory, the microeconomic mode reanimates a logic that paradoxically served both to distinguish the liberal individual from the primitive savage and to identify that which was universal in all human beings. However, as the example of slavery suggests, life-interest dissolves the oppositions that define the liberal individual, with the result that the universal function of natural law tropes eclipses their hierarchical function. The racialized and racializing opposition between civilization and savagery continues to appear in the microeconomic mode, but it does so precisely in order to indicate the absence of—and often the yearning for—the hierarchies of life that this opposition once guaranteed. That we encounter structures of yearning rather than relief suggests the way in which the microeconomic mode speaks from and to the position of those human lives identified with the liberal individual as a category rather than of those who were never considered to merit that status.

We can get a sense of how this doubled gesture works by examining the trope of the shipwreck, which is both a prominent setting in the microeconomic mode and one of the primary occasions in which natural law dictates were seen to apply during the heyday of natural law theory.[57] In the first of two famous historical cases, Avramescu recounts, a group of sailors who killed and ate a shipmate to avoid starvation were tried and found not guilty in 1737, in effect because they were seen to have been occupying a realm of extreme necessity in which only natural law applied. In the latter case, which took place in 1884, the sailors from the *Mignonette* were found guilty of a similar charge, a shift in approach that Avramescu attributes to the growing perception that the sea was governed not by natural law but by English positive law.[58] Thus, the same natural law that could be evoked to mark out entire continents for conquest and domination could also be applied to the actions of civilized men who found themselves both outside the arena of positive law and subject to the pressures of self-preservation, which rendered positive law's normative strictures inapplicable.[59]

As the depiction of cannibalism in the microeconomic mode makes clear, this mode reactivates aspects of the universal approach to human nature propagated in natural law theory, specifically the view that in the right circumstances we all revert to so-called savagery. However, because the subject of life-interest embodies a fusion of the compulsive attachment to life with the cognitive evaluation of interest, this recognition of universal savagery simultaneously gestures toward a history in which civilized Man understood savages to be safely and decisively Other. For example, Yann Martel, the author of *Life of Pi* (2001), has recounted that the novel's cannibalistic plot was in part inspired by the court case of the sailors from the *Mignonette*, and the name given to the tiger in the novel is in fact that of the captain of the *Mignonette*, Richard Parker.[60] Like Pi, the sailors on the *Mignonette* had no choice but to act in relation to self-preservation, but they were still judged as autonomous agents who could be held responsible for choices made in that context. In assigning this choice to the charming child Pi, the novel insists on the inherent humanity of life-interest even as it underscores the weight that these actions have placed on his conscience. By recasting Pi as an animal acting on instinct rather than an agent motivated by rational will, the competing versions of his story indicate simultaneously the essential nature of life-interest and a wishful invocation of now defunct hierarchies of life—in this case, those that place the human over the animal. Cannibalism in the microeconomic mode thus indicates the grotesque fusion of human agency and human life within a regime of life-interest—literalized in the choice to sustain oneself by consuming another human being—as well as the resurgence of an approach to self-preservation that presumes no one is immune to becoming savage.

Likewise, in Cormac McCarthy's *The Road* (2006), cannibalism has become widespread in a context that resembles a Hobbesian war of all against all, but we encounter this world via a protagonist who attempts to distinguish between himself as civilized Man—one of the "good guys," in the character's parlance—and the cannibals.[61] In the father's bald attempt at categorization, we witness his stubborn attempt to preserve a hierarchy between civilization and savagery in the face of what has become a single self-preserving mass of desperate humanity. We can identify the racialized quality of this attempt in the clichéd imagery associated with the cannibals in the novel, which seems borrowed from a *National Geographic* photographic spread on tribal customs: "deranged chanting," "crude tattoos etched in some homebrewed woad," and the preservation of a severed head under a cakebell.[62] However, the father clutches at the distinction between the good guys and the bad because he cannot help but recognize that, when it comes to preserving his son's life, there are no good choices left to him. The novel's obsession with cannibalism indicates both its admission that life-interest necessarily leads to savagery for everyone and its nostalgia for the sort of racializing assemblages that promised civilized white men that they were categorically distinct from man-eating savages.

In the microeconomic mode, then, subjects are forcibly returned to the primal scenes of preliberal natural law theory, but they arrive there trailing the wreckage of the liberal individual as a category. As I will discuss in chapter 5 in particular, this wreckage may be seen to present opportunities as well as challenges to those populations that were never granted full inclusion in the category in the first place. In a sense, the white man serves as the central protagonist in the microeconomic mode because his conflation with the liberal individual renders his changing status the means by which the ebbing of that form of political subjectivity can be measured. Which is not to say that his continued centrality is not thereby reinforced. Indeed, live models that feature white male protagonists often enact and rely on a persistent attachment to distinctions among savage and civilized life—on the presumption that it is particularly disturbing to see white men reduced to mere cannibals, slaves, and beasts—at the same time that they insist that no human being can now escape the first law of nature. We can see the effect of this double vision in the distinctive temporal signature of the microeconomic mode, its suggestion that the liberal subject of right has been left behind even as all humans have been stripped back to the most "primitive" and intrinsic features of human existence, including the white men formerly guaranteed an escape from that fate.[63] The subject of life-interest belongs to a present in which the emergence of life-interest both threatens an alien future and activates a living essence that has historically been associated with a primeval past. Whether the live model in question is a castaway tale or a postapocalyptic dystopia, this doubled temporality manifests itself in the recourse to natural law tropes to define a form of political subjectivity that, unlike Hobbesian Man, supersedes rather than precedes the liberal individual. In their association with the premodern past to which non-Europeans have routinely been consigned, the cannibals, savages, and beasts of prey that populate the microeconomic mode embody in themselves this doubled vision; they remind us of the long ascendancy of the liberal individual even as they document its demise.

PART II

Sovereignty

Chapter Three

SURVIVAL GAMES

In direct contradiction to the conventional understanding of the word, no modeling process creates the live model, and that is what makes it appear simultaneously so authoritative and so strange. Watch enough social complexity and primary resources drain away, and the live model seems simply to emerge, fully formed, as if it had always been present beneath the distracting detail of everyday life: this is the wager on which natural law narratives like those of Thomas Hobbes and John Locke are based. In this chapter, I examine a form that closes the distance between map and territory from something like the opposite direction: the survival game. As its name suggests, the survival game as a form encapsulates the abstraction and extremity that constitute the microeconomic mode in a fashion that is reminiscent of the live model. In contrast, however, survival games feature and interrogate the role of human intervention in bringing the subject of interest to life. Even when games seem to arise *sui generis* without an identified designer or external referee, the word "game" signals an arena in which the goals, choices, and consequences one encounters are by definition delimited by human design or convention, reduced in relation to an external, less processed form of experience. Rather than dissolving this secondary status in the fashion of the live model, survival games combine this sense of restriction, estrangement, and artificiality with life-and-death consequences. They codify the elemental vectors of life and death within a structure that is necessarily a product of human design—that is clearly culture, not nature. Whereas live models claim to reveal that human life in pure form takes the shape of a model, survival games expressly act upon life by locating it outside the full range of dynamics available in the nongame world and inside an arena in which self-preservation is deliberately threatened. Survival games retain the sense that life-interest is found, not made, but, unlike live models, they do not purport to leave it as they find it.

In this chapter, I consider what the constitution, range, and remarkable ubiquity of survival games across popular culture since the late 1990s tell us about the function of life-interest in the present. Although it appears in various guises throughout the twentieth century, the survival game has become commonplace in the twenty-first century, giving shape to works as diverse in tone, ambition, and audience as the reality TV series *Survivor* (1997 to the present), Michael Haneke's art-house film *Funny Games* (1997), and postapocalyptic video games such as *Left 4 Dead* (2008).[1] These texts form part of the much larger array of game texts in the microeconomic mode that populate contemporary culture. From bug-eating and other gross-out contests on reality TV series such as *Fear Factor* (2001 to the present) to the otherworldly isolation endured by occupants of the houses in *Big Brother* (2000 to the present), innumerable twenty-first-century game narratives fill an abstracted field of game play with "extreme" physical and psychological experiences. Although I locate the survival games I consider within this larger web of game tales in the microeconomic mode, I concentrate on works that I argue most clearly engage the effects of life-interest: games in which strategy plays a central role and characters comprehend rightly that the way they play the game will make the difference between death and life. In contrast to contests focused solely on strength, endurance, or a physical skill, strategy games chime with the microeconomic imagination because they showcase the role of individual rational decision in determining game play. This rubric thus excludes works such as *Funny Games*, in which the point of the film is precisely that there is no strategy that could have an effect on the outcome of the so-called game, but also video games such as *Left 4 Dead*, in which it is the individual at the controller who plays the game but the avatar whose life is at risk. While there are obviously still suggestive elements in the texts that I exclude here—that you cannot win in *Funny Games* while you can win in *The Hunger Games* (2008) tells us something about how both think about agency—my concern is with games that present the most complete engagement with life-interest.

As its different representational signature suggests, the survival game asks different questions about this turn to life-interest than the live model does. By locating the subject within a structure that expressly propagates and channels interest in life, the survival game form foregrounds that which is specifically foreclosed by live models: the harnessing of interest by an external force. The survival game *activates* the subject of life-interest, as an effect of—as evidence of—a highly specific form of power. In so doing, I suggest, it operates in a fashion importantly distinct from the widespread process of gamification or the increasing perception that everyday life activities operate and are best approached as games.[2] Whereas gamification emerges from a regime of immaterial labor that disperses individuals into constantly shifting and measurable flows of affect and action, survival games reverse this process.[3] They spool the subject up into a tightly wound bundle of predictable, ferocious, undeniable interests related to each person's status as a live human organism. They do so, I will argue, not as an exercise in nostalgia but rather a means of exploring the painful ways in which the individual persists as a unit of domination, despite that individual also being (equally painfully) dissolved into countless shifting streams of data for the purposes of capital. The survival game imagines how it is that, for example, the same subject who unravels into flows of information can also be an individual whose one and only life is irreversibly blighted by a bad credit score or a felony conviction or an industrial accident—that is, by permanent consequences that attach to a single, identified agent. The aesthetic signature of the survival game encodes the conviction that, in the twenty-first century, this is what the direct, showy, physical application of power over human beings is *for*: to ensure that we remain individual life units piloted by conscious subjects who have no choice but to keep making choices. Ultimately, I argue, it is the emergence of this power as a new form of sovereignty that the survival game stages, over and over, in its countless contemporary incarnations. This form of sovereignty registers not through a decree over life and death but instead through the capture of decisions that people cannot help but make in the interest of their own lives.

*   *   *

In the game narratives of the 1980s and 1990s, the game form operated primarily as a way to examine the power and danger of simulation as a technologically advanced mode of representation. To take a classic example, in the 1983 film *WarGames*, the hero of the film hacks into the American nuclear defense computer and begins to play a strategy game called Global Thermonuclear War. However, the computer system takes the game as real and prepares an actual attack on the USSR, and the teenage hacker finds himself racing to prevent the ultimate in real-world consequences. Despite its seeming engagement with game-theory models of Cold War brinkmanship, gaming in this film thus has more to do with simulation than strategy. The problem in *WarGames* is not that a computer might outthink a person—or that Russia might outthink America—but rather that a digital realm might control the material realm. We can trace a similar concern with the relationship between simulation and direct experience in countless virtual reality narratives from the 1980s and 1990s, in which the hero or heroine inevitably learns that dying in the virtual reality game will mean dying in real life as well.[4] What unites these game narratives is an interrogation of the threat that simulation might engulf, overwrite, or render irrelevant the plane of direct, material experience. In effect, these late-twentieth-century game narratives provided the vernacular version of the obsession with the power of representation over reality that characterized postmodern theory, or what in the theoretical register was variously described as the medium as message, the precession of the simulacra, or the loss of true historicity.[5]

In survival games, characters never have any doubt that to die in the game is to die in real life because survival games are carved out of real-world space in the first place—and that is what makes them appear as a shocking violation to those forced to play.[6] Of course, many types of games, including most sports, likewise involve direct action by and upon bodies, and some of these possess serious physical consequences. But these games are still characterized by a voluntarism and freedom absent in the survival game. In effect, survival games are games that have been stripped of the element of play. Whereas a game is "an activity defined by rules in which players try to reach some sort of goal," the word "play" in particular carries with it a sense of freedom that is linked to its status as fiction, its lack of direct consequence for the players.[7] In Roger Caillois's definition, activities that qualify as play are "(1) free, (2) separate, (3) uncertain, (4) unproductive,

(5) regulated, and (6) fictive."[8] Survival games retain the separation, uncertainty, and regulation that Caillois identifies, but they lack precisely the sort of freedom that is crucial to play. As Caillois puts it,

A game which one would be forced to play would at once cease being play. It would become constraint, drudgery from which one would strive to be freed. As an obligation or simply an order, it would lose one of its basic characteristics: the fact that the player devotes himself spontaneously to the game, of his free will and for his pleasure.[9]

In survival games, so-called players do not play out of their own free will or for their pleasure, nor is their action spontaneous.[10] Instead, they are forced to participate in the game through coercion or emotional blackmail, and their choices within the game itself are presumed to be compelled by the unavoidable attachment to life. The life-and-death consequences of game play likewise eradicate the fictive nature of the game by tethering the separate realm of the game to the ultimate in real-world consequences: murdering or being murdered. The perception of wrongness that accompanies the survival game—the sense that life and death should never be treated as "just a game"—arises from this use of a form usually defined as free and fictive to organize content characterized by unwilling players, intrinsic motivations, and catastrophic, permanent results.

This friction between form and content distinguishes the survival game from gamification, which instead depends on the perception that existing experiences resemble or already function as games. Rather than being self-justifying in the fashion of games proper, gamification brings to the fore gamelike features in a system that exists for reasons other than the experience of playing a game. For example, the recent corporate turn to gamification as a management style proposes that existing structures of competition and reward that motivate employees will be more effective if their resemblance to a game are recognized and enhanced. In general, when gamification proselytizers acknowledge the distinction between the game and the nongame realm, it is in order to argue that this distinction should be decreased by recognizing how much like a game the experience in question is and enhancing those gamelike features.[11] Survival games also collapse human life and the game form, but they do so in a way that requires and reinforces the distinction between existence inside and outside the game. If the teenagers in *Battle Royale* (2000) already experienced daily threats to life, then there would be no tension between the game as a voluntary, created realm and their unwilling insertion into game play as a zone with fatal consequences.[12] Rather than arising from the autotelic purposes of game play, the survival game would simply be a formalization of a preexisting dynamic with its own justification and goals. Instead, *Battle Royale* turns on the irony involved in transforming teenagers' banal experiences of friendship, love, and betrayal into a gory, hyperviolent fight to the death. Rather than highlighting the resemblance between game and nongame spaces, survival games make the difference between everyday existence and an arena of life-and-death competition signify. They do so because they approach the "life" contained within game play differently than the proponents of gamification do. Gamification encompasses "life" meant as all the various behaviors and experiences in which humans ordinarily engage, while the survival game concerns "life" in the sense of "life and death," or the sheer unfolding of biological existence that must be sustained if the individual is not to be snuffed out.

In order to trace what is important about this difference, I want to begin with a novel that explores the relationship between the survival game and gamification: Gillian Flynn's *Gone Girl* (2012). The novel opens in small-town Missouri, where a young wife, Amy, has gone missing and her husband, Nick, is suspected of having murdered her. As we learn the backstory that has brought them to this pass, the novel takes shape as a canny fictionalization of the real-world growth of immaterial labor within post-Fordist capitalism. Since her early childhood, Amy's parents have been cowriting and publishing books for children based on her life, called the Amazing Amy series. Rather than cherishing her for her own sake, they seem to have taken Gary Becker's analysis of parental motivations as their instruction manual; they treat Amy's existence as an investment that can be made to pay dividends, and they reap the financial rewards accordingly.[13] As Amy puts it, "I'd never really felt like a person, because I was always a product."[14] Shortly after Amy and Nick's marriage, however, Amy's parents confess that they have blown through their money as a result of profligate living, the waning market for their books, and the 2008 stock market crash. After writing them a check for the bulk of her trust fund in order to clear their debts, Amy can no longer support Nick, who has lost his job as a writer due to the casualization of journalism in the Internet age, so they move from Manhattan to Nick's hometown, North Carthage. A plot point concerning the local mall neatly signals the town's emblematic status as a postindustrial backwater. Having gone bust, the mall now houses an encampment of men who became homeless after they were laid off from the local plant. Although these processes involve different trajectories and scales, Amy and Nick's arrival in North Carthage is determined by a confluence of monetization, flexible employment, financialization, and Web 2.0. In rendering these processes concomitant aspects of its initiating situation, *Gone Girl* invites readers to observe what they all have in common. They represent different aspects of the same transition from industrial to immaterial labor, which turns the most ephemeral, minute, and personal aspects of human behavior into forms of capital.[15]

What makes *Gone Girl* revealing is what it does with this observation: uses it as fuel for a mystery-thriller potboiler complete with withheld information, shocking twists, and a killer on the loose.[16] These generic conventions give the novel access to narrative possibilities foreclosed in the social-realist vein, and that imaginative reach extends its analysis in directions very different from those offered by contemporary cultural theory. The hinge between the novel's social-realist and thriller registers is the gamification of love, which both brings Amy and Nick together and triggers the thriller plot. As is made clear in the title of the most well-known dating handbook of the last twenty-five years—*The Rules: Time-Tested Secrets for Capturing the Heart of Mr. Right* (1995)—love has increasingly been presented to women as a game that one must play to win, and this understanding amounts to a significant shift in the ideological import of romance as an ideal.[17] Rather than being expected to enjoy the contingency signaled by the phrase "falling in love," women are advised to set out to catch Mr. Right, a process that requires understanding and finessing previously unwritten rules of the game.[18] Although this approach seems to undercut the demand that women in particular be surprised by love lest they be classed as gold diggers or desperate cases, *The Rules* makes clear that winning for women involves keeping secret one's actual interest in catching a man, since any sign that one is on the hunt will only cause Mr. Right to sense that he might be trapped and flee.

By only slightly exaggerating the sort of approach recommended by *The Rules* and its ilk, *Gone Girl* recounts the way in which its heroine, Amy, sets out to transform her personality in order to seem worth dating by her Mr. Right. After meeting Nick at a party, Amy intuits that he is looking for an incarnation of what she calls "the Cool Girl." Beautiful but low-maintenance, self-confident but undemanding, sexually uninhibited but otherwise like one of the guys, the Cool Girl can be recognized by her professed love of football, poker, cheap beer, threesomes, and anal sex (222). Winning Nick requires that Amy convince him that she is the Cool Girl of his dreams, who of course would never be so uncool as to modify her behavior to catch a man. Amy has no qualms about leveraging her persona in this way because her experience of familial love was much the same; the key difference is that in this case she assumes she will profit from the venture herself. Through this account of the game of love, *Gone Girl* demonstrates the way in which gamification encourages women to see love as the product of individual agency—as the result of sensible and strategic action in one's own best interest. Once Amy successfully becomes the Cool Girl and wins Nick's affections, however, she comes to the outraged realization that playing love like a game is an inherently self-canceling project. Remaking herself as someone to whom Nick will commit turns out to mean that Amy has foreclosed the possibility that she will be loved for herself, since it is not Amy that Nick has chosen but the Cool Girl she has been impersonating. Not only is winning in this scenario indistinguishable from losing, but it is specifically Amy's capacity to game the system that has caused her to wind up with a booby prize. Precisely because it creates such a clear and instrumental path to the goal of love, the power of Amy's will is the source of her self-injury. When finding love turns into just another act of individual will, *Gone Girl* suggests, it leads to suffering agency for the woman involved.

This realization sparks the novel's thriller plot because, as readers discover in the novel's central twist, Amy is actually a psychopath who cannot bear to have her will thwarted or her amazingness denied. In part 1 of the novel, we read a series of diary entries by Amy cataloging her relationship with Nick from their first meeting in Manhattan to his gradual shift to selfish indifference and finally violent outbursts. At the start of part 2 of the novel, however, we abruptly find a very different account of the recent past. In first-person, present-day narration, Amy gleefully informs the reader that "diary-Amy" is a fake, created to cast suspicion on Nick. Instead of being a victim of forces beyond her control, Amy turns out to be a monster whose villainy is directly tied to her superlative capacity for goal-directed action. From secretly crafting her faux diary over months to slicing into her own arm to leave her blood at a staged crime scene, Amy reveals herself to possess a creepy but not at all supernatural ability to achieve her objectives. As she advises readers, "'You just have to decide to do it and then do it. . . . Discipline. Follow through. Like anything. Nick never understood that'" (388). What enrages her about the results of her Cool Girl campaign is not that she has missed out on real love but rather that her feat of discipline and follow-through somehow failed to garner the results it should have.

For Amy, this failure means that Nick won the game of love despite clearly being the inferior player, and she finds this denial of her superiority intolerable. In Nick's words, Amy "needs to win. She's less pissed off that I cheated [on her] than that I picked someone else over her. She'll want me back just to prove that she's the winner" (355). Amy doesn't want to get her way in order to get the things she wants; what she wants is to get her way, and the other rewards that follow are welcome but generally superfluous. Her ultimate interest is in coming out on top, in having her interests always and everywhere triumph over everyone else's. As a villain, she embodies rational interest taken to a ludicrous yet logical extreme, and that is why her capacity for evil emerges fully blown when she encounters the problem of suffering agency. Suffering agency belies the inherent good of successful action in one's own best interest, and Amy rightly understands herself as that value incarnate. In her "psycho bitch" guise, she embodies the furious, spiteful energy of someone who has found herself betrayed by a system whose precepts she has followed with unimpeachable fidelity (271).

In order to reverse this defeat, Amy does something only a villain could do: she forces Nick to play a survival game of her own design. She fakes her own death in a fashion that will cast suspicion on Nick and then leaves a series of clues for Nick to solve seemingly based on details of their relationship, which he can solve provided he has been paying attention to their interactions. Not only does Nick have no choice but to "play the Missing Wife game," as he calls it, but he also reminds the reader that, given that Missouri is a death penalty state, this game is life or death for him (42). In order to humble Nick on the same ground where she found her will thwarted, Amy designs her survival game to resemble the gamification of love, but this time as viewed from the heterosexual male perspective. Repeated across countless sitcoms and romcoms, this is the narrative in which women are game players who baffle men by turning communication into guesswork and minor interactions into symbolic relationship landmarks. Amy's sly twist is that, in this case, the clues actually refer to Nick's affair with a much younger woman, and with each riddle he solves, he digs himself in deeper with the police. When she gets Nick to play the survival game she has created, Amy successfully traps him in an all-consuming structure that threatens to be fatal for him but is a voluntary and delightful fabrication for her. As the title of *Gone Girl* suggests, it is Amy's successful disappearance from the field, her ability to watch from the wings as Nick plays out a game that she has created, that proves her ultimate triumph—not only over Nick but over gamification at large.

In portraying the survival game in this way, *Gone Girl* illuminates its crucial power as a mechanism for sorting human beings. Amy uses the survival game to materialize a division between those with the power to legislate a self-contained realm governed by rules of their own design and those who cannot help but treat these fabricated, arbitrarily imposed rules with all the seriousness reserved for matters of life and death. This division is what makes the survival game designation not simply a category error. In the survival game, the game form's characteristic distance from necessity persists in an amplified form for the game's designers, even as it is eradicated for the game players, who must inhabit the game whether they like it or not. The power that attaches to the game designer arises from the capacity to make others pursue tremendously important ends through pointlessly inexpedient means—to make them play out their real lives in a toy world, like lab rats running a maze. Yet this form of power over others specifically requires that subordinated subjects continue to take agential action. In fact, given the deadly stakes involved, the survival game heightens the import of each action in a way that intensifies its status as a performance of individual agency. Amy proves herself the ultimate winner not only because of her supreme capacity to act in her own best interest but also because her revenge depends on Nick's (gratifyingly lesser) capacity to do the same. She doesn't take away his ability to choose; she *captures* his capacity for choice, and that is how she performs her dominance over him. She relocates his will inside a set of life-and-death parameters whose very existence expresses her will, and, in so doing, she proves that hers is the meta will. Or, to put it in more familiar terms, she proves that her will is sovereign. But what the survival game designer decrees is not who lives or dies but rather the terms by which players may either win or lose their lives. Sovereign is he—or she—who decides on the rules of the game.

Because it locates the survival game within a mystery-thriller plotline that centers on the real-world game of love, *Gone Girl* reveals something crucial about the relationship between this form of sovereignty and the gamification process that accompanies the shift to immaterial labor. As I have suggested, both the survival game and gamification collapse gaming with life itself, but they do so with opposing results. Survival games sort characters into those who create the game and those who are forced to play for their very existence, while gamification implies that life is already akin to a game for all involved, which means that game play is simply the most expedient form of action. The novel's revelation of Amy's monstrous nature might be expected to undercut her critique of gamification, especially given that the critique appears in the second part of the novel, voiced by Amy in her role as unmasked psychopath. Yet Amy's sneering dissection of contemporary dating mores in this section is too well observed and too resonant for it to read as merely her insanity talking. Women readers may not go as far as Amy in attempting to win the game of love, but there is a reason that the Cool Girl phenomenon has been widely discussed since the novel's publication.[19] Furthermore, *Gone Girl* pointedly does not contradict the specific indictments of her parents and Nick that Amy mounts in this section. Even when the novel is focalized through Nick, he never becomes significantly more sympathetic than he appears in Amy's version, even when Amy herself becomes profoundly less so.

This framing means that Amy's critique of the gamification of love still belongs to the novel's realist vein even as her insane response to it becomes the primary engine of the novel's genre fiction status, both authorized and pathologized by its mystery-thriller conventions. Amy's takedown of the Cool Girl provides the conceptual switching point between the novel's two generic and epistemological registers: one that purports to represent the world as it is and one that features the shocking acts of individuals who interrupt everyday life with evil machinations. One result of this conjunction is to undercut the reader's identification with the feminist ire in the novel's satire of heterosexual dating habits, by making it the motivation for an over-the-top form of revenge that readers cannot be expected to endorse.

More importantly for my specific purposes here, however, this trajectory suggests that the relationship between gamification and the survival game is one of causation rather than equivalence. That is, the survival game in *Gone Girl* is not a meditation on or metaphor for the process by which each human life becomes a locus of capital but rather an example of the profound, outsized measures required to set oneself outside—above—that process. The survival game is Amy's answer to the question, what does it take to achieve sovereignty over the countless games in which people act in their own best interests?

To get a sense of how this form of sovereignty operates and why it carries such imaginative power in the present, I want to turn now to a set of works that represent the survival game genre more fully than *Gone Girl* does: the *Saw* horror franchise, particularly the prototypical first film.[20] Whereas *Gone Girl* foregrounds the relationship between the survival game and the overarching process of gamification, the *Saw* films present the survival game as the only one in town for their unfortunate characters. In the first two films, the primary villain is a man known as Jigsaw, but, as one of his victims points out, Jigsaw cannot be considered a serial killer because he never actually kills anyone. Instead, Jigsaw presents his victims with the capacity to decide their own fates; as he puts it, "Live or die. Make your choice."[21] Victims encounter this choice when they find themselves caught in situations or mechanisms created by Jigsaw—referred to as "traps" in the fan culture surrounding the series—that for the most part require victims to make decisions between saving their own lives and an option that seems almost worse than death.[22] In the central trap of the first film, for example, two people wake up with their legs shackled to opposite sides of a grimy bathroom. Between them is a body lying in a pool of blood, holding a revolver and a tape player. They learn from audio tapes they find that one of them, Lawrence, must kill the other, Adam, before six o'clock, or Lawrence's wife and daughter will be killed and he will be left in the bathroom to die. Adam and Lawrence soon realize to their horror that the other, unspoken option is to use the saws provided to cut through their own legs, and the voice on the tape tells them, "Let the game begin."

Because his victims technically may live if they choose accordingly, Jigsaw's game makes a claim to futurity that punishment by death does not.

The painful option he offers always relates to a past moral failing—in the opening scene of *Saw II*, a voyeur must cut out his eye if he wants to live, for example—but the process is expressly meant to shape his victims' future actions rather than simply torment them for past actions. As Amanda, his only surviving victim, puts it in *Saw*, undergoing one of Jigsaw's tests made her "a better person." In a fashion familiar from *Gone Girl*, *Saw* demonstrates the villain's masterful control of the game through this ability to predict and shape the actions of the players despite being invisible on the field of play. The climax of the first film hangs on the revelation of just this quality. In the film's final and most startling twist, the supposedly dead body on the floor between Adam and Lawrence suddenly moves and comes to its feet, and we realize this seeming corpse was Jigsaw all along, lying inert while his schemes unfolded around him.[23] Jigsaw is such a terrifying force because, unlike the horror villains that have come before him, he can be as passive as a dead man and still ensure that events transpire exactly as he wishes. He embodies the power to control others by capitalizing on rather than foreclosing their capacity to make choices in their own best interest.[24]

Although Jigsaw and his successors manufacture some choices that involve close emotional ties, most traps feature the sort of grotesque, excruciating mutilations heralded in the title of the franchise. Given the historical importance of spectacular forms of torture to the assertion of sovereignty, it is not surprising that an exploration of sovereign power would involve such vivid and unpleasant displays of bodies undergoing physical torment. But unlike the spectacles of penal torture famously described by Michel Foucault in the opening pages of *Discipline and Punish*, torture in the *Saw* franchise arises not only from the physical pain involved but also from its status as the victim's selected option.[25] The criminals in Foucault's account are only required to undergo torment and die, but the victims in *Saw* are required to choose between two appalling options and enact the slightly less appalling one themselves. The fact of having to choose and to enact one's choice is as much a form of torture as is the ultimate result.

In turning choice into a form of torture, these survival games generate and enforce suffering agency of the most agonizing kind. When Lawrence succeeds in sawing off his own foot, he proves he can subordinate supremely excruciating immediate sensations to his commitment to achieving his other, chosen option: life for himself, his wife, and his child. Because only the most profoundly focused will could carry someone through an action that is so abhorrent, agency and suffering become mutually reinforcing for the *Saw* victim: the more suffering he inflicts on himself, the more he proves his capacity for agential action—and the more agency he demonstrates, the more self-inflicted suffering results, and so on. The result of Jigsaw's power in *Saw* is not a decree over life or death but the manifestation of an individual who enacts total commitment to his or her own life-or-death choice. Jigsaw's ability to induce this form of focused will is what leads Amanda to align herself with his mission and become his apprentice. Amanda is a semi-suicidal cutter and heroin addict when she finds herself caught in one of Jigsaw's traps, the infamous and terrible "reverse bear trap," and she discovers in the process that she is utterly determined to live—so determined, in fact, that she is able to perform amateur surgery on a conscious, screaming stranger in order to extract the key that will spring the trap in which she is caught. Unless they wish to die, Jigsaw's victims must likewise enact this unwavering pursuit of life, carried through in the face of the most overwhelming internal opposition. The question is, as the tagline for the first film put it, "How much blood would you shed to stay alive?" The more blood that is shed, the stronger the attachment to life. What Jigsaw aims to trap in his elaborate and unspeakable devices is a purified and magnified expression of life-interest.

As *Saw* makes exceptionally clear, this project requires physical torment because bodily pain and injury are uniquely permanent, inalienable, and individual experiences. Lawrence cannot change his mind about having amputated his own foot or assign the outcome of that decision to anyone else. Instead, because his consciousness is necessarily tethered to his existence in a single living human body, he must experience the results of whatever choice he makes about his physical being, for as long as he continues to draw breath. Jigsaw relies on and ritually enacts the belief that there is no greater guarantor of the link between choice and consequence than the fact that each human being necessarily has only one life to live and one body in which to live it. Whatever we choose to do to our bodies, we will have to endure ourselves. And there is thus no more powerful mechanism for isolating a single, individual will than its inevitable location in a single living human organism, which possesses largely predictable responses to physical torment and imminent death.[26] In general, we can expect that people will want to avoid pain, retain all their limbs, and escape with their lives, but the sensations and consequences that adhere to each of those possibilities unfold within each human being. Short of science fiction measures, one body's physical pain or deadly injury cannot be shared with, transferred to, or expropriated by another. And the more unbearable an act is, the more conscious we are of who exactly will and will not have to do the bearing. Whereas atrocity in Foucault's account of penal torture serves as a measure of both sovereign power and the vile nature of the prisoner's crime against the sovereign, here atrocity operates as a means of drawing a line around individual experience. Torture by choice is a universally applicable mechanism, but what it produces is a form of individuation. By engaging the living body that houses each individual will, this form of sovereign power identifies, activates, and amplifies the victim's singular, nontransferable experience as a vector of life-interest.

When it depicts life-interest in this fashion, the *Saw* franchise offers a way to understand the fixation on horrific bodily mutilation across the microeconomic mode, which appears everywhere from *The Road* (2006), *127 Hours* (2010), and the *A Song of Ice and Fire* (1996 to the present) series to numerous works I do not discuss in detail here. When Jigsaw designs his victims' options based on their intense and inescapable interest in staying alive, escaping pain, and preserving bodily integrity, he forcibly conjoins their physicality to their status as agential actors. He manifests interest as life-interest by bringing costs and benefits to bear that are inseparable from each victim's status as a living organism, options that victims must then choose between and endure from inside the container of their own skin. And once this fusion between bodily existence and agential choice takes place, it makes an awful kind of sense that, for example, Lawrence leaves behind a portion of his body when he chooses against one of his interests. Because his biological being has been made identical to his capacity for choice, acting against one of his interests in favor of another requires physically partitioning the life-interest housed in his own flesh. That foot is a manifestation of life-interest in an entirely non-metaphorical way.

Although it shares a focus on the intersection of cognition, choice, and life itself, this is a vision of the contemporary subject profoundly at odds with that familiar from the accounts of immaterial labor associated with gamification. In its guise as an engine for perpetual reevaluation and modification of behavior based on available information—the sort of constant minor recalibrations in response to new data that Amy enacted in order to become Nick's ideal woman—interest in general can be seen to fit neatly with the emphasis on flexibility and self-transformation associated with immaterial labor. In this version of interest, the importance of human being itself has to do with the real subsumption of life by capital, which monetizes every element of our existence from our DNA to our status as symbol-creating animals.[27] Yet, as imagined in the survival game, the subject of interest is instead all fixity and no flow. Decisions in this regime are expressly conceived as binary and permanent—life or limb, him or me—and individuals necessarily each perceive themselves as single specific life forms. By incarnating interest as life-interest, the survival game turns the subject of interest into a single, locatable, and forcibly unified individual.

If, as I have suggested, the survival game operates as a means of imagining the form of sovereignty that accompanies the real subsumption of life by capital, then this is a power that works by manifesting discrete individuals out of the constantly modulating flows of data that make up the regime of immaterial labor. Rather than decreeing their status as living or dead, juridical person or mere human life, this form of sovereignty produces concrete and irreversible acts of individual will related to each individual's living being. Instead of harnessing the flux of life in the form of immaterial labor, it seizes on the singularity of each human body's life-interest in order to bring concrete individuals into its crosshairs. Alongside the capture of life, understood as the sum total of human behavior, we find a forcible realization of the indelible link between an individual and a single life, understood as an irreplaceable unit of organic existence subject to decay and death. Whereas the control society requires that life be broken into its smallest components, which become one of an infinite number of elements within modulating streams of information-as-capital, the sovereignty imagined in the survival game gathers life up into human body-sized parcels. It sutures our interests to our living bodies in a fashion that ensures that we will be self-identical and singular containers for overwhelming and predictable interests, interests that in turn reinforce our status as bodies that each house only one unique human life. When it makes individuals legible as bounded units of congealed life-interest, sovereign power keeps the microeconomic subject from being washed away by the flows of post-Fordist capital. In contrast to other incarnations of sovereign power over life, this form produces an enforced experience of ourselves as individual living organisms housed in vulnerable, mortal bodies.

The survival game form emerges in the twenty-first century as a way to imagine the type of sovereign power that correlates to the subject of life-interest, but it doesn't impose a necessary perspective on that power. That is, while survival games provide a tool for thinking about sovereignty over life-interest, the thoughts that emerge are not identical. Thus far I have deliberately focused on the confluence of elements in my examples in order to trace the survival games' key features as an aesthetic formation. However, I want to turn now to two examples that exploit the elasticity of the form to offer very different arguments regarding sovereignty over life-interests. The first, *The Hunger Games* series of novels, argues that this form of sovereignty can be easily derailed because the subject of life-interest is merely an imposed construction that can be displaced by selfless action. The second, the novel cycle *A Song of Ice and Fire* and its television adaptation, *Game of Thrones*, explores the crisis that results if we recognize sovereignty as an interest in its own right—a problem that the series suggests can only be resolved through magical means.[28] Together these examples demonstrate the capacity of the survival game to perform arguments for and against the existence of the subject of life-interest, and for and against the desirability of sovereign power over this subject. Although neither series can find grounds to challenge life-interest except through narrative sleight of hand, their accounts reveal the perceived flaws and limits of this form of sovereign power.

In *The Hunger Games* series' near-future version of North America, the government of Panem periodically requires formerly rebellious districts to turn over children selected by lottery to compete in a televised kill-or-be-killed survival game, from which only one champion will emerge alive. However, rather than being conscripted into the survival game, the heroine of the series, Katniss, joins up in order to save the life of her younger sister, Prim, when Prim's name is drawn in the lottery. In beginning with an act that directly denies the compulsive attachment to self-preservation on which the survival game depends, the series declares its intention to drive a wedge between its heroine's private motivations and the goals and choices anticipated and encouraged by the logic of game play. In large part, the series produces this effect by displacing the rhetoric of near-impossible choices on which the legibility of interest usually depends. As I have argued, the microeconomic mode makes interest palpable by generating abstracted, high-stakes situations in which the benefit of choosing one option is only slightly greater than the cost paid: you can catch a man but that means he won't love you, you can save your life but you'll lose your leg, you can stay alive but you'll have to cannibalize someone else. In contrast, Katniss's choice to volunteer in place of Prim is an obvious and easy one, despite its extreme and painful consequences. She never exhibits any attachment to the option she abandons—letting her sister enter the survival game—because she values her own life so much less than she does Prim's safety. Katniss makes her choice in an instant because, when the benefit so greatly outstrips the cost, the cost hardly weighs in the balance. She suffers as a result of this exercise of agency since the games are of course unbelievably harrowing, but the exercise of agency in what is arguably her most consequential choice is not itself a site of suffering.

Given the lessons in unpleasantness provided by works such as *The Road* and *Saw*, it is easy to imagine how Katniss's protective love for others might instead have been activated as an interest and thus turned into a source of suffering agency for her. She could have been required to choose between killing her sister and causing her sister perpetual agony, for example, or between killing her sister and killing her ally, Peeta, and so on. Instead, her love for Prim and later for Peeta is activated to compel her into the game and to cause her suffering—for example, when the President of Panem makes sure that Katniss understands that Peeta is being tortured because of her choices—but that love never becomes completely encompassed by the codifications and binary choices of game play. Were Katniss to be forced to choose between two outcomes both prompted by her need to protect others, then the Capitol would have proven this other-directed motivation to be no more than another form of interest; the proof would be in its capacity to make Katniss actively weigh and choose whom she is ultimately more interested in protecting. Even if the choice were motivated by protective instincts in that she judged one person less able to bear the pain than the other, the active process of decision would transform her self-sacrifice from a counter to the Hunger Games, capture of interest into another manifestation of that capture. Because Katniss's commitment to loving self-sacrifice is never transformed into suffering agency in this way, the series can insist on a division between the motivations it associates with game play—subterfuge, narrow self-interest, betrayal—and those embodied by Katniss, Peeta, and Katniss's sister, Prim: an unwavering commitment to putting the welfare of others before that of oneself.

Once we accept this account of sovereignty over interest, the apparent power imbalance between those who would be sovereign and the populace they desire to rule becomes inverted. While interest is required by the game designers if they are to manifest their power via the survival game, Katniss seemingly proves that people need not be interested provided they can retain the ability to put others before themselves, even in the face of profound pressure to focus on one's own self-preservation. In effect, the ineradicable quality of interest becomes attached to sovereign power, which must have interested subjects if it is to function, while its subjects, as exemplified by Katniss, can eschew interest if they so choose. (That this choice to deny self-interest does not itself register as a form of action in Katniss's own best interest indicates the series' success in disavowing the framing power of the microeconomic imagination of choice.) This transformation reaches its apex in the climax of the first novel, in which Katniss forces an impossible choice upon the game designers themselves. At the last moment, the Capitol rescinds an amendment that had promised two tributes from the same district might together win the games, rather than only one emerging alive as the victor. Faced with the necessity to kill or be killed, Katniss pulls out a handful of berries so poisonous that they are fatal almost instantly when ingested. When they realize that both Katniss and Peeta plan to commit suicide together rather than complete the games on the Capitol's terms, the gamemakers face their own impossible choice: allow the games to finish with the hugely popular final tributes both dead or allow Katniss and Peeta to win the game in a way that defeats the Capitol's own plans. In forcing the Capitol to choose the only slightly lesser of two evils, Katniss foists upon the rulers an experience of suffering agency that they never manage to invoke in her. It is seemingly sovereign power that is hostage to interest, not Katniss herself.

Although the narrative depends upon our acceptance of this false distinction between Katniss's motivations and those that can be understood as interested, this acceptance is encouraged and sustained by the conventions of the romance genre, specifically those regarding the heroine's relation to interiority. As feminist critics have argued, romance narratives require the heroine to be almost comically dense regarding her own feelings and those of the male love interest.[29] By not knowing either how she feels about the hero or how he feels about her, the heroine is rendered by definition innocent of either wanting his affections, which would require that she understood how she feels, or attempting to capitalize on what he is beginning to feel for her, which would require that she understood how he feels. Instead, as perhaps most famously enacted by *Pride and Prejudice*'s Elizabeth Bennett, the heroine goes about her business with no sense either that the hero is falling in love with her or that she is falling in love with him. In *The Hunger Games* trilogy, this convention protects the series' primary romantic plot from being engulfed by the logic of game play. Although Katniss and Peeta pretend to be in love in the first and second novels to win advantages in the arena, the distinction between real love and self-serving playacting is only reinforced by this pretense, which rests upon a distinction between instrumental and non-instrumental approaches to love. In fact, Katniss at first has no idea that Peeta's playacting is no such thing since he actually does love her, and after this realization she is still in the dark regarding her feelings for him. Rather than it seeming implausible that she cannot see Peeta's love when it is blindingly obvious to the reader, this implausible obliviousness is ratified as a recognizable feature of Katniss's generic status as a romantic heroine. As a result of her incapacity to know her own mind, Katniss cannot instrumentalize Peeta's real feelings in order to win the games since she isn't aware of them; nor can her feelings for him also be activated as a site for the suffering agency, since she does not decide what she feels about him until a period outside the chronology of the series' main plot, narrated in retrospect in the flash forward of the final novel's conclusion. The same conventions that evolved to protect the romance heroine from being read as motivated by self-interest rather than love operate in *The Hunger Games* series to protect Katniss's primary function as a romance heroine—choosing the right mate—from being transformed into yet another interested choice coded as game-play.

In attempting to enforce this boundary between Katniss's motivations and those of interest, the series necessarily transforms the perceived relationship between sovereignty and interest. Not only does Katniss's loving protection of others escape full codification within game play, but also this failure delimits the conceptual and geographic reach of interest as a form of rule. By conflating the Capitol, game play, and narrowly self-serving notions of interest, the series indicates that sovereignty over life-interest can be escaped provided one leaves the political realm behind. This escape comes to fruition in the series' flash-forward epilogue, in which we find Katniss, Peeta, and their children living a happy rural family life on the outskirts of the realm controlled by the new government. In offering this vision of a back-to-the-land existence purged of the problems of interest, the series regenerates the opposition between sovereignty and survival that other survival games collapse, but it can only do so by forcibly denying aspects of both. Living outside the complexity of contemporary existence becomes aligned with love, peace, and community, while the common-wealth becomes the frightening arena in which survival and self-interest reign supreme. If sovereignty is now revealed to rest on a certain kind of interest, *The Hunger Games* trilogy argues, then that revelation only makes it clear that government itself must continue to be understood as the problem, not the solution.

Taken in sum, the series' argument thus functions by realigning and repurposing rather than rejecting the connection among interest, self-preservation, and sovereignty that I have been tracing in this chapter. *The Hunger Games* trilogy engages the same elements as survival games that insist on the intransigent qualities of life-interest, and that is what gives its version both its extraordinary sense of currency and its seeming authority to challenge the engulfing logic of game play. Yet its challenge is specious in that, as I have suggested, Katniss's loving commitment to others is not categorically distinct from interest but only made to appear that way, in part through the conventions of romance on which the series depends. *The Hunger Games* series relies on magical thinking because it invites us to believe the baseless argument that it isn't possible to turn love into just another move in the game—that if the Capitol's game designers can't successfully gamify love, then it cannot be done. That this reasoning depends entirely on an illusory opposition between self-sacrifice and interest is something the series implies we will find in our own interest to ignore.

In *Game of Thrones*, the failure of sovereignty arises for exactly the opposite reason: rather than life-interest being reduced to simple self-preservation, which can be set aside in favor of saving the lives of others, interest frames every possible aim, including that of becoming sovereign. Whereas works such as *Gone Girl* demonstrate the way in which the survival game proves the game designer's sovereignty over a world ruled by interest, *Game of Thrones* depicts a survival game motivated by the fierce interest everyone has in becoming sovereign. Rather than existence outside the survival game being a measure of sovereignty, sovereignty becomes the prize promised to the competitors in a life-or-death game. As one character puts it, "When you play the game of thrones, you win or you die."[30] Once sovereignty becomes merely the ultimate interest motivating competitors, however, it seemingly becomes impossible for true sovereignty to be achieved since sovereign power over interest requires legislating rather than playing the game. The title of *Game of Thrones* encapsulates a logical conundrum: by definition, no one who plays this game can achieve the sovereignty that is the game's ultimate prize.

To some extent, we might understand this conundrum as merely a rehearsal of the logical contradictions that have been argued to haunt the concept of sovereignty in general.[31] Yet what *Game of Thrones* points to is the more specific incarnation of this problem created by the seemingly unlimited scope of interest as an explanatory frame. Once every motivation comes to be understood as an interest, there is no reason why the goal of being sovereign cannot be treated as an interest like any other. But if sovereignty is treated in this way, it becomes subject to the same potential capture via individuals' life-interest that we have seen in survival games such as *Saw* and *Gone Girl*. That is, the problem is not just that no one playing the game exists outside of it in a way that would enable them to design and set its parameters; the problem is also the very fact that sovereignty is an interest, which means everyone who tries to set themselves outside of the field of play as sovereign can be pulled into the game through their inevitable embodiment of life-interest.

In order both to explore and resolve this conundrum, *Game of Thrones* relies on an unprecedented generic hybrid. It combines—or, more specifically, places side by side—a hyperviolent, sexed-up survival game that plays out through political intrigue and a conventional fantasy narrative featuring destiny, heroism, and magical powers. We can get a sense of how crucial this co-presence of fantasy and game is from the way in which HBO packages its canny television adaptation of the novels. The title sequence takes its form from one of the defining elements of fantasy as a literary genre: the detailed map of fantasyland. Maps are crucial to fantasy because the genre's imagination is fundamentally spatialized; in fantasy, space is both moral and magical, and there are good and evil places as much as good and evil people. But the map appears here in a kind of toy-model guise that suggests less a document one might use to navigate a landscape than the play space of an elaborate board game; the individual kingdoms and houses seem not so much geographical destinations, fictional or otherwise, as pieces to be won.

Within the series itself, the spatial imagination of fantasy as a genre is reworked to distinguish the survival game and fantasy genres and to place them in telling relation to one another. Part of what makes *Game of Thrones* read as cutting-edge fantasy is that it tropes the spatial imagination of the genre by localizing the conventions of fantasy itself. In the north and across the sea, both readers and characters find themselves squarely in the landscape and generic conventions of a portal-quest fantasy: a journey in which a hero or heroine has to learn the conventions of a magical realm and his or her destiny within it.[32] Across the sea, for example, the rightful queen of the seven kingdoms, a teenager named Daenerys, raises dragons, withstands fire, and is marked in various ways as the one destined by birth and magical abilities to reclaim the Iron Throne of Westeros. But in most of Westeros itself, where at least half the action is set, characters and readers occupy a more or less rational world governed by the same physical laws as our own. Westeros once contained dragons and other magical elements, the novels imply, but these are now the stuff of legends and most people scoff at the idea that they could return. In segments set within Westeros, the generic form is less that of fantasy than a sensationalist realist novel (in the text version) or big-budget quality drama of a certain type (in the TV version), concerned with intrigue, romance, sexual decadence, betrayal, inheritance, and lust for power; remove the crowns and swords, and you might at first glance be in a world little different from television series such as *House of Cards* or *The Sopranos*.

There is nothing new about narratives focused on such Machiavellian battles for power, and arguably that familiarity explains their ubiquity in the present moment. It is less troubling to see every motivation as a form of interest when the people concerned are expected to be selfish and lacking in empathy—that is, self-interested in a straightforward way. What *Game of Thrones* dramatizes is something rather different, however: a world in which even the most genuinely caring or otherwise morally valorized motives are revalued and flattened within the calculus of game play. For example, when Lady Catelyn betrays her son's side in the civil war in an attempt to save her daughters' lives, her son excuses her actions by attributing them to the irrationality of love, "which can lead us to great folly, but we follow our hearts."[33] Lady Catelyn asks herself ironically, "*Is that what I did?*" because her son's self-serving interpretation ignores her well-calculated plan to get her daughters back, which might have worked had it not been thwarted by her brother's stupidity; rather than being driven willy-nilly by foolish love, she judged the cost of losing an advantage in the war to be less than the benefit of ensuring the safety of her children, and she made her move accordingly.[34] Although we can witness a similar flattening of motivation in live models such as *The Road*, which erodes the distinction between selfless and selfish forms of parental love for children, the survival game form creates this perception of leveling by transcoding rather than deconstructing moral distinctions. Rather than understanding her actions as inhabiting a separate realm or register in which love rather than will to power pertains, Lady Catelyn sees herself as simply approaching the same war of succession as her son in the way that makes the most sense for her. Her love for her children functions merely as another interest with effects within the game.

Even when characters don't understand the effects of their own actions in this way, the significance of these actions for the series' narrative trajectory and for the other characters lies in their relation to the survival game. When Lady Catelyn's naïve young daughter, Sansa, fancies herself in love with the loathsome Prince Joffrey in the first novel, her romantic notions provide Queen Cersei with the chance she needs to enact her own strategy, with the result that a foolish preteen crush becomes a decisive factor in the game of thrones' first round. Despite the fact that Sansa's own motivations have little connection to the ruthless will to power that structures the game's ultimate goal, her interests become transposed into the logic of the game and utilized accordingly. Of course, characters' actions might be seen to contribute to any tightly constructed plot in a similar way. No matter what their various desires and goals, all the major characters in *Romeo and Juliet* contribute to determining its tragic conclusion. The difference is that, in *Romeo and Juliet*, the events belong to the text's created world, whereas in *A Song of Ice and Fire*, they belong to a game that happens inside but is not identical to the created world. Instead, the novels display over and over the process by which an action, occurrence, or desire comes to produce a result within the game, even for those who do not consider themselves players.

This transposition process lies at the heart of the series' initiating plot, which occupies the majority of the first novel and creates repercussions that echo through the tens of thousands of pages that follow. The current king, Robert Baratheon, convinces his old friend Ned Stark to relocate to the capital and serve as the Hand of the King, a decision that thrusts Stark, his wife, and his children into the center of the game of thrones. That he fails to understand how thoroughly they now inhabit this game space leads to Ned's death and various forms of tragedy for his wife and children when he underestimates Queen Cersei's ruthlessness and determination to win. Even though there is no plot in the Westeros sections that does not play a role in the game, the game remains distinct from the fictional universe writ large precisely because their collapse into one another is so dramatically and repeatedly enacted within the text in this way. Rather than simply creating a world that is a game, *A Song of Ice and Fire* thematizes the process by which a game engulfs the world.

This engulfing process is spatial—enfolding the ripples of every possible action within Westeros—but also temporal, in that it involves continual speculation regarding the future. Because even actions not intended as game play still operate as such, successful play requires comprehending the motives of others and predicting what they are likely to do next. In order to plot successfully, one must also plot the course that others are likely to take based on what they are likely to want. Sansa's crush on Joffrey contributes to the game's unfolding in large part because Cersei correctly reads Sansa's character and thus can both foresee and reframe the choices Sansa encounters. Although there are battle sequences and consequential victories by various armies, this need to predict and manipulate the actions of others constitutes the primary field on which the war for sovereignty unfolds. In this focus, the game of thrones resembles other strategy games, but it also renders the prediction process much more difficult. Because of the capacity of the survival game to engulf and recode any motivation into its own logic, consequential actions are not necessarily motivated by the goal of winning the game. Instead, players will pursue whatever interest they find primary, and those actions will create ripples for other players that still need to be anticipated, contained, or turned to some advantage. Despite her intense commitment to her son's cause, for example, Lady Catelyn still belies his expectations by putting the lives of her daughters ahead of his attempt to win the civil war and become king. Even when it comes to trusting a mother not to betray her child, the inability to predict what others will see as in their own best interests can lead to catastrophe for players of the game.

The series is littered with similar highly consequential instances of misplaced trust, many of which cause the death of those on the "good" side of the war; in one character's succinct summation, "Trust would get you killed."[35] As a result, characters who do stay alive tend to do so because they place little faith in those around them, a fact that is conveyed by repeated declarations of distrust. A few examples from the second novel suffice to suggest the dizzyingly multidirectional nature of this mistrust: " 'Balon Greyjoy is not a man to be trusted' "; "Tyrion did not trust Varys, though there was no denying his value"; " 'I trust no one,' Cersei snapped"; " 'The Spider spins his secret webs day and night,' Grand Maester Pycelle said ominously. 'I mistrust that one, my lords.' "[36] As the sheer number of such declarations suggests—some fifty in the second novel alone—distrust is not a one-time act of negation but rather an ongoing process of suspicion, analysis, and calculation. Players in the game of thrones survive by gleaning what lies behind others' outward actions and making shrewd guesses regarding their opponents' actual goals and plans. In this survival game, winning requires that players be able to parse and predict human behavior, and "trust" only happens after an examination so searching that it seems to contradict the very definition of the word.

This is precisely the sort of game that game theory, a key contributor to the microeconomic imagination, was designed to master.[37] In the prisoner's dilemma, the classic game theoretical scenario, two prisoners are each separately given an option to inform on the other for a reduced sentence, but the reduction only holds if the other player doesn't choose to "defect," as it is called. If neither of you defects, you both receive only a minor charge. Trusting the other player not to defect can have a huge benefit, but only if (a) she is trustworthy and (b)—and this is the crucial point—she trusts you. If your partner assumes that you will defect, she will likely do so as well. The prisoner's dilemma is a succinct encapsulation of a world in which the presence of other people results in the need for constant evaluation not only of one's own best interests but, crucially, of what those others are likely to think is in their best interests. Because we can expect that people will "defect"—that is, alter their plans and actions when it benefits them to do so—as situations evolve and each player reacts, everyone's calculation of their own and others' interests becomes locked in a perpetual feedback loop. And because people's interests will affect the game even if they do not seem related to achieving the game's stated goal, these interests must also be expected to vary infinitely in kind as well as over time. Normal versions of trust are forms of futurity that stop this endless cycle; trust is in effect a belief that people will behave in the future in ways that are consistent with either our own evaluation of them in the present or their own statements of intent. Once the survival game renders everyone a subject of life-interest, however, trust becomes replaced by continual doubt in a kind of serial, paranoid version of sociality in which there is no exit from or cessation of the prisoner's dilemma for all involved.

As I discussed in the previous chapter, several of Hobbes's contemporary commentators have analyzed the resemblances between the prisoner's dilemma and the decision confronting Man in the state of nature. For Hobbes, sovereignty provides an external check on this process of perpetual and mutual suspicion by enforcing peace and allowing individuals to cease fearing one another. In the game of thrones, however, it is this very position for which the game is being played. Or, to put it another way, the commonwealth *is* the state of nature in the game of thrones, and that is the problem.[38] As a result, there appears to be no end to the iterative cycle of allegiance, ascendancy to power, destabilization, betrayal, dethroning, and so on—a fact that registers on the level of form through the novels' incredible and seemingly unending proliferation of families, characters, villains, and subplots over thousands of pages and numerous volumes.[39] Because of the game of thrones' internal logical contradiction, stopping this process requires that someone achieve sovereignty, but sovereignty can only appear to be achieved by someone who is not playing the game for which sovereignty is the prize.

Within the series' realist plot, characters attempt to resolve this chicken-and-egg dilemma by activating the intrinsic, unbearable quality of others' life-interest through gruesome and shocking acts of violence. To give just a few examples, a twelve-year-old girl is stripped naked and beaten bloody by knights, a nine-year-old girl witnesses repeated torture, a woman has her face bitten off by a man, countless people are flayed alive, and one character has his hand chopped off and is then forced to wear the rotting appendage around his neck. What is notable about these acts is that, unlike the sort of interested behavior analyzed by game theory, they rarely serve instrumental purposes in terms of advancing the goals of the characters in question. Unlike Jigsaw's use of life-interest to elicit acts of profound will by his victims, the villains in *A Song of Ice and Fire* frequently appear to be motivated by pure attachment to violence against others. Prince Joffrey doesn't have Sansa stripped and beaten in order to get information out of her but because he likes using his power to cause pain. Even in the repeated torture that nine-year-old Arya is forced to witness, which is ostensibly undertaken in order to gain valuable information, it is all too clear that the torturer enjoys his work in a way that is not strictly required by the information-gathering process.

We can understand the purpose of this behavior if we place the dynamic of life-interest alongside the analysis of sadism offered by feminist theorist Jessica Benjamin. In this view, sadism is a cultural commonplace because individuality has been conflated with a masculine posture of "over-differentiation," which takes extreme form in order to negate the inevitable, underlying dynamics of resemblance, mutual dependence, and intersubjective fusion.[40] Because this over-differentiation is under continual threat from the actual mutual dependency we experience in infancy and intermittently throughout our adult lives, sadism is required to shore up the falsehood of a fully individuated self. Sadism functions to deny interdependence because when we cause pain rather than empathizing with it, we insist on our fundamental distinction from the body in pain, on our bounded separateness. While Benjamin understands reciprocal responsiveness as a positive experience that is denied by the culture at large, the microeconomic imagination makes a certain type of reciprocal responsiveness the norm in the form of endless calculation of and response to the perceived interests of others. The need for separation that sadism fulfills becomes particularly pressing in game theory's *mise en abyme* of unending mutual assessment. In causing his victim pain, the sadist blocks this reciprocal relation by making interest solely the problem of the other, for whom the interest in escaping pain becomes all encompassing. To paraphrase Elaine Scarry's famous argument regarding torture, we might say that to experience pain is to have an interest while to cause pain is to master interest.[41] Acts of intense, gratuitous violence against others appear to make the sadist momentarily sovereign over life-interest rather than simply another subject of it.

If sadism is one of the best answers realism can offer to the endless cycle of mistrust that constitutes the prisoner's dilemma, then it is perhaps no surprise that *A Song of Ice and Fire* turns to fantasy or that this turn has proven so appealing. What makes fantasy so potent in this context is its reinvigoration of otherwise outmoded notions of supernatural agency in the guise of magic and destiny. As a genre, epic fantasy privileges the trope of the "true king" who is marked out by genealogy as the bringer of ulti- mate peace, and the crowning of this king conventionally supplies the necessarily happy if long-delayed ending to epic fantasy cycles. In *A Song of Ice and Fire*, the fantasy plot takes shape for the most part outside of Westeros and concerns the fate of Daenerys, a young woman who is both the legitimate heir to the throne of Westeros and possessed of a magical affinity with dragons that signals her chosen status. Daenerys's dragons prove that she is the rightful queen, but they also prove that she belongs to a fantasy plot that guarantees that the rightful heir will eventually triumph. Not only does Daenerys operate outside the physical and generic space of Westeros's realist game of thrones—another girl gone from the field of play—but she also occupies a genre that possesses the means to make one person's eventual sovereignty appear inevitable, total, and permanent.

Even for those not fated to be sovereign, the dynamics of agential action become transformed by fantasy's focus on bringing into being a world that is foreordained. For characters with magical abilities, human choice becomes both agential and destined in that they are aligned with a larger pattern that serves the ultimate good. To act in keeping with destiny requires that the heroine make the choices that she is supposed to, but the choices and actions importantly still remain hers alone. In the *A Game of Thrones* novel, Bran, a child who becomes paralyzed in the first book, is, like Daenerys, strongly associated with the portal-quest fantasy conven- tions of the series and hence most marked by destiny. We can get a sense of destiny's ability to balance agential action and overarching pattern from this description of a vision Bran has after his disabling accident:

Now you know, the crow whispered as it sat on his shoulder. *Now you know why you must live.*

"Why?" Bran said, not understanding, falling, falling.

Because winter is coming.

Bran looked at the crow on his shoulder, and the crow looked back. It had three eyes, and the third eye was full of a terrible knowledge. Bran looked down. There was nothing below him now but snow and cold and death. . . .

Now, Bran, the crow urged. Choose. Fly or die.

Death reached for him, screaming.

Bran spread his arms and flew.[42]

The paranoid speculation, sadism, and seriality without end that constitutes the game of thrones is replaced here with a kind of attunement to the path that the hero should follow but must choose for himself. Destined action is future-oriented not because it assesses what others will do in their own best interests but instead because to act in keeping with destiny is to realize a preexisting design or prophecy, to bring about the future that is meant to be. For example, queen-in-exile Daenerys is more than capable of making mistakes—like most of the good characters of Westeros, she suffers as a result of misplaced trust—but the actions she takes in the cause of reclaiming the throne are presented as part of a destined series of events that ultimately will restore order to an out-of-balance world. If action in one's own best interests turns everyone into a permanent opponent, destined action ultimately leads to harmony, to a permanent end to the game. Destined action thus offers the fantasy, in both senses of the term, that individual choice can be purged of the negative consequences associated with suffering agency at the same time that it manifests a form of agency that is global in its consequences.

Although the series remains unfinished, we can expect that, in the end, Daenerys will achieve sovereignty and end the game of thrones because, when it comes to designating true sovereignty, fantasy conventions overpower those of realism. In realism, there is no such thing as the one true king or queen, destined by birth to return to power and put an end to all struggle, and that is why the series requires fantasy if it is to be able to declare a winner in the game of thrones. Once sovereignty itself constitutes the field of play, the series suggests, it is impossible to imagine a final end to the game without calling on forces that exceed simple human agency since every mere human action simply becomes enfolded within the logic of the game. By organizing human life according to an overarching pattern that we do not create, fantasy's confluence of magic, destiny, and true birth provide a means of designating a predetermined and perfect end to the game that is unavailable within the apparatus of realism. Fantasy counters the engulfing logic of life-interest, which threatens to encompass the possibility of sovereignty itself, with a universal and total reach of its own.

Taken together, *The Hunger Games* and *Game of Thrones* indicate both the reach and the inherent instability of sovereignty over life-interest as a basis for governmental power. On the one hand, both texts indicate that there is no external locus to the operation of a sovereignty based on our inherent experience of life-interest. Both the *A Song of Ice and Fire* and *The Hunger Games* series can only find a limit to this operation by activating a kind of magical thinking—quite literally, in the case of the former set of texts. On the other hand, the *A Song of Ice and Fire* novels indicate that there is something inherently iterative about this form of sovereignty: given that it is not the exercise of sheer force but rather the capture of life-interest that differentiates the sovereign game designer from the mere game player, there is a continual danger that the game designer's own interest will be captured and codified as game play as well. This is precisely the possibility that *The Hunger Games* relies on in order to produce a form of suffering agency for the Capitol rather than Katniss. In its drama of sadism and suspicion as a process without end, *A Song of Ice and Fire* instead offers a means to understand the obsessive replication of survival games across the field of popular aesthetics. Unlike the sovereign power to kill or let live, sovereign capture is not a constitutive threat but an ongoing process. It must be continually reinforced and reenacted if we are to understand ourselves as governed through our status as specific and unfolding individual units of life.

I want to conclude by considering briefly what the relationship I have traced here among life-interest, sadism, torture, and sovereignty reveals about the type of stories that have been told regarding the American use of torture in the war on terror. As my analysis thus far will have suggested, the link between torture and the microeconomic mode is overdetermined. In its archetypal form, torture offers what might be the ultimate version of the abstraction and extremity that characterize this mode: through the stripped-down confrontation between the torturer and the tortured, torture aims to produce interests in the victim so profound that they white out and render irrelevant everything else in the world.[43] In what is tellingly called the "economic model" of torture, the actions of torturer and victim specifically involve "the give and take of question and answer, of pain and information, of possible costs and benefits."[44] This economic logic becomes particularly explicit in the ticking-time-bomb scenarios through which American torture has been fictionalized and debated in the twenty-first century.[45] Exemplified by works such as the film *Unthinkable* (2010), the ticking-time-bomb narrative features a reluctant American torturer who must face the impossible choice between overcoming his own intrinsic and deeply held distaste for torture (presented as simply a feature of the American psyche) and letting innocent Americans die.[46] In effect, this scenario stages an evaluation in which the moral cost of torturing is measured against and found to be worth the huge benefit of the saving of thousands of innocent lives.

Although the ticking-time-bomb scenario makes elements of the economic model unusually explicit, it is specific in shifting the terms of this model from the painful interests of the tortured to those of the torturer.[47] Whereas in Scarry's archetypal scenario torture that eradicates agency turns the victim's pain into the torturer's power, torture in the ticking-time-bomb trope transforms the victim's pain into the torturer's pain. That is, in facing an unbearable choice that requires subordinating one profound interest to another, the torturer manifests his own version of suffering agency. As the American torturer, H, puts it in *Unthinkable*, "This is war. This is sacrifice"—in this case, his sacrifice of his own humanity for the lives of his countrymen, who are under imminent threat by three hidden nuclear bombs planted by the torture victim, Yusuf. Because H finds it agonizing to perform torture on Yusuf, every scream requires that H steel his will to maintain the path he has chosen. And once the torturer endures his victim's agony while also causing it, his will becomes writ large. Yusuf simply withstands being tortured, but H withstands torturing himself. This is a position, the film makes clear, that no one wants to occupy. When his good-cop foil, Agent Brody, tries to stop H from torturing Yusuf's wife in front of him, H offers instead to transfer the unappealing position of suffering agent to her by making her take on the choice he faces: "Do you want to know where the bombs are or not? It's my responsibility! You want me to win, or you want him to win? . . . So you made a choice, you want him to win?"

H does in the end win the information he seeks by preparing to torture Yusuf's children in front of him—this we learn is the film's particular unthinkable thing—but H never turns Yusuf into the helpless, shattered nonagent familiar from the archetypal *Nineteen Eighty-Four*-style torture narrative. As I have argued in this chapter, when suffering agency activated by life-interest operates as the guarantor of individuality, torture can be seen to manifest its victims' agency rather than eradicating it. In this view, the victim has chosen to be tortured because he or she could end the process easily by revealing the information required. *Unthinkable* reinforces this perspective by reminding viewers over and over that Yusuf has put himself in this position deliberately and prepared himself to withstand torture as a result of his commitment to his cause. Even at the moment in which the tortured individual capitulates, he is not seen to have abandoned his position as an agent but rather confirmed it by making one of the most consequential sort of choices imaginable. Yusuf may be denied the liberal rationality that *Unthinkable* associates with full personhood, but he is nonetheless presented as fully qualified and capable as a subject of life-interest. When H gets Yusuf to reveal the location of the bombs, he does so not by crushing Yusuf's capacity for choice but instead by giving Yusuf the necessary incentives to choose freely the option that H himself prefers Yusuf to choose. *Unthinkable* asks us to believe that, while H holds his agonized course with greater commitment than his victim, Yusuf also remains a suffering agent to the end.[48]

Of course, there is an obvious political utility in imagining the torturer as an equal victim in an almost-equal battle of wills with his victim. Yet I want to suggest that its depiction of the victim as a subject of life-interest suggests that the ticking-time-bomb scenario has a more specific function, which may explain some of its more puzzling features. Not only does it appear as a point of public debate almost immediately after the destruction of the World Trade Center, well before there is any official acknowledgment of the United States as engaging or needing to engage in "enhanced interrogation techniques," but also the torture that was eventually revealed to be perpetrated by the United States in the war on terror bears very little resemblance to the dynamic that drives the ticking-time-bomb scenario. Even leaving aside the spurious value of torture for actual information-gathering purposes, the actions and circumstances captured in the Abu Ghraib photos, for example, suggest little of the battle between almost-equal interests depicted as unfolding between H and Yusuf. Instead, what we know of actual U.S. torture more obviously suggests the unilateral and self-gratifying exercise of power that Scarry and others identify as the goal of torture in its archetypal form.

However, the early, repeated, and erroneous recourse to the ticking-time-bomb scenario makes a different kind of sense if we understand its purpose otherwise: not as a means of mediating the actual use of torture in the war on terror but instead as a way to negotiate the uncanny, powerful, and disturbing resemblance between the act of the suicide bomber and the form of individuality guaranteed by life-interest. Not only is interest in the microeconomic imagination by definition nonfalsifiable and incontestable—it's in my interest to blow myself up if I say it is—but the suicide bomber also pays for his or her choice in the very currency that underwrites agential action in the present, the embodiment of life-interest. Considered from this perspective, it is difficult to refute the logic that leads one individual to judge the benefit of making a fatal strike against one's enemies to be worth the cost of losing his or her life. In fact, once self-preservation operates as the clearest sign of interest, acting against self-preservation in order to achieve another objective becomes a profound expression of suffering agency, of the commitment to attain one interest at the expense of another held almost equally dear. And, unlike the self-sacrifice of the soldier who flings himself into the breach to save his comrades, the emphasis on premeditation in depictions of suicide bombing puts the focus on the calculated trade-off that brings a subject to see something else as more valuable than continuing to live. In fact, the very bafflement that is so frequently expressed regarding this choice highlights its status as a decision, as a process of weighing and selecting among options that is presumed to exist but in this case confounds the observer. When the confluence of life and choice operates as the medium of individual will, deliberately and consciously turning suicide into a weapon in one's own cause may come to seem one of the most cogent and agential acts a subject can take.

To be clear: my point is not that this logic has any bearing on the actual motivations of any actual political actors or torturers outside the fictions of American torture apologia. Rather, I am suggesting that the ticking-time-bomb trope is in part an attempt to engage and revalue a perceived resemblance between the suicide bomber's instrumentalization of life-interest and the dynamics of living choice that guarantee individuality in a regime of immaterial labor. If the "terrorist" appears to triumph through an über-potent expression of life-interest, then it becomes imperative to imagine an assertion of American sovereignty over this particular form of power. A narrative focused on torture by choice offers itself as the ideal means to conjure this victory because, as *Saw* in particular makes clear, the product of torture by choice is a supreme expression of life-interest. In order to both activate and overcome the life-interest of the terrorist, however, the ticking-time-bomb scenario revises the narrative familiar from *Saw*. It is not sufficient in this version for the torturer to force the victim to subordinate one profound interest for another since it is the terrorists' capacity to master their own life-interest that constitutes the threat to be eliminated. Rather, in order to prove his power, the torturer must demonstrate that he can best the victim on the same ground on which the suicide bomber has gained the advantage: the enactment of suffering agency.[49] That is why H is not outside the game, a sovereign designing its rules, but inside of it, a player fighting to win; that is why he must be both torturer and self-torturer. In order to stage the defeat of an enemy who has weaponized life-interest, the ticking-time-bomb scenario proves that its hero can withstand more suffering for his agency than his opponent can.

Chapter Four

SOVEREIGN CAPTURE

In chapter 2, I offered a theorization of life-interest by reading it in relation to the role played by self-preservation in natural law theory, liberal biopolitics, and the set of methodologies that contribute to the microeconomic imagination of choice as essentially allocative, rational, and individual. Here, I shift my focus to consider life-interest not in relation to its theoretical antecedents but rather in the context of the contemporary theorization of control, which provides a framework for thinking through the relationship between life-interest, sovereignty, and discretization. In my discussion of survival games, I argue that they model a form of sovereignty that both accompanies and interrupts the movement from the individual to the "dividual" that Gilles Deleuze identified as one effect of the control society.[1] In its relentless focus on the human individual as a bounded, rational unit of life, the microeconomic mode would seem to work in direct opposition to accounts of life in control, which often point toward the modulations of becoming and the permeation of affects across bodily boundaries as defining features of the control era. Yet, as I suggest here, both becoming and affect are crucial to the way in which life-interest is instantiated in the microeconomic mode. In the first part of this chapter, I read sovereignty over life-interest in relation to both the process of discretization and valorization associated with control and the classical version of monarchical sovereign power. In combining features of each, I suggest, sovereignty as imagined in the microeconomic mode calls into being a version of both becoming and affect steeped in limitation, lack, and loss. Finally, I turn in conclusion to the relationship between the microeconomic mode, affect, and horror. Horror provides the affective signature of the microeconomic mode, I suggest, because it yokes the physical embodiment of each individual's vital flesh to the threat of suffering and death.

As I began to suggest in the previous chapter, sovereign power over life-interest resembles classical monarchical sovereignty in uniting judgment, force, and the vulnerable status of human life. In Michel Foucault's famous formulation, monarchical sovereign power is defined by the capacity to "take life or let live," to consign some subjects to life and others to death.[2] Because sovereignty necessarily acts without reference to determinate judgment, sovereign decisions inevitably create rather than align themselves with such distinctions—the most foundational of which is the distinction between those who are subject to the law and those who create law but are not subject to it.[3] Acts of sovereign decision thus couple judgment regarding foundational conceptual demarcations with the power to render such judgments absolute and final. As in the decision to kill or let live, the application of force upon the body is crucial to the display of the absolute nature of the categorical distinctions instantiated by the sovereign. Vengeance upon the body of the condemned man "affirm[ed] the dissymmetry of forces" and "revealed truth and showed the operation of power."[4] From prolonged torture to the severing stroke of the executioner's sword, literal slices into and through the subject's body carve into flesh the distinction between the monarch's immense power and the subject's puny mortal being, between the guilty and the innocent, between the suspicion of wrongdoing and its reality, between falsehood and truth.[5] In what Foucault calls "the right of the sword," the demarcating power of sovereign decision becomes materialized in the cut through living flesh.[6]

Sovereignty over life-interest also entails a confluence of supreme will, living flesh, and conceptual demarcation, but, as manifested in the survival game, sovereign power cuts not through living flesh but rather through the dense, everyday texture of the preexisting social field. What is carved out through sovereign decision is the game itself, the delimited arena in which all human action is either transcoded into the life-or-death logic of game play or rendered irrelevant. By combining the epistemological and visceral right of the sword with this act of forcible transcoding, the survival game fuses sovereign power with one of the central but elided processes of control: the act of capture. Through a set of interlocking metaphorical transfers among the biological, ecological, and technological registers—traced in illuminating detail by Seb Franklin—control comprehends all human behavior as a self-regulating, quantitative system of one kind or another. In the control society, Franklin points out, "all of life—or, at least, all that matters about life—appears already fully digital and thus intelligible as value-creating labor."[7] What is foreclosed in this world view is capture, or the "instrumental practice [of] the digital rendering of the world."[8] Capture is the means by which the teeming, uneven, variegated field of human behavior becomes rendered in a uniform, binary language from which value can be extracted. If control presents the world as always already digital, then capture describes the disavowed practice of discretization and quantification that makes such a presentation possible.

When human action is recoded as a game composed of binary, life-and-death choices, we are confronted with a recognizable if highly unpleasant form of this combined digitization and valorization of life. The survival game reflects the perspective of control in its assumption that individual life and binary choice are always already fused; without this fusion, there would be no guarantee that players would participate in the game. Yet the survival game does not disavow but rather spectacularizes the work of capture, such that the usually implicit violence of selection and discretization becomes a showy testament to the power of sovereign will to carve up the fabric of the world. Each human is tethered by the game to the twin vectors of individual life and choice, trapped in a wrenching series of binary, life-or-death, them-or-me decisions. If we understand the imposition of the survival game as a violent, overpowering act of discretization—what I will call sovereign capture—then we must understand this act not as a break with the logic of control but rather as a highly specific version of that logic, one focused on the coalescence of power, binarization, life, and the bounded body of the individual human being. Or, to put it another way, we might say that sovereign capture is the version of control addressed to the individual as itself a living binary switch: the choice between life and death as the ultimate 1 and 0.

The result, as I began to suggest in the previous chapter, is a very different view of the process of discretization and valorization usually associated
with control. As Franklin demonstrates, what we see from the vantage
point of control is a "cybernetically modeled world, [a] flat ontology of black
boxes" that emerges from "fractal processes of exclusion and erasure."[9]
This is the view reflected in the network diagram: a two-dimensional
representation of the routes and switches through which information travels. From this perspective, each individual human being appears as just
another black box whose inner workings are irrelevant since only the
binary signal that issues from the black box registers as information within
the network. Each human action constitutes a choice that sends one signal
rather than the other along the network chain, and what happens within
the human-as-black-box to generate that signal is invisible and inconsequential. However, as Franklin indicates, this opacity does not render the
individual immune to interference but rather the reverse. Once the individual subject is conceived as essentially a switching circuit, it becomes
possible to envision this subject as an eminently "programmable object."[10]
This vision, Franklin argues, is exemplified in the cycle of *Bourne* films,
which center on an amnesiac who discovers he has been programmed as a
sleeper agent. A black box even to himself, Jason Bourne has been subject
to "implanted memories and behavioral patterns" that demonstrate the
"literal programmability (biological and/or psychological)" of the human
body as hardware.[11] Through this literal act of programming, the films gesture toward "the historical production of the social actor as intelligible
through the principles of informatic control."[12]

In contrast, what we find in the microeconomic mode is something
more like the view from inside the black box, and from this position choice
appears utterly agential rather than preemptively programmed. Whereas
human decision registers in the network diagram only via the transmission of a binary signal, the microeconomic mode obsessively renders the
agonized process by which the subject of life-interest moves from the recognition that a choice must be made to the enactment of that choice. As an
aesthetic form, the microeconomic mode dilates on the human cost of
moving that switch to either 1 or 0. In effect, both the network diagram and
the microeconomic mode represent the same ethos of control from radically different vantage points. What from one perspective looks like

agency—a supremely individual act in one's own best interest—looks from another perspective like programming: the shaping of context to encourage a decision that the switch is better moved in one direction than the other, even as the subject remains entirely free to choose. Each choice is necessarily both a signal shaped by its context within the network and an act of agency for the subject in question. The distinct aesthetic registers that house the programmable object and the suffering agent respectively both index and manage the seeming contradiction between these two facets of control.

We can see this dual process at work in the third film in the franchise, *The Bourne Ultimatum* (2007), in which Bourne finally finds out the truth about how he came to be an agent for the Treadstone program.[13] Rather than having been somehow seized and programmed against his will, Bourne learns, he volunteered himself for the initiative. This decision, the film demonstrates via flashback, was not merely a matter of signing on the dotted line but instead had to be manifested through exactly the sort of unbearable choice that I have argued indicates suffering agency. In a scene marked by all abstraction and extremity that define the microeconomic mode, we see Jason Bourne in close-up being questioned by the program's leader. He points out that Bourne "hasn't slept in a long time," that "this can't go on" and thus it is "time to make a decision." In other words, viewers learn that Bourne has for some time been in the agonized state of enduring indecision that produces the context for suffering agency. As he is disparaged by the project head for this hesitation, it becomes clear that Bourne has been given a kill order, but he must decide whether he is willing to obey without having any context that would enable him to decide for himself whether the order is justified; he will get no answers to his questions about who the man is and what he did to merit summary execution. He cannot enter the program—cannot be programmed—until he freely chooses to be controlled by someone else, to entrust his will to another. This drawn-out, tormented, morally charged act of choice could not be further from the automatized, desubjectivized, machinic precision with which Bourne executes his opponents in his guise as a programmable object. When he finally decides to shoot without knowing why, Bourne indicates through an act of suffering agency that he has chosen to be an instrument rather than an agent. By temporalizing the relationship between suffering agent and programmable object in this way, *The Bourne Ultimatum* narrativizes the causal link between these two facets of control even as it presents them in opposed aesthetic registers.[14]

Without such a narrative link, these two registers can appear not merely unrelated but diametrically opposed. In a sense, the survival game is itself a version of this narrative linkage: it tells a story that explains how we might be both programmed and agents, compulsorily coded into a game not of our own making but nevertheless choosing each move we make. However, even in the survival game, the perspective of the microeconomic mode remains radically different from that of the network diagram. Not only is the emphasis on the individual act of choice rather than the programmable context, but also this choice always turns on the specific unit of a single living human body. If, as I argue in chapter 2, the subject of life-interest has displaced the liberal individual who possessed a right to life, then we might understand the view captured in the survival game as that of the subject governed by control. This is not the birds-eye map of the network but rather a glimpse from inside each living human switch. Sovereign capture of individual life-interest is what results when the political subject and sovereign power are both reimagined according to the discretization and valorization of life itself that defines control. The network diagram is a manifestation of the conviction that capital is identical to life; the microeconomic mode is an attempt to conceive what becomes of the liberal individual when that conviction has reshaped our understanding of human being. If, as Deleuze and Félix Guattari insist, the molecular and the molar operate simultaneously, then the subject of life-interest is the molar form that human being takes in tandem with its molecularization by control.[15]

As my description of *The Bourne Ultimatum* suggests, the distinction between these two perspectives registers in large part through their very different approach to the relationship between living flesh and digital form. The body of the programmable object is sleek, speedy, and nearly immune to pain; it moves faster than the eye can see, faster than any normal reflex could be. The body in the microeconomic mode, I have argued, is all too mortal, a site of vulnerability not only to the actions of others but, most painfully, to acts of one's own will. In this section, I consider the relationship between this form of physicality and the concepts that have been central to the theoretical interrogation of living being in the control society: becoming and affect. Although they have primarily been theorized in relation to the same dynamic of dividual, molecular flows of data that are interrupted by sovereign capture, both becoming and affect are central to defining what it means to be a subject of life-interest, albeit not in a way entirely predicted or encompassed by central theorizations of either term. By identifying the work of affect in constituting the self-perception of interest in and as continued becoming, however, it becomes possible to comprehend one of the aesthetic signatures of the microeconomic mode: its reliance on the affective work of horror as a genre.

In Jasbir Puar's influential account, becoming forms one element of the malleability of the body within control, its reconfiguration as "parts, affects, compartmentalized capacities, and debilities, as data points and informational substrates."[16] As she puts it,

In Deleuzian terms, becoming is the "I" cascading into the impersonal, the stripping of all registers of signification that make each body succumb to subjectification over "signifiance." Becoming . . . is a "wholesale deterritorialization of the human," and a "becoming imperceptible"—a divestment of codes, of signification, of identity and a process of taking on the register of the impersonal. Becoming is . . . about allowing and reading more multiplicity, multiplicities of the impersonal and of the imperceptible. Importantly, becomings have no static referent of start point, end point, or climax; they have no narrative. Becoming is awash in pure immanence, never coincident with itself, marked only by degrees of intensity and duration.[17]

Although Puar makes clear that "becoming has become a zone for profit for contemporary capitalism," she contrasts the multiplicity, immanence, and nonlinearity of what she calls "becoming trans" with the capitalist biopolitical capture of the body's capacitation in "trans becoming," which puts "the subindividual capacities, the nonhuman capacities, the prosthetic capacities, the molecular capacities and the hormonal capacities" of becoming in the service of a linear telos.[18] If the result of trans becoming is a productive, capacitated subject, then becoming trans "would be a politics of manifesting beyond what control can control."[19] In both cases, however, becoming is understood to describe the status of the body in relation to control, and this is a body that is nonunitary, impersonal, multiple—its boundaries traced and submerged by the same unceasing tides of vital information.

For Puar and co-author Ann Pellegrini, the "affective turn" refers both to the central example of this form of bodily becoming and to a varied grouping of theoretical investigations that have shifted critical attention to the intersection of becoming and control. Informed by intersections of bioscience and philosophy, "this conception of affect poses a distinction between sensation and the perception of the sensation. Affect, from this per-spective, is precisely what allows the body to be an open system, always in concert with its virtuality, the potential of becoming."[20] Understood as a physiological surge in intensity within the autonomic system, affect exists outside the reach of cognition or the qualifications of emotion; it travels between bodies without subjective intention or will. Although it appears as a newly dominant instrument and vehicle of control, affect is also under-stood as an organic property of human being—one that in itself jams the mechanisms of subjective coherence, full self-presence, bodily integrity, and rational cognition. As such, it forms a crucial element in the series of oppositions that for Puar define the distinction between disciplinary and control societies: "from self/other, subject/object construction to micro-states of subindividual differentiation; . . . from will to capacity; from agency to affect; from subject to body."[21]

From one perspective, it seems that nothing could be further from this deterritorialization of the human into impersonal cascades of affect than the subject of life-interest, who is tortured by conscious choices that must be made in relation to the absolute finitude of a single living body. Affect is impersonal, precognitive, and de- or subindividual; life-interest is self-determined, rational, and fixated on the temporal and physical boundaries of each mortal human organism. While becoming is necessarily productive within control societies—even debilitation or death generates data to be valorized and circulated—life-interest is negotiated in a closed system in which each benefit comes with a cost almost too horrible to be endured. Interest necessarily gestures toward an essential remainder to every choice since it signals the option whose benefit most outweighs its cost in the sub-ject's estimation of what is in his or her own best interest. And, finally, whereas agency appears to be displaced as a value within the operations of control, life-interest understands the sheer fact of ongoing life as the incar-nation of agential action.

Yet the microeconomic mode does not simply privilege the subject over the body, individuality over becoming, or rational agency over precognitive affect. Instead, in each case, it transforms our understanding of the former term by forcibly grafting it onto the latter. For the subject of life-interest, there is no longer a separation between agential action in the service of one's own best interest and the consciousness of oneself as confined to a mortal, vulnerable organism. As I suggest in my reading of the *Saw* films, the subject's body in effect registers as congealed interest, as living testament to agency put in the service of preserving and continuing life. Rather than being defined in relation to categories of identity, this subject is stripped of social markers and oriented toward the simple preservation of life and the needs of bodily being. When life-interest is activated, in other words, the vital substrate of life shifts from a background activity of biological persistence to the central conceptual focus of cognition and activity. Life-interest rests on and propagates the realization that without this vector of bodily unfolding, without the ongoing process of life itself, the individual in question would cease to be. Or, to put it from the opposite direction, we might say that life-interest is what becoming becomes when it is itself the object of active, ongoing choice.

What becomes of this becoming is a specific kind of "impingement," to borrow Brian Massumi's description of the effects of affect. In his well-known account, Massumi defines affect in relation to "one's 'sense of aliveness' [as] a continuous, nonconscious self-perception."[22] Although it is only "the perception of this *self-perception*, its naming and making conscious, that allows affect to be effectively analyzed," this analysis can only proceed provided "a vocabulary can be found for that which is imperceptible but whose escape from perception cannot but be perceived, as long as one is alive."[23] This is not to say that affect and consciousness do not have a relation but rather that affect does not itself become conscious. Massumi describes this relation in a gloss on affection in the philosophy of Spinoza:

It is only when the idea of the affection is doubled by *an idea of the idea of the affection* that it attains the level of conscious reflection. Conscious reflection is a doubling over of the idea on itself, a self-recursion of the idea that enwraps the affection or impingement at two removes. For it has already been removed once by the body itself. The body infolds the *effect* of the impingement—it conserves the impingement minus the impinging thing, the impingement abstracted from the actual action that caused it and actual context of that action. This is a first-order idea produced spontaneously by the body: the affection is immediately, spontaneously

doubled by the repeatable trace of an encounter. . . . Conscious reflection is the doubling over of this dynamic abstraction on itself. The autonomic tendency received
secondhand from the body is raised to a higher power to become an activity of
the mind. Mind and body are seen as two levels recapitulating the same image/
expression event in different but parallel ways, ascending by degrees from the
concrete to the incorporeal, holding to the same absent center of a now spectral—
and potentialized—encounter.[24]

For Massumi, what appears to be compelling about affect is this combination of infolding and spectrality. Because it registers on the autonomic level
each minute aspect of our encounters with the world, affect demonstrates
the permeability, changeability, and multiplicity of our bodies; because it
does so in a way that can never be grasped in itself, it carries the utopian
trace of that which cannot be fully named or known. Yet, as Massumi's
description also indicates, affect produces forms of consciousness even if it
does not itself become conscious. What makes the heart beat faster is only
infolded in this effect—the impingement minus the impinging thing—but
the recognition of anxiety is nevertheless "recapitulating the same image/
expression event in different but parallel ways, ascending by degrees from
the concrete to the incorporeal." Something about affect escapes thought,
but something also arrives: "the perceptions that are [affect's] capture."[25] It
is because of this capture that perceptions have the shape and intensity and
direction that they do. Affect escapes, but precisely via that escape it also
works.

In the microeconomic mode, we can see this work in the predominance
of horror as both autonomic reaction and generic form. Across the countless contested definitions of horror as a genre, the confrontation with
human mortality appears as a consistent feature, alongside the threat of the
partial or total destruction of the human body.[26] Horror is the aesthetic
vehicle through which our affective sense of aliveness becomes captured as
an involuntary and overwhelming perception of our vulnerability to death,
decay, physical torment, and destruction of bodily integrity. Crucially, the
means by which horror produces this perception is itself lodged in affect,
in a fashion that distinguishes it from most other genres.[27] Linda Williams
places horror (alongside pornography and the tear-jerker) under the
umbrella of "body genres," or genres in which "the body of the spectator is
caught up in an almost involuntary mimicry of the emotion or sensation

of the body on the screen."[28] In horror—"a genre that derives its very name from the affect it seeks to elicit"—these physical reactions are often specifically autonomic.[29] Goosebumps, hair that stands on end, the "startle effect": these all happen without conscious thought as we embody reactions that mimic those of the characters represented.[30] In a fashion that resembles Massumi's description of the "punctual" experience of affect "typically as a form of shock," horror makes the body react before we perceive our own fear.[31] Horror not only represents our essential physical vulnerability as living bodies but also enacts that vulnerability by producing physical sensations in us over which we have no control. That is, horror is an affective genre, and the perceptions that result from it are themselves tied to a consciousness of the affective as a register—of our liveness, vitality, and processual life, evoked precisely through the threat to its ongoing unfolding.

For the subject of life-interest, this perception of vitality under threat cannot be separated from the burden of agential action. Fear, revulsion, disgust, and terror arise in the microeconomic mode not only from the threat of death but more specifically from what individual characters will do in relation to that threat. From the Hobbesian state of nature to the *Saw* films, self-preservation leads to a nightmarish realization of what each human is capable of when survival itself is at stake.[32] The horror of the microeconomic mode resides thus in the inescapable interest the subject has in survival, which both arises from our usually impalpable vital becoming and drives us to take actions to protect and preserve that vitality. Suffering agency is not always horrific, but, in the microeconomic mode, horror is most often tied to the extremes to which life goes to preserve itself. While the infolding of affect remains precognitive and impersonal, horror operates here as a specific capture of that affect, one that returns us simultaneously to the limit of our mortal flesh and the seemingly limitless lengths to which we will go to preserve it. Agency, affective becoming, and horror merge in an agonized perception that we have no choice but to choose that which will keep us alive. Life-interest makes it impossible to separate consciousness and life, becoming and bodily finitude, agency and affect—and that in itself appears as a source of horror.

In my discussion of life-interest in chapter 2, I suggest that the subject of life-interest occupies the position once inhabited by the liberal individual who was possessed of a right to rather than an interest in life. If, as I argue there, we can understand this transformed approach to individual life as part of the large-scale subsumption of the subject of interest by the subject of right, then this subsumption is itself an aspect of control: it is the subject of interest rather than the subject of right who can be conceived as a switching circuit toggling between binary choices. However, because it unites the preservation of life itself with the agential negotiation of finitude, life-interest brings together an emphasis on bodily becoming that is as alien to theories of social construction as its fixation on individual agency is to the affective turn. Life-interest is a product of control, but its operation as such can only be grasped by putting aside some of the expectations that theory has produced regarding what control entails. The microeconomic mode suggests that the individual in the control society is neither an atavistic holdover nor a disciplinary distraction—but it is also no longer classed in relation to a form of liberal subjectivity in which the body signifies as a possession. Instead, the subject of life-interest is a single unit of bodily being, a discrete packet of vital agency sliced from the field of life. In its gory pageantry, the survival game operates as a testament to this discretization, the horror of which is captured as a manifestation and measure of sovereign power.

PART III

Thriving

Chapter Five

PARTIAL FICTIONS

Life-interest signifies as a universal human property, as a given fact of human being, but that does not mean its attendant miseries are universally distributed. Yet this unevenness is disputed across the microeconomic mode, which insists over and over that the privileged are as driven by life-interest as anyone else. Because no human can be categorically immune to the perils that define existence as a living body, activating life-interest simply requires a greater departure from everyday experience when it comes to the privileged—hence the exceptional and even outlandish scenarios often faced by the white male protagonists that populate the microeconomic mode. We are all creatures of life-interest, the microeconomic mode insists, but in some cases it takes a dramatic alteration in circumstances to prove it. We can see this process at work, for example, in the disaster film *The Impossible* (2012), based on the true story of a white middle-class Spanish family who found their vacation in Thailand turned deadly by the 2004 Indian Ocean tsunami.[1] By showing its well-heeled holiday makers facing the same fight for survival as the country's native inhabitants, *The Impossible* feeds on the fear that there is nothing necessary or categorical about the distribution of life-interest as a form of suffering. What is revealed as impossible is the guaranteed escape of any human being, no matter how privileged, from the excruciating choices that accompany life-interest. In a sense, one of the functions of the microeconomic mode is to insist upon this universal existential vulnerability, to remind us that life-interest is applicable to all. It is more difficult to make the opposite argument—that only some, usually racialized inhabitants of the global North experience survival as routinely threatened—within the microeconomic mode because this mode specifically forecloses systematic or social analyses. Without those registers, it is difficult to document the way in which life-interest operates as an exceptional cataclysm for some and a daily horror for others. The experiential partiality of life-interest is rendered invisible by a mode designed to insist on the underlying presence of life-interest as a universal and defining feature of human being.

In light of this function, a set of aesthetic and conceptual challenges confront any attempt to represent or interrogate the distribution of life-interest as registered in the microeconomic mode. This mode is the language in which life-interest can be communicated, but its parameters specifically exclude the forms of social determination that lead some humans to face consistent and nonhypothetical threats to their survival. I refer to texts that concentrate on this contradiction as partial fictions. These works focus on the particular means by which the experience of life-interest comes to be primarily activated for one part of a divided field of humanity. As a result, the microeconomic mode gives shape to only part rather than all of their represented worlds, and this partial invocation in turn serves as a formal rejection of the implicit argument embodied in the microeconomic mode: that suffering agency is a universal facet of human life itself. The unequal distribution of threats to survival registers in these works primarily as a narrative horizon that neither characters nor readers can traverse but beyond which human lives are seemingly enabled to flourish. Through this formal cleavage, partial fictions thus signal both the seemingly inescapable and defining power of life-interest even as they suggest that this apparently universal quality is localized in specific areas and populations. The same formal and epistemological limit that renders the characters' life-world an inescapable totality also serves as the text's primary indication that this experience is paradoxically not as total as it seems. This cleavage in both population and narrative form is itself depicted as the product of partiality—as a result of a preferential distribution of resources that turns mere survival into a constant effort for some and an unquestioned given for others.

In so doing, partial fictions document the challenges that life-interest poses to long-standing liberal and radical critiques of the conceptual and material organization through which, as Sylvia Wynter puts it, "Man" comes to be "overrepresented" as equivalent to human being.[2] In general, partial fictions share with both liberal and radical forms of critique a focus on the profoundly uneven distribution of human suffering that exists alongside the celebration of supposedly universal human attributes. For liberal thinkers, of course, this situation arises from the incomplete and narrow boundaries that have historically defined the category of Man, a situation they suggest shifts over time as formerly excluded humans come to be incorporated into the category. For radical theorists focused on the actual forms of dispossession, disposability, and domination produced by global racial capitalism, the overrepresentation of Man is itself a key means by which racial capitalism has been propagated and justified.[3] In liberal critique, the false universality of Man is contingent and correctable while in radical critique it is definitive and integral—but in both cases this supposedly universal category hides a deleterious form of invested particularity. Partial fictions share with these critical discourses a focus on exposing the deeply unequal life-worlds both sustained and masked by falsely universal definitions of the human.

Beyond this shared gesture, however, the particularities of the microeconomic mode mean that partial fictions encounter both possibilities and difficulties not encompassed by either the liberal amelioration or the radical rejection of the false universals that define Man. Put simply, the subject of life-interest is not Man as understood by liberal individualism, and that is the problem that takes center stage in so many texts in the microeconomic mode. As I suggest in chapter 2, the subject of life-interest fuses the rational self-will of the liberal individual with a compulsive, inalienable attachment to life, which turns agential selfhood into an embodied burden rather than a mark of Man's superiority over other animals and inferior humans. In producing this shift, life-interest appears to dissolve a constitutive division between those humans considered qualified to act as liberal individuals and those abjected from that category.[4] As I argue in chapter 2, we can register this perceived shift in the countless narratives in the microeconomic mode focused on white men diminished to the status of savages, cannibals, and slaves. That is, the universalizing engine of life-interest might be understood to operate in two complementary directions: while it draws formerly exempt white men toward the compulsions associated with being a living body driven to survive, it also extends the inevitable burden of agential choice even to genres of the human formerly classed as irrational, animalistic, or both. Moreover, to the extent that the conceptual universality of life-interest hides a partial distribution of life-interest in practice, it is now the dispossessed segments of the human population rather than those formerly designated Man who would seem to most exemplify this new purported universal.

This complex realignment affects liberal and radical critiques of Man in different ways. For approaches ostensibly aimed at rendering liberal humanism truly universal, I suggest, life-interest appears as a kind of blockage, a short-circuiting of several of the key liberal arguments aimed at recognizing the universal value of the human. Captured with particular clarity in the United Nations' Universal Declaration of Human Rights (UDHR), these gestures concatenate "faith in fundamental human rights" with "the dignity and worth of the human person," a conception of human equality that in turn rests on a Kantian conflation of personhood and dignity.[5] In the narrative logic of the UDHR, it is because humans as a group are possessed of "inherent dignity and . . . equal and inalienable rights" that each human being can claim "the right to recognition everywhere as a person before the law."[6] Within this tautological logic, one can make claims based on universal human rights by demonstrating one's essential dignity as a person.[7] As many theorists have demonstrated, this concatenation of normative concepts remains fused to forms of violence that unfold at the intersection of liberal epistemological demarcations and material force upon flesh.[8] Just as the inscription of legal personhood in state and federal law cannot be separated from the institution of chattel slavery in the Americas, the genesis of human rights as a global norm cannot be separated from the post–World War II hegemonic order from which it emerged.[9]

As the novels I examine here indicate, however, life-interest renders both personhood and expressive interiority irrelevant and turns agency into a punishing absolute rather than a sign of true belonging to the genre of Man. Rather than celebrating the elevated attributes of the liberal individual, the microeconomic mode emphasizes what humans share with other animals (a commitment to survival) and renders what purportedly does make them unique (their capacity for rational choice in their own best interests) an endless horror. Moreover, partial fictions indicate that life-interest cannot be made to function as a principle of abstract, disinterested equivalence in the fashion of liberal humanism, despite being framed as a universal human attribute. Rather, because it necessarily involves both survival and choice in one's own best interest, life-interest throws into relief the invested nature of choices that determine who has the resources to thrive—in other words, exactly those material concerns often elided within the liberal human rights paradigm.[10]

This emphasis on the material capacity to thrive presents a different set of opportunities and obstructions when read in relation to radical critiques of racial capitalism. On the one hand, life-interest resonates with such critiques in raising the role of vested interests in distributing access to both the category of personhood and the physical means of survival. When the resources required for thriving are center stage, it is harder to mask that, as Grace Kyungwon Hong puts it, "the promise of universal incorporation offered by . . . developmental narratives is contradicted by the material histories of racialized and gendered difference upon which the property system is based."[11] In its emphasis on bodily needs and foreclosure of abstract equivalence, the microeconomic mode can also appear to gesture toward the asymmetrical access to resources produced by global capital. Particularly when it renders human life just one more resource to be consumed, the microeconomic mode can seem to echo important work that traces the production of new forms of disposable life in contemporary capital.[12] On the other hand, however, the microeconomic mode is defined in part by its profound antihistoricism, which means that the historical and geographical contextualization crucial to radical critique are necessarily inaudible in this mode. The global historical extraction of resources through dispossession and disposability by definition cannot be expressed or interrogated within the terms of the microeconomic mode. As *The Impossible* makes clear, the emphasis in this mode is not on the historical complexities that generate such uneven access to thriving but rather on what happens when extremity and abstraction render such complexities inconsequential. Not only is this antihistorical approach to survival inimical to radical analyses of global domination, but it can also appear to give credence to key facets of what Wynter calls "Man2"—a bio-economic version of Man that naturalizes global racial hierarchies as an expression of evolutionary selection.[13] By emphasizing binary choice in relation to survival and outside the context of historical determination, the microeconomic mode may seem to chime with a survival-of-the-fittest logic that represents inequality as an inevitable feature of life itself.

The partial fictions that I analyze in this chapter navigate these crosscurrents from quite disparate points of entry. In Dave Eggers's *What Is the What: The Autobiography of Valentino Achak Deng: A Novel* (2006) and Kazuo Ishiguro's *Never Let Me Go* (2005), the incompatibility of the claims of liberal humanism and the burdens of life-interest take center stage. *What Is the What* attempts to revise the human rights bildungsroman so that it can accommodate a context in which agency and self-determination have become more problem than solution and cost–benefit analysis rather than recognition of universal personhood guides individual action. In attempting to manage this transformation, however, the novel racializes the production of life-interest in the United States in a fashion that exonerates and continues to elevate those most aligned with the genre of Man. *Never Let Me Go* instead presents the privileged as exemplary subjects of life-interest and explores an emerging distinction between the unique person who deserves dignity and the ontologically distinct life to which one is attached. The guiding question of the novel—one to which it cannot find a positive answer—is whether there is any escape from being guided by individual cost–benefit analysis once we accept interest in life as the quintessential human imperative. In Jesmyn Ward's Hurricane Katrina novel, *Salvage the Bones* (2011), we find a sustained critique of the resonance between narratives of life-interest and the survival-of-the-fittest model incarnated in Man2. Unlike the other partial fictions I examine here, *Salvage the Bones* reads the survival logic of the microeconomic mode in relation to the natural world, but it deploys this naturalization to demonstrate the role of human intervention in creating its characters' inability to thrive. In its thorough engagement with the parameters of the microeconomic mode, the novel offers the most far-sighted interrogation of the consequences of life-interest for radical critiques of racial capital that I have encountered.

Although these novels do not coalesce into a single form in the fashion of the live models and survival games I analyze in chapters 1 and 3, respectively, their struggle to address life-interest produces a shared aesthetic signature nevertheless. In each of the partial fictions I examine here, the narrative is shaped by a conspicuously inapt choice of genre, which creates a disjunction between form and content that signifies in its own right. In *What Is the What*, the human rights novel becomes a means to appropriate the voice of the protagonist and argue against his status as an agent capable of acting on his own behalf. In *Never Let Me Go*, a biotech-based sci-fi scenario provides the frame for an elegiac counterhistory of the recent past. Finally, in *Salvage the Bones* we find the coming-of-age novel repurposed to tell a story about the inherent violence of biological development. By foregrounding the repurposing of generic registers in this way, these novels stage the distance between long-standing critiques of the genres of Man and adequate responses to the emergent justifications of injustice enabled by a regime of life-interest. That they enact this generic gap rather than moving beyond it indicates the extent of the conceptual and aesthetic shift required to manifest demands for social justice in relation to a subject defined by life-interest.

What Is the What is based on the real-life history of Valentino Achak Deng, a Sudanese "Lost Boy" who was separated from his family at the age of nine when war came to his village.[14] As did thousands of other young boys during the 1980s civil war, he walked hundreds of miles through a violent landscape shorn of food and shelter toward supposed safety, first in Ethiopia and then in Kenya. Not only was the fate of the Lost Boys publicly discussed as a human rights crisis, with important and visible UN intervention, but also the novel is marked in various ways as a human rights bildungsroman.[15] It is largely composed of a first-person narrative of human rights abuses; its implied reader is designated as heretofore uninformed about the extent and geopolitical causes of these abuses; and the contribution of its profits to charitable endeavors links the existence of the text to the need for ameliorative action on behalf of those who have suffered such abuses. Although there are numerous critiques that can and have been made regarding the constraints and efficacy of the human rights bildungsroman, *What Is the What* is revealing for my purposes because it remains wedded to characteristic narrative technologies of the human rights novel. As a result, the novel demonstrates what becomes of this representational apparatus when the human rights abuses in question amount to a form of suffering agency and the choice to recognize such abuses involves individual cost–benefit analysis. As I will suggest, *What Is the What* attempts to envision a response adequate to both of these shifts, but it does so by rely-ing on familiar narratives that position liberal whites as enlightened enough to move beyond self-interest.

In the fashion of partial fictions, the novel insists that suffering agency is distributed to some portions of the population rather than others, and it mirrors this unequal distribution in its divided narrative form. The por-tions highlighting suffering agency focus on Achak's experiences as a Lost Boy, and, although they make up the bulk of the novel, they are conveyed via a frame narrative set in present-day America that highlights the gulf between his personal history and that of the Americans around him. After briefly describing the idyll that is Achak's life in the village before the civil war erupts, the framed narrative recounts Achak's journey across a land-scape that has turned deadly in ways that defy enumeration. The Lost Boys are variously killed by raiders, used as cannon fodder by their own side, stalked and eaten by lions, starved and dehydrated, worked to death as slaves, felled by a variety of illnesses, and turned into living blood banks for injured soldiers. In one disturbing passage, Achak is so close to death that he wakes to find a vulture perched on his leg, ready to begin its feast.[16] Moreover, Achak and the other Lost Boys encounter this deadly landscape without the interpretive tools of either historical context or social typology. Not only has the social world of their villages been decimated, but, because of their youth, they also lack the knowledge or experience to comprehend the details of the conflict around them. Without an understanding of what motivates the people he meets, how strangers might want to use him, or even what country he inhabits, events for Achak and his reader are rou-tinely abstracted to whatever can be gleaned of their immediate, apparent causality. In their relentless journey across a landscape of abstraction and extremity, the Lost Boys endure horrors strikingly similar to that of the father and son in *The Road*, but they inhabit a historical reality that, as pre-sented by the novel, has itself come to embody the microeconomic mode.

What Is the What depicts the Lost Boys' stumbling efforts to keep alive in this deathly landscape as a form of suffering agency, even in the absence of a dramatic choice regarding equal and overwhelming interests. Because of the Lost Boys' youth and dire circumstances, they suffer continually from being left to care for themselves despite having neither the materials nor the knowledge required to do so. When Achak is living at the Pinyudo refugee camp, for instance, he and the other unaccompanied minors are told to build their own shelters with a few inadequate pieces of wood, and Achak describes the results in a way that makes clear how inadequate their efforts are:

When I arrived here in the U.S., one of my old friends from the camps bought me a gift, a set of Tinker Toys. The thin dowels were so like the sticks we used to construct our first shelters in Pinyudo that I had to laugh. Achor Achor and I built a facsimile of our Group Twelve home on our coffee table and then we laughed some more. It was so similar it stunned us both. (301–2)

Required to function as grown men capable of producing shelter for themselves, the unaccompanied minors can only produce results appropriate to children playing with toys, an untimeliness underscored by the fact that they only encounter the toy version much later, as adults. Even in the more stable world of the Pinyudo camp, which provides a brief respite from the Lost Boys' wanderings, life as an unaccompanied minor means suffering in large part because one has no choice but to act as an agent—too soon, too completely, and with too few resources to make the effort any less than an exercise in near failure.

In exploring such experiences of suffering agency, *What Is the What* indicates the inadequacy of human rights rhetoric to capture contexts in which self-determination has been demanded rather than denied. This inadequacy is particularly clear when Achak encounters situations that are commonly addressed as human rights' abuses, such as the use of young boys as child soldiers. When Achak is at Pinyudo, the army commander there makes a speech calling the Lost Boys "the seeds" of the new nation of Sudan, and this phrase soon becomes a telling nickname (332). In order to bring the new nation into being, the Seeds are expected to undergo harsh military training aimed at making soldiers from emaciated boys, whose ranks are then decimated by either the war they are sent to fight or the brutality of the training itself. Even when a totalitarian, militarist regime plans their every move and treats them as disposable tools, the unaccompanied minors suffer not only from a lack of autonomy but also from the demand that they function as men rather than boys. Given no choice but to manifest a power they do not have in the service of a cause they do not understand, the Seeds are required to perform as if already fully grown. Their designation as the Seeds indicates the self-defeating and untimely nature of this demand: they are expected to be capable of generating the very nation that preemptively harvests their lives in the process. Rather than needing their inherent equality recognized and enabled, what Achak and the other Lost Boys need most is a release from the presumption of parity voiced in the demand that they operate as the equals to men at full strength—that they perform simultaneously as suffering agents and convenient tools.

The obvious release from this horror would seem to involve Achak being protected and nourished like the child he is. However, *What Is the What* demonstrates that suffering agency undermines this possibility as well. Not only does the agency involved in their suffering make presumptions of essential human equality more damaging than helpful to the Lost Boys, but the suffering involved in this agency also seems to mark them out as categorically not worth helping. Achak recounts that, even in the increased comfort and structure of the camps, the unaccompanied minors occupy the "lowest rung" of the dispossessed, and his narrative includes many accounts of the contemptuous treatment that results from this status (225). In one such episode, Achak and his crew of near-starving children are sent to perform heavy labor for a woman at Pinyudo, and they ask her for a drink of water after completing the work. She refuses to help them and implies that they should be well aware that they have no claim to anyone's assistance: "Is this a joke? Get out of here, mosquitoes. Drink from a puddle!" (328). The woman's insulting name for the Lost Boys encapsulates the link between their obvious deprivation and their lowly status—a link repeated when they are called "insects" by a soldier who chases them off rather than protecting them (224). Just as their sticklike, rickety bodies make them resemble insects, their lack of thriving provokes the sort of revulsion and disdain elicited by such creatures. As children attempting to survive with little assistance and less hope of succeeding, their self-guardianship is necessarily torturous and inadequate; this manifest lack of thriving then renders them abject and thus unworthy of assistance; and this same judgment makes it highly unlikely that they will be helped to thrive. Although it is not uncommon for humans who appear near death to be presented as abject, the novel presents the Lost Boys as trapped in a cycle of abjection that is specifically tied to their untimely and inadequate efforts as self-responsible agents. It is because they struggle and fail to help themselves—because of their suffering agency—that they are seen as unworthy of help from others.

It is this form of suffering agency, I want to suggest, that *What Is the What* attempts to reverse in its most troubling distortion of the human rights bildungsroman genre: its narrative ventriloquism. In his foreword, Deng explains that the narrative is told by Eggers in an "approximat[ion]" of Deng's voice and was "pronounce[d]" a novel because Deng simply could not remember all the details from events that took place when he was so young.[17] In other words, this is an account of human rights abuses told by someone who did not endure them, in which "many of the passages are fictional."[18] To the extent that telling the story of one's personal development constitutes the tautological act of "narrative self-sponsorship" that defines the human rights bildungsroman, this approach would seem to rob Deng of the very manifestation of personhood promised by the act of narration.[19] Yet the rhetorical violence of this act rests in part on the presumption that telling one's own story guarantees a form of agential personhood that has previously been denied. As presented by the novel, the Lost Boys' suffering arises not from a lack of agency but rather from the premature and excessive demands placed upon them as agents. To insist that Deng demonstrate his worth as a human being by writing his own autobiography would, in this view, only add yet another demand for self-sponsorship to what has already been a crippling and criminal burden. Perhaps more crucially, self-sponsorship by definition cannot reverse the crucial judgment encapsulated in the Lost Boys' designation as insects, which declares them unworthy of assistance precisely because they were left to fend for themselves in a war zone with predictably poor results. By speaking on Achak's behalf, the novel counteracts not only the suffering agency that defines the Lost Boys' struggle to survive but also the perceived lack of value that attaches to lives for which and about which no one cares.

This intervention obviously smacks of paternalism, and in a sense that is precisely its point. The novel draws on the Lost Boys' particular experience of suffering agency to model social justice as a kind of fostering in both the general sense of promoting life's flourishing and the specific sense of the voluntary and temporary acceptance of parental responsibility for children not one's own. As a non–biologically determined form of responsibility for children otherwise lacking guardians, fostering figures a complex relationship among vulnerability, protection, and choice. It signals on the one hand that we cannot demand every life be always already responsible for itself, and on the other that there is no universal standard that enables us to demand that this guardianship be undertaken by any particular individual. Children are widely understood to require some form of guardianship, but fostering is conventionally undertaken by volunteers, not conscripts. By placing Achak's sufferings as a child-agent on a continuum with his struggles to thrive as an adult in the United States, the novel positions acting in loco parentis as both the literal counter to the Lost Boys' experiences and as one possible response to the unequal distribution of suffering agency among adults. The Lost Boys, as children in the camps, desperately need actual foster parents; furthermore, the very existence and form of *What Is the What* indicates that, as an adult, Deng has sought the more oblique forms of fostering embodied in the novel itself. Given that the proceeds from the book go in part to fund a college education for Deng, who was in his late twenties at the novel's time of publication, readers who purchase *What Is the What* have in effect already cosigned the extension of this fostering to vulnerable adults struggling to thrive by helping to underwrite an expense often paid by a college students' parents. Although fostering is thus positioned as a tidy counter to the usual prioritization of the survivors' action on their own behalf, the conflation of the Lost Boys' childhood needs with adult Achak's needs also indicates a troubling failure of imagination—as if the only form of care the novel can envision is that of a typically hierarchical helping hand.

The extent of this failure becomes clear if we attend to the way in which the novel works to reframe the model of cost–benefit analysis through which subjects of life-interest can be expected to make decisions. As I will suggest, these efforts collapse into exactly the sort of white-man's-burden trope whose specter is raised by Eggers's paternalistic fostering. Central to this reimaging of choice is the decision to listen to Achak's story, which presses upon the reader through the novel's chronotopic structure. In the twenty-four hours described in the frame narrative, Achak recounts his autobiography as an internal monologue directed to those around him, including a hospital receptionist, his neighbors, and so on. Over the course of this day, Achak is robbed and beaten in his apartment, dismissed by the police, denied care at the hospital, and then treated to friendly, willfully superficial chit-chat at the gym, where he works facilitating the self-care rituals of others. Achak's continued struggles to thrive in America and the obliviousness of those around him become the context in which the reader learns of the history that has shaped him. By funneling the entirety of his extraordinarily painful history through the keyhole of this twenty-four hours, the novel's pointedly lopsided chronotope positions Achak's past as an overwhelming yet invisible weight still borne daily in the present. Confronted with the oblivion of those around him, Achak recounts his silent protests: " 'You do not understand, I would tell them. You would not add to my suffering if you knew what I have seen' " (29). Yet, even if it is true that knowing his story would alter the behavior of those around him, Achak has no ground to demand a hearing beyond "what he has seen"—that is, beyond the content of the very story those around him have chosen not to hear. Rather than his history eliciting care, the choice to care is required to make his history signify. In positioning readers in this narrative gap between the unbearable weight of Achak's story and the pointed ignorance of his social world, the novel asks us to consider what might be required to close this gap, to elicit a different kind of choice.

As an answer to this question, the novel offers its eponymous parable, a Dinka origin story about the first man and woman. Tellingly, the parable of the What stages the problem of action that must be undertaken in the radical absence of crucial knowledge regarding costs and benefits. That is, a choice must be made before the stakes can be fully understood and weighed. As Achak's father tells it, the story of the What begins when God makes cattle as a gift for the Dinka. However, God also offers the first man and woman another choice besides the cattle:

The man and woman thanked God for such a gift, because they knew that the cattle would bring them milk and meat and prosperity of every kind. But God was not finished. . . .

—God said, "You can either have these cattle, as my gift to you, or you can have the What." My father waited for the necessary response.

. . . Sadiq said, helping out, —What is the What? he said, with an air of theatrical inquisitiveness.

—Yes, yes. That was the question. So the first man lifted his head to God and asked what this was, this What. "What is the What?" the first man asked. And God said to the man, "I cannot tell you. Still, you have to choose. You have to choose between the cattle and the What." Well then. The man and the woman could see the cattle right there in front of them, and they knew that with cattle they would eat and live with great contentment.

So the first man and woman knew they would be fools to pass up the cattle for this idea of the What. So the man chose cattle. And God has proven that this was the correct decision. (62)

In Achak's father's version, the Dinka were correct to make this choice because God gave the What to the Arabs instead, which explains their lack of fertile land. However, the later dominance over the Dinka by the Arabs in the civil war disproves his interpretation, and the numerous other guesses regarding the What that circulate in the novel underscore its fundamental mystery. The total and categorical nature of this absence is reflected in the tautology of the novel's title. From the position of the individual choosing, there is no way to designate the option at hand except in its own opaque terms, such that the only designation possible simply reiterates the question: the what? Only by choosing the What can you learn what it is.[20]

As this description suggests, the parable of the What functions as an abstracted version of the choice that confronts the people who encounter Achak in his daily life in America. Like the Dinka, these people face a decision that involves distribution and access to the means of thriving. Moreover, in both cases, the decision can only be made in the complete absence of information regarding one of the options involved. In the case of Achak's story, potential auditors cannot know what it will cost them to listen until they do so. Of course, it is certainly likely those around him might decide that the risk potentially involved in opting for the unknown What is not worth whatever potential benefit might be forthcoming. In effect, this is the choice made by the Dinka in the parable and seems to be the choice made by most of those Achak encounters over the course of his day. Yet, by demonstrating the possibility of choosing the radically unknown in such elemental circumstances, the parable of the What reveals this ignorance not as a mere continuation of the status quo but rather as an active choice not to know. Achak's potential listeners choose between the known and the What exemplified by his story, whether they note the choice or not. Although the novel thus insists that the existence of Achak's story necessitates a decision from those around him, this choice crucially cannot be made based on an evaluative comparison of the two choices at hand since the knowledge required to perform a cost–benefit analysis can only be gained after the fact.

Like the Dinka, *What Is the What* argues, we can only know what we have chosen once we choose; we have to leap without being able to look both ways. In modeling the choice to allow Achak's claims to reach us in this way, the novel turns the epistemological chasm between his experience and those of his potential interlocutors into a means to prevent this decision from being subject to cost–benefit analysis.

This solution is remarkably tidy, but it unfolds in practice via a predictably racialized distribution of decision that reveals the novel's commitment to a version of liberal individualism associated with whiteness in particular. That is, *What Is the What* revises the language of choice as an instrument of social justice, but it envisions these choices as best enacted by the usual suspects. Most obviously, Phil Mays, the upper-middle-class white man who becomes Achak's sponsor, emerges as the novel's ideal incarnation of the choice to listen despite not knowing the cost. Although Phil originally intends only to donate money to the Lost Boys' cause, he capitulates to becoming Achak's mentor once he allows Achak to present his case. Phil is so moved that, in the aftermath of the meeting, Achak "watched as [Phil] got into the car. . . . He sat down behind the wheel, put his hands in his lap and he cried. I watched his shoulders shake, watched him bring his hands to his face" (173). Indeed, once he decides to listen to Achak, Phil appears to have so little ability to resist being driven by empathy that Achak "feels terrible" for "the poor man" as Phil "struggles" not to take on more than he planned—as if Achak knows that the power of his story is too strong to resist (172). In suggesting that recognition of Achak's suffering leads Phil to capitulate, *What Is the What* evokes the concatenation of narrative empathy, recognition of shared humanity, and performance of ameliorative action that is a mainstay of human rights discourse.[21] Because we feel for others in the way that is encouraged by first-person narratives, the argument goes, we will recognize their human dignity; in seeing this shared status, we will come to see others' oppression and pain as an unacceptable violation of their dignity that must be eradicated. In keeping with this framework, Phil's capitulation to sponsorship is presented as inevitable once he decides to listen to Achak since Achak's story generates an empathic reaction that Phil cannot help but heed. Once he chooses to hear Achak, Phil reacts as a liberal individual who has no choice but to do what is presented as the right thing.

That which enables Phil to listen in the first place, however, seems to be his privileged access to resources. The importance of this factor becomes clear when we compare his role in the novel to that of the African American characters who feature in the opening scenes. The frame narrative begins when Achak opens his apartment to an African American woman who says she needs help after a car accident, but it soon transpires that she and her partner in crime, an African American man, have concocted this story in order to rob Achak. He is pistol-whipped, tied up, and left with a young African American boy, Michael, whose treatment of Achak is dehumanizing in a way that resembles Achak's treatment as a child during the civil war. When Michael drops a phone book on Achak's head, Achak feels that the boy sees him as a bug to be crushed—in other words, much the same view as expressed by the woman at Pinyudo who told him to drink from a puddle. Although Achak recognizes that the boy's own situation hardly seems to a good one, this exculpatory narrative positions those who are themselves in need as unable to make the leap into empathy that Phil exemplifies. Rather than firsthand knowledge of hardship rendering another person's hardship legible, the characterization of the boy and the adult robbers indicates that dispossession is destructive of empathy. Those in the boy's situation, who have almost nothing, can only be expected to act from their own interests, whereas those who have more than enough, like Phil, can choose to open themselves to the empathy elicited by others' stories, and thus continue to function as liberal individuals.

In keeping with what Jodi Melamed calls "neoliberal multiculturalism," this division relies not on a notion of race founded in biological determinism but rather on an invocation of cultural difference. Whereas racial liberalism simply used culture as a stand-in for race, Melamed argues, neoliberal multiculturalism deploys "economic, ideological, cultural, and religious distinctions to produce lesser personhoods, laying these new categories of privilege and stigma across conventional racial categories, fracturing them into differential status groups."[22] *What Is the What* offers a version of this logic from a putatively sympathetic perspective. In the terms of the novel, blackness as such is not what strips Michael and the robbers of their capacity for empathy; rather, the sort of cultural context in which blackness is most often found—one shaped by poverty and criminalization—makes it unlikely that they will feel concern regarding the struggles of others. As in more avowedly conservative versions of this argument, it is an exception that proves this rule: the novel's one sympathetic African

American character, Mary Williams, turns out to have been raised in a milieu shaped by wealthy white donors. Mary is head of the Lost Boys Foundation and the daughter of former Black Panthers. After her parents fell prey to addiction and incarceration when she was a teen, she went to a camp for underprivileged youth sponsored by Jane Fonda. Mary was eventually adopted by Fonda, and Fonda and Ted Turner's wealth underwrites her efforts on behalf of the Lost Boys. Of course, given that Mary-as-character is based on the real-world Mary Williams, her biography is not invented for the purposes of the text—which may also be the case for the story of Achak being robbed in his apartment. Whether or not it is based on real-world events, however, the novel sends a particular message by making its inciting incident a violent, self-interested act perpetrated by African Americans. As the first and worst thing to happen to Achak in the novel's framing narrative, this act comes to exemplify the way in which Achak's present-day existence continues to be damaged by others' actions in their own best interest.

In adopting this approach, *What Is the What* maps the uneven distribution of life-interest in a fashion that chimes with neoliberal multiculturalism as described by Melamed. Although the majority of Americans that Achak encounters in the frame narrative range from self-absorbed to overtly selfish, the only characters in the frame narrative who undertake violent actions motivated by an interest in survival are African Americans. Because their association with life-interest is explained by cultural context rather than by race per se—in other words, whoever struggles to thrive becomes aligned with life-interest whatever their phenotype—this racialized distribution of interest mirrors the way in which "neoliberal multiculturalism overlays conventional phenotypical racial categories with new systems for ascribing privilege and stigma, interjecting flexibility into race procedures."[23] In *What Is the What*, the distribution of privilege and stigma remains along familiar racialized lines, but this distribution now indexes the extent of one's capacity to act outside of the constraints of life-interest. Or, put another way, we might say that escaping determination by life-interest emerges as a new signifier for proving one's alignment with universal values of "freedom," as opposed to the "monocultural," close-minded views associated with failed multicultural subjects; like those monocultural subjects, subjects of life-interest do not have the capacity to get beyond their own, purportedly narrow view.[24] Although *What Is the What* attempts to reformulate human rights rhetoric to address the burdens of suffering agency, it accomplishes this shift only by arguing that the prosperous segment of the American population remains aligned with liberal individualism because that population remains untouched by the depredations of life-interest. That prosperity itself might emerge from or serve life-interest is something the novel chooses not to imagine.

Never Let Me Go unfolds within just this imaginative gap, by envisioning a world in which power and privilege enable rather than render moot the compulsions of life-interest. In so doing, the novel foregrounds exactly the question *What Is the What* attempts to forestall: what becomes of liberal arguments for justice when it is subjects of life-interest who decide on the value of those arguments? The narrative centers on a group of friends who are raised in relative comfort in a boarding school called Hailsham, where they are encouraged to develop and display their artistic talents. As the reader gradually learns, however, all the students at the school are clones produced and raised to serve as organ donors for nonclone humans. Their humane upbringing constitutes a radical experiment by their do-gooder guardians, who aim to prove that, reared properly, the clones will demonstrate through their artistic creations that they "ha[ve] souls."[25] Although it is often read as a parable of our biocapitalist present and future, the novel is identified by a frontispiece as beginning in "the late 1990s," when the clones are adults and have begun donations, which indicates that the period retrospectively narrated by the novel begins in the late 1970s and ends before the end of the century—that is, the period in which neoliberal governance in Britain became ascendant.[26] Given that a system of clone slavery obviously did not emerge and become accepted during those decades, we must read *Never Let Me Go* as counterhistory, positioned to tell us something about what did happen in those years by telling us about something that did not.

This sense of inhabiting an alternate and to some degree illusory reality constitutes the novel's signature poetics. The narrative cleavage that defines partial fictions here places us in a kind of epistemological bubble, confined within a worldview we are nevertheless told is inaccurate or incomplete. The novel is narrated by a clone named Kathy, who recounts her personal history from the vantage point of her present job as a "carer" for "donors" who have their organs extracted from them until they die or "complete" (3, 203). The human society that has created and perpetuates this system of clone slavery is obscured by a Russian doll-like series of contained conceptual landscapes, which Kathy and, by extension, the reader inhabit. On the level of narration, Kathy shares with Ishiguro's other first-person narrators a penchant for self-deception, especially the tendency to retreat to memory when confronted with pressing realities in the present, and these qualities entrap the reader within a description of Kathy's life that is clearly shaped by wishful thinking. Her memories are in turn fixated on Hailsham, which makes up the clones' whole world when they are children and frames their understanding of their situation. Hailsham itself was created as a utopian alternative to the brutality encountered by other clone children and operated on the principle that the clones possess souls, a view clearly not shared far beyond its walls. As this description suggests, the novel communicates through a type of counterfocal narration, although in a fashion more sweeping than what is usually meant by the term. Rather than simply directing our attention to a focalizing character, *Never Let Me Go* foregrounds the way in which its nested perspectives each operate as screen or substitute for a less illusory or more representative account of the world. In each case, readers are prompted to recognize the existence of an epistemological frame that the novel both acknowledges as a limit and refuses to transgress. We crane our necks to see what is beyond this horizon—to counter the novel's focus—precisely because it has so pointedly directed its own gaze away.

This counterfocal poetics forecloses the possibility of a direct comparison between the clone and nonclone worlds, but the one clear fact we do possess about nonclone society is sufficiently telling: it has gone to extreme measures in order to satisfy individual interest in life. As the former cofounder of Hailsham, Miss Emily, explains to Kathy and Tommy near the conclusion of the novel,

by the time people became concerned about . . . about *students* . . . well, by then it was too late. . . . How can you ask a world that has come to regard cancer as curable, how can you ask such a world to go back to the dark days? There was no going back. However uncomfortable people were about your existence, their overwhelming concern was that their own children, their spouses, their parents, their friends, did not die from cancer, motor neuron disease, heart disease. So for a long time you were kept in the shadows, and people did their best not to think about you. And if they did, they tried to convince themselves you weren't really like us. That you were less than human, so it didn't matter. . . . Here was the world, requiring students to donate. While that remained the case, there would always be a barrier against seeing you as human. (257–58, italics in original)

According to this account, the designation of clones as less than human is generated by the interest individuals have in believing them to be so, and, by extension, the interest nonclones have in keeping their own loved ones alive. Although Miss Emily catalogs a number of diseases that can now be cured, there is notably no mention of the car accidents or war wounds that would presumably also create a need for donations. What activates extreme measures here is not an external threat to survival but the internal unfolding of human life itself, which inevitably involves aging and the development of disease over time. In registering interest in life as a largely unspoken but overriding cause, Kathy's veiled, oblique narration effects a kind of canceled version of the microeconomic mode. Or, to put it from the opposite direction, this partial fiction places the microeconomic mode on the far rather than the near side of its structuring narrative fissure.

Tellingly, this veiled account of life-interest seems to eschew both bioethical fears regarding human replication and the trope of the uncanny double, the aesthetic vehicle through which such fears have routinely been envisioned.[27] There is never a suggestion in the novel that the clones might displace or otherwise undermine the agency of the specific originals from which they have been copied, and the only potential confrontation between a clone, Ruth, and her "possible" (the woman from whom she may have been copied) fizzles to a disappointing conclusion when it becomes clear that the resemblance between them is not as great as Ruth and her friends first suppose (160).[28] The value attached to the clones likewise has nothing to do with their status as doubles for existing people. Instead, the clones serve as reservoirs of spare organs for the nonclone population—and not even reservoirs for their specific originals. The only indication we get of the clones' origins, in a bitter speech from Ruth, suggests that the clones have been copied from those in "the gutter"; in other words, people who would presumably lack the means to commission a clone for their own eventual organ-replacement needs (164). In contrast to the sort of hypothetical arguments frequently made in bioethical circles about the dangers and seductions of cloning technology, which imagine what would transpire if we had the ability to re-create dead or dying loved ones, these clones are manufactured to supply parts rather than replace wholes.[29]

As with the novel's other counterfocal aesthetic maneuvers, this reworking of the clone narrative indicates what is relevant in part by gesturing toward what is not. Despite appearing primed to stage concerns about the uncanny or unethical status of human duplication, the clone system in *Never Let Me Go* turns out to be driven not by the possibility of replacing specific human beings with copies but by the *impossibility* of doing so. When it presents us, against our expectations, with a society that ignores the capacity to duplicate loved ones in favor of preserving the particular living human beings to which people are already attached, the novel insists on the difference between genetic and ontological sameness—between possessing the same biological blueprint and being the same living organism. Even a clone who is biologically identical to someone's son or mother or husband can never be the same life, understood as a unit of organic existence unfolding from inception to death, and the clone system in *Never Let Me Go* is designed to preserve the specific, singular, finite lives in which people are already invested. By presenting the clones as organ donors for existing humans, the novel turns their status as biological duplicates into a means of illuminating the nonduplicable, ontologically distinct quality of each human life. The persistence of the clone narrative beyond its usual relevance throws into relief the emergence of this new understanding of human uniqueness in which the double as such possesses no value and poses no threat. In the realm of life-interest, it seems, there is no longer any such thing as an uncanny double.

In characteristic fashion, the novel traces the import and consequences of this shift by examining the model of human uniqueness that has been displaced. Through their attempt to prove that the clones have souls and hence cannot be considered less than human, the guardians indicate that they have staked their claim on behalf of the clones on the expressivist version of dignity ensconced in human rights rhetoric, which emphasizes the free development and manifestation of each human's personality.[30] This version of personhood combines a Kantian notion that essential human dignity is based on rationality with an expressivist view arising from the Romantic conviction that "each human being has some original and unrepeatable 'measure.'"[31] Once dignity and equality arise from the uniqueness of each human's interiority (or soul, in the novel's terms), this uniqueness can be manifested by plumbing and expressing one's inner depths. Because of the "power which has been ascribed since the Romantic period to the creative imagination," art serves as the crucial means by which it is possible to demonstrate that one possesses this unique subjective core.[32] The guardians proceed according to this long-standing cultural concatenation of personhood with uniqueness, uniqueness with imaginative interiority, and art with the manifestation of that interiority.

As this description suggests, however, expressivist individualism is fundamentally a qualification of life: it views the human as a container for an unrepeatable combination of properties. A person is unique because there is no one else who is exactly *like her*, and that is why the duplicate/clone constitutes a threat. In contrast, a single human life is unique because there is no one else who actually *is her*, who exists as the same organic being who persists from birth to death. Unlike the person, whose uniqueness can be undermined by uncanny duplication, the individual life form is defined by its absolute, ontological specificity as a single unit of being. You might replace your daughter with a genetically identical version, but you would not thereby resurrect the actual dead original. And, given that the clone-slave system is designed to save the particular, specific beings to which people are already attached, it is irrelevant within this system whether the clones are merely robotlike duplicates of true individual humans or actually soulful persons possessed of distinctive interiority. Neither can replace the actual being of the beloved because there is no replacement. The problem the guardians at Hailsham encounter is not that the clones, as duplicates, fail to meet the standard of personhood but that personhood is no longer the standard. This, I think, is why the novel must be set in the years leading up to its own publication: it traces the parameters and consequences of a change that has already taken place in the historical reality outside the novel. Through this temporalization, the novel suggests the dilemmas that appear to preoccupy the text—the tensions between originality, uniqueness, and intrinsic human value on the one hand, and the copy, the inhuman, and the machinic on the other—already belong to the past, however futuristic they may at first appear.

In light of this shift, the clones' disparate struggles with their status as duplicates become legible as another counterfocal maneuver, a map of the blind alleys created when the notion of the person outlives its power to qualify the human. Kathy's close friends Tommy and Ruth embody opposing and familiar tropes related to unique personhood, as indexed by creativity. Tommy is sincerity incarnate and produces art that expresses the tragedy of his situation, while Ruth resorts to manipulative fantasy and consumerist mimicry to make herself seem special. Even her imagined future as an office worker, which seems to express something akin to a sincere desire, is based on a magazine advertisement she finds "near a puddle" (225). The distinction between Tommy's artistic depth and Ruth's shallow copying could not be clearer, but it is just as clear that this distinction makes zero difference in terms of their shared designation as disposable lives. Although apparently more radical, Kathy's appreciation for duplication leads to much the same designation: "Here in my bedsit, I've got these four desk-lamps, each a different color, but all the same design—they have these ribbed necks you can bend whichever way you want. So I might go looking for a shop with another lamp like that in its window—not to buy, but just to compare with my ones at home" (204). Kathy's enjoyment of these copies transgresses notions of uniqueness as an inherent value, but the necks that can be twisted "whichever way you want" also remind us of the passivity of the clones, their status as objects to be manipulated and used. When personhood becomes a defunct value, it seems, it is neither beneficial to display expressivist individuality nor revolutionary to disdain it. Neither unique creativity nor routinized duplication have bearing upon the nonclones' interest in preserving absolute ontological specificity of discrete life forms.

Although the clone system appears from one angle to be based on the forms of recognition associated with human rights—the clones are treated as disposable objects because their personhood isn't recognized—this system thus attests to the utter eradication of these categorical norms in the face of survival situations: the clones are treated as objects because once the lives of loved ones are at stake, it is no longer seen as relevant whether clones are persons or not. That is, subjects of life-interest will predictably choose in favor of *the specific lives in which they are interested.* In insisting on this consequence of a regime of life-interest, *Never Let Me Go* offers something like the opposite perspective from *What Is the What.* Not only does the dominant class here ferociously pursue its own best interests, but also the fostering of lives provided by this class directly and obviously serves their interests at the expense of those being fostered. It is the dominant class rather than the dispossessed who enact the demise of the liberal individual as a standard and guiding principle. Obviously, viewing this demise as loss requires a conviction that liberal critique was at any point an effective tool of social justice—a view not really supported by the novel itself. The ability of Miss Emily and her partner, Madame, to write off the clones once their initiative fails suggests that liberal ideals can quickly give way to actions in one's own best interest when circumstances are pressing. In that sense, what the novel documents is less the loss of personhood as an effective lever for social change than the loss of the faith that it could be so used. It is the wrenching loss of just this faith that we witness at the climax of the novel, when Tommy and Kathy confront Madame and Miss Emily and learn the truth about Hailsham.

In terms of the clone system, this shift means that the line between valued and disposable lives has been decided by individual interest in specific human beings. The nonclones have apparently deemed the cost of clone lives well worth the benefit of a loved one's continued existence. To be marked for survival in this regime, you must be valuable not inherently, as a person with dignity is valued, but rather valued *by someone*, by a subject with the power to choose based on that value. You must be a life that someone else cannot imagine relinquishing. This, of course, is precisely the situation that Kathy fantasizes for herself in the scenario that gives the novel its title. As a young girl, we learn, Kathy becomes obsessed with the love song that gives the novel its title. While pretending to be a mother holding a child, she listens to the song over and over and sings along with its chorus: "*Oh baby, baby. Never let me go*" (266, italics in original). When Kathy playacts a mother holding a baby and singing to it "never let me go," she dramatizes a situation in which a powerful adult enacts the most profound kind of attachment to another life and is poised to resist any intervention that would separate her from this treasured, vulnerable being.[33] Like a mother who wants to keep her child an infant in her arms forever, the nonclones in this system refuse to let the passage of time separate them from their loved ones, who otherwise will move closer to illness and death with each year that passes. The lyrics Kathy sings plead for just this sort of fierce form of attachment even as she enacts that commitment for herself by cradling the imaginary child. What would keep Kathy alive is precisely someone who would not relinquish her to death, but there is no one who to clings to her life in the way nonclones cling to their loved ones—no one who refuses to let her go. So, wrenchingly, Kathy playacts both sides of the

process, her words issuing the plea to be kept (alive) while her actions embody
the sort of unwavering attachment that marks out those chosen to live.

Although she attempts in this way to hold on to her own life, Kathy's
actions are expressly fantasy, and a fantasy whose importance she cannot
entirely admit to herself. Throughout the novel she enacts this sort of mental resistance to exterior reality, from her attempt to preserve her childhood
connections with Ruth and Tommy as they grow apart to her retreat into
memories of their shared past once she is an adult carer. In each of these
cases, Kathy refuses to acknowledge the changes that unfold with the
passage of time, even as time's passage brings her and those she loves ever
closer to death. In part, I think, we can read the insistently interior rather
than material quality of this resistance as a result of Kathy's formation
and enclosure within the expressive doctrine of personhood, which insists
that imaginative interiority is the measure and meaning of Man. Yet I think
the seemingly pointed futility of her interior resistance also points toward
the difficulty of imagining a more thorough exit from the world life-interest has wrought. When we ask *How can Kathy fail to try to save herself?*, we
rephrase Miss Emily's own rhetorical question in defense of the clone system: "How can you ask [nonclones] to go back to the dark days?"—that is,
the days in which people's loved ones died of now curable diseases (257). To
assume that the temporal finitude of her own life must necessarily spur
Kathy to action is to reiterate the same view that has judged her life as forfeit:
the view that it is only natural to act to save ourselves and those we love.
Were the clones to embrace and trumpet their own equal status as ontologically unique lives driven to survive, that would amount to an endorse-
ment of this emergent paradigm, not a form of resistance to it. There is no
politics of recognition in *Never Let Me Go* because there is nothing to recognize—that is, nothing beyond the ascendancy of life-interest as the
defining feature of human life. This is the problem incarnated in the novel's counterfocal poetics: in its nested series of alternate, wishful, delusional
worlds, *Never Let Me Go* stages a struggle with the facticity of life-interest
and the horrors that emerge when it is the subject of life-interest who distinguishes disposable from valuable life.

In *Never Let Me Go* the choice made to harvest from and kill the clones
is a given: it is both temporally prior to the narrative's unfolding and

conceptually axiomatic. As Miss Emily puts it, "Here was the world, requiring students to donate" (258). The problem the novel lays before its readers is the perceived impossibility of challenging this judgment once life-interest defines human life. In Jesmyn Ward's *Salvage the Bones*, the unquestionable givenness of such decisions becomes the target of sustained interrogation through an exploration of decisions made by an African American family living on the edge of survival in rural Mississippi, in a fictional town named Bois Sauvage. Set in the week leading up to Hurricane Katrina, the novel is narrated by fifteen-year-old Esch Batiste, who lives in the woods with her drunken father, her three brothers, and her brother's prized pit bull, China, who is a celebrated champion in local dogfights. Emotionally hobbled by the death of their mother several years before, the children scrabble to gain a subsistence-level existence from their family land, known as the Pit. The clearing gained this name after Esch's grandfather allowed its clay to be excavated by white men, who used it to build the foundations of their houses. The white men paid for the dirt, but the transaction was still manifestly unequal: they wound up with houses on solid foundations while Esch's family wound up in an eroding hole. That the Pit was dug in Esch's grandfather's generation creates a clear analogy between this transaction and the way in which the disposability of African American lives continued to fuel white American flourishing in the Jim Crow era.

Because Esch's experiences are largely confined to the all-black community in and around the Pit, these causal social factors remain largely off-stage even as their effects are registered as defining elements of her existence. That is, her world is abstracted to the minimal elements required for survival in the fashion that defines the microeconomic mode, but her experience is still designated as particular in a fashion that renders *Salvage the Bones* distinct from the live models I discuss in chapter 2. The governing assumption of works such as *127 Hours* or *The Impossible* is that anyone in the protagonists' position would suffer the same way they do; the governing assumption of *Salvage the Bones* is that in reality only some people are made to do so. As in *What Is the What* and *Never Let Me Go*, the particular distribution of life-interest manifests itself in *Salvage the Bones* through the formal dynamic of cleavage and foreclosure that defines partial fictions. Like the clone enclave, the Pit is the product of inequality, of a division between those who amass resources and those from whom they are taken, but those who benefit from this cleavage likewise remain largely offstage. In effect, the world of Bois Sauvage appears complete unto itself because it has been so successfully partitioned from the larger world, which as a result becomes foreclosed. The deprivation of Esch's world is what creates its perceived wholeness, an irony captured in the name of the Pit. The very fact that so much of the story takes place in the Pit indicates that there is an outside, elevated world that is invisible to those who have been forcibly located both spatially and materially below its level.

In *Salvage the Bones*, however, the relationship of this cleavage to life-interest is the reverse of what we find in *Never Let Me Go*. Whereas Hailsham's pursuit of personhood acts as a counterfocus to a regime of life-interest, the poetics of *Salvage the Bones* are hyperfocal rather than counterfocal. The events in the present day of the novel are largely spatially contained in Bois Sauvage and the Pit itself and temporally contained in the week leading up to and including Hurricane Katrina. And, unlike the first two novels I've discussed here, *Salvage the Bones* concerns itself with the consequences of life-interest for radical critiques of racial capital rather than liberal critiques aimed at expanding the definition of Man. Central to this effort is the novel's resignification of the defining features of the microeconomic mode, including its exploration of a closed system in which each benefit carries with it a cost. In *Salvage the Bones* this closed system becomes a way to insist that the prosperity of some necessarily comes at the expense of others, who then lack the resources required for thriving. The novel figures this inverse relationship through an invocation of the material world as a living fabric that includes plants, animals, humans, and the built environment, each of which requires resources to persist. This approach, I argue, targets the capacity of life-interest to give new fuel to aspects of a long-standing argument for domination as itself natural, which Wynter describes under the rubric of "Man2." For Wynter, Man2 refers to the "bio-economic subject" who emerges in the nineteenth century as the top of a Malthusian hierarchy of races.[34] The conception of Man2 naturalizes racial capitalism by positing racial domination as the outcome of evolution and evolution as a measure of one's "master[y] of natural scarcity."[35] In a precise and ingenious reimagination of the microeconomic mode as mirrored in forces that exceed the agency of human beings, *Salvage the*

Bones turns the logic of life-interest into an argument against the view that there is anything natural about the ideal of Man2 or the selection of disposable lives.

The framework for this argument is a particular idea of what we might call the natural world, understood here to encompass the view that biological, geological, and meteorological forces link living beings on the planet together in a complex field of cause and effect. In the novel, this conception of the natural world emerges as a single living system through a dense web of repeated, visceral imagery that is applied variously to humans, animals, landscape, and buildings. Blood, fingers, red, pink, meat, bone, skin, fish, chicken, line: these words recur countless times and concatenate in constantly shifting patterns across the prose of the novel. Esch's father's face is compared to "chicken skin" as he sleeps, while a few pages later her brother Randall enters their house between its "thumb and pointer finger," which "clench" behind him (184, 193). China's "mouth is wet and pink as uncooked chicken" (128); an injured man's hand "slaps [a] door wetly, his fingers trailing red like fishing line" (34); Esch's brothers' friend Big Henry later tries to "rub the blood off his hands," which has "pinked and spread over his skin like a jellyfish" (132). The result is a fictional world that appears to verge on the monistic, in which the humans, animals, and their surrounding environment seem to be assembled from the same few living materials, combined and recombined.[36]

As in the cost–benefit logic of the microeconomic mode, this living system can only grow in one area by shrinking in another. And because living beings form part of this closed system of finite resources, there is in effect no becoming of one life without loss to another. When Skeetah, Esch's brother, kills and roasts a squirrel, for example, she tastes in the meat the animal's own struggle for life: "I bite and I am eating acorns and leaping with fear to the small dark holes in the heart of old oak trees" (49). The description of the movement from living flesh to dead food inscribes the process by which life feeds on life in order to survive: energy transferred from the acorns, whose reproductive potential is lost when eaten, to the squirrel, to Esch. In this vital system, there is no possibility of every life flourishing equally because lives necessarily exist at the expense of other lives. Growth in one area is death in another; becoming requires and produces lack. As with the concept of life-interest itself, the preservation of life is inseparable from loss, trade-offs, and foreclosed possibilities in the vital system that makes up Bois Sauvage. Or, to put it another way, *Salvage the Bones* figures the choices that result from life-interest not as a feature of exceptional situations—a description that includes every other text I examine in this volume—but rather as a feature of existence as a life on this planet as conveyed through its particular conception of the natural world.

By setting the choices among lives within this framework of material finitude, the novel resignifies analogies between the environmental and the economic that are a long-standing feature of the postwar approach to nature.[37] Whereas such analogies can be used to justify the ascendancy of the bio-economic subject Man2 as the outcome of an inevitable and natural competition for resources, the novel deploys its conception of the natural as a tool to expose and challenge the everyday choices that cause some lives to survive rather than others, including the choices that consigned the Batistes to the Pit. Precisely because life exists at the expense of other life, *Salvage the Bones* suggests, violence inheres in the false perception that anyone fosters all lives equally—a perception that we learn is necessarily untrue and very likely masks a highly interested choice.

The novel explores this danger through Esch's brother Skeetah and his fixation on the dog, China. Through the novel, Skeetah focuses on channeling as many of the family's resources as he can into feeding, doctoring, and protecting China and her litter of puppies, born in the novel's first scene. On the last day before the hurricane hits, Skeetah chooses to spend most of the family's scant money for hurricane provisions on two large, expensive bags of high-end dog food, despite the fact that he knows his sister is pregnant and the entire family near starving. When his father and siblings protest his bringing China and the puppies inside before the storm, he defends his decisions by arguing, "Everything deserve to live" (213). Esch makes the myopia of this view evident when she recounts its repetition, in the final words of the chapter: " 'Everything,' Skeetah says, and looks through me" (214). In looking through Esch, Skeetah refuses to see the reality of his own selective choice. He is not giving "everything" an equal chance but instead choosing China's life over those of his father and siblings.

By juxtaposing the distribution of scarce resources with Skeetah's argument on China's behalf, the novel insists on the inadequacy of liberal critique to address the realities of material access to thriving. When Skeetah argues that a nonhuman animal is part of the "everything" that deserves to live, he echoes the liberal gesture by which the category of protected lives expands to include those humans originally excluded by the genre of Man. Here the extension appears more radical since it extends the category to include species beyond the human.[38] However, as Esch's description of the squirrel suggests, *Salvage the Bones* presents some lives as necessarily resources for other lives, such that there is no way to enable every life to flourish at the same time and to the same extent. For this reason, there is no way in the Pit to create an equal distribution of resources without first determining which lives should be considered part of the group to be given equal portions. Even if resources are divided with one's best effort at equality, the status of all lives as themselves necessary resources for other lives means there must be an initial division between the fostered and the fuel. Everything may deserve to thrive, but not everything can.

Given this framework, there is no choice but to make a choice when it comes to the distribution of resources. Skeetah both refuses to acknowledge this choice and makes his decision in the only way possible within the microeconomic mode: as a result of his own individual cost–benefit analysis. Of course, cost–benefit analysis does not negate the possibility of acting in a loving, self-sacrificing, or compassionate way, but it does negate the possibility of divorcing those actions from a process of calculation related to oneself—a process that is by nature destructive to the idea of personhood upon which human rights rhetoric rests. To be a person is to be recognized as an end in oneself, but, crucially, there is no action that can be undertaken by a subject of life-interest that is not defined by the end of individual interest. When the subject of life-interest asks *Is it in my interest to see this life as a person?*, the life in question has already been treated as less than an end in itself by being evaluated according to the role it plays in another individual's interests. And once every life is simply a resource to be distributed according to interest, there is no barrier to granting animal lives more consideration than human lives, provided one is more interested in the animals'. Thus, it is no surprise that Skeetah treats his family's lives as resources to be used to foster China's, most obviously and grotesquely when he jokes that he should feed his father's severed fingers to the dog since "that's free protein" (187). Once human lives are just another resource to be apportioned, there is no reason not to see a chunk of human flesh as animal fuel rather than vice versa.

As Skeetah's example suggests, refusing to recognize either the necessity of choosing or the content of one's choices is exactly what enables accumulation for some at the expense of others. Skeetah's problem is not only that he chooses to feed China but also that he refuses to see that doing so starves Esch and his other siblings. To ignore this zero-sum game is to refuse to note the inherent violence in one's accumulation and distribution of resources.

The novel extends this critique to historic acts of dispossession through metaphors of willful blindness that echo Skeetah's refusal to see Esch. Esch's white neighbors, for example, inhabit "a blind house with closed eyes . . . painted bright blue, the kind of bright blue I've seen on the lizards that live in the seams of our walls" (71). Boarded up before the storm, the same neighbors' house has "no glass left peeking through cracks, only plywood closed smooth and tight as eyelids" (208). Whereas the neighbors' house is blind in its perfect imperviousness, Esch's home is penetrated even in its seams by living creatures and remains open to vision—a permeability that becomes itself a kind of seeing. As Gloria Fuentes puts it in one of the novel's headnotes, "And my body is an endless eye / Through which, unfortunately, I see everything" (vii). As the use of the house as metaphor for sight suggests, this is a materialized, corporeal form of vision that emerges from physical presence. Life in the Pit renders the either/or quality of thriving visible not because only those in extreme privation face such choices but rather because enforced proximity to privation makes the embodied reality of these choices more difficult to unsee.

In this way, the novel deploys the zero-sum logic of its natural world to suggest that the thriving of some, like the white neighbors, comes at the expense of the lives of the Batistes and others in their position. Because it represents this either/or approach to thriving as a feature of the natural world, *Salvage the Bones* may appear in danger of depicting dispossession as itself natural—as unfolding according to the bio-economic, Malthusian logic that underpins Man2. Instead, however, the novel deploys this vision in order to assert the centrality of human agency in producing the uneven distribution of resources that results from negotiating this either/or choice. That is, making a choice regarding thriving may be unavoidable, but the content and consequences of the choice are not. To insist on the role of human agency and the possibility of change, the novel invites readers to notice the difference between the naturalized results of structural violence and the violence that inheres in the living fabric of the world.[39] In one extended comparison between these two different vectors of violence, Esch's father and his son Randall try to use a tractor to pull down a chicken coop for boards to cover the windows of the house, while in the nearby shed Skeetah tries to get China, who has been sick since birthing the puppies, to eat. Randall is driving the tractor as his father struggles to work loose some wire caught in the engine, and his father's instructions to Randall to start and stop the tractor intermingle with Skeetah's to China to eat and behave. The passage communicates through a form of complex intercutting and repeated imagery worth quoting at some length:

The red puppy creeps forward, rounds China's bowl, noses her tit. China is rolling, rising. The rumble of the tractor is her growl. Her toes are pointed, her head raised. Skeetah falls back. The red puppy undulates toward her; a fat mite. China snaps forward, closes her jaw around the puppy's neck as she does when she carries him, but there is no gentleness in it. She is all white eyes. She is chewing. She is whipping him though the air like a tire eaten too short for Skeetah to grab.

"Stop!" Skeetah yells. "Stop!"

Randall puts the tractor in gear, switches it to park, but the small hillock the coop is on pulls the tractor back as the engine idles.

"No!" Daddy calls. Daddy flings his hand free. There is oil on it. He holds to his chest. His shirt is covered in oil. Daddy's jaw is slack. He is walking toward the light of the shed. The oil on his T-shirt turns red. The sound coming out his open mouth is like growling.

"No!" Skeetah calls.

The blood on Daddy's shirt is the same color as the pulpy puppy in China's mouth. China flings it away from her. It thuds on the tin and slides. Randall comes running. Big Henry kneels with Daddy in the dirt, where what was Daddy's middle, ring, and pinkie finger on his left hand are sheared off clean as fallen tree trunks. The meat of his fingers is red and wet as China's lips.

Skeetah kneels in the dirt, feeling for the mutilated puppy; he knocks into metal drums and toolboxes and old chainsaws with his head and his shoulders.

"Why did you?" Skeetah wails.

"Why?" Daddy breathes to Randall and Big Henry standing over him, the blood sluicing down his forearm. They are gripping Daddy's wrist, trying to stop the bleeding. Skeetah is punching the metal he meets. China is bloody-mouthed and bright-eyed as Medea. (129–30)

Were this violence an accident in its usual sense—an act with no willed cause—then the answer to the father's plaintive question "Why?" would be "No reason." From the perspective of the microeconomic mode, in which every factor that led to the situation is ruled irrelevant, this nonanswer would be assumed since we would read the factors delimiting the father's choices as irrelevant contingencies. If we read instead from the perspective the novel encourages, in which we see the Pit as divided from the larger landscape through the unequal distribution of resources, then the father's accident is not underdetermined but overdetermined. Why does the father lose his fingers? Because he needs boards to cover the windows before the storm and he can't buy any. Because his yard is filled with trash because he has too few resources to abandon anything that might be useful, no gas to haul it away, and no money to pay to use a landfill. Because some people are enabled to prepare for Katrina with ample resources and the time and will to use them, and some people are left to prepare with broken tools and the labor of their children. As a brutal, seemingly unintended yet structurally produced act of severing, the slice through the father's hand is both a product of and metonym for the larger division of resources in which it occurs.

In comparison to this predictable outcome of structural violence, China's act remains genuinely inexplicable, not so much unmotivated as motivated in a fashion that escapes even explanations based on predictable biological impulse. As the commonplace phrase "maternal instinct" insists, the understanding of mothers as driven by their very physicality to care for their offspring is one of the abiding examples of behavior presumed to be so innate as to be unavoidable. The mother who kills her young raises the possibility that, even at the heart of this most inextirpable of purported instincts, there is something in the organic operation of existence that remains arbitrary and unknowable. When contrasted with China's sudden and surprising violence, the long-standing, predictable, and unilateral deprivation that defines life in the Pit appears too consistent to be anything but the result of human intervention upon the world; it is *meant* in a way that China's random violence is not. China's actions indicate that even the biological realm cannot be reduced to a battle among lives for resources and survival, since her violence serves neither, while the father's so-called accident indicates that what looks like a mere fact of life is actually a product of underlying human intent. If the either/or choice among lives leads to the foreclosure of universals in a regime of life-interest, then China's inscrutable violence shows up the very partial approach to life that may result, in which human choices aggregate to structural violence that is then naturalized as the unforeseeable effect of randomness, complexity, and contingency.

Salvage the Bones insists upon the choices involved in creating domination and dispossession by contrasting such concentrated effects of structural violence with the impartial distribution of both destruction and growth in its natural world, exemplified by China's violence and, most importantly, the hurricane itself. As part of the zero-sum logic of the novel's natural world, Katrina enacts its own version of cost and benefit, one in keeping with its extreme power:

Her chariot was a storm so great and black the Greeks would say it was harnessed to dragons. She was the murderous mother who cut us to the bone but left us alive, left us naked and bewildered as wrinkled newborn babies, as blind puppies, as sun-starved newly hatched baby snakes. She left us a dark Gulf and salt-burned land. She left us to learn to crawl. She left us to salvage.

What Katrina has taken away is everything daily, the ordinary and purportedly unbroken operations of the natural and built environment—and, crucially, she destroys the nearby prosperous town of St. Catherine even more thoroughly than Bois Sauvage. What she has given in exchange is rebirth as a kind of revelation—in effect, the baptism that the Batistes' family name implies. She reveals the world stripped back to a naked, newborn, bewildered state and the existence of a power great enough to produce this state. In contrast to the structural violence that left the father without his fingers, that left African Americans in the path of the storm and denied them the resources to rebuild, Katrina figures the natural world as contingent, impartial, and possessed of an inherent if mysterious reciprocity, one that does not distribute costs and benefits in predictable fashion. As the novel's headnote from Deuteronomy puts it, "I kill and I make alive, I wound and I heal, neither is there any can deliver out of my hand" (ix). In contrast to the speciously naturalized and highly partial effects of human cost–benefit analyses, which deliver the same populations to destruction again and again, the forces of the natural world sow damage and growth in a fashion that does not align with the patterns of power and privilege.

Katrina demonstrates that, in contrast to structural violence, natural violence is genuinely impartial and unwaveringly reciprocal: it does not demand that costs always be paid by the same people, who themselves gain no benefit, and its division of those to be killed and made alive, wounded and healed, arises from an unfathomable power distinct from the disavowed patterns of human domination.

Ultimately, this imagination of Katrina enables *Salvage the Bones* to reframe the either/or choice between lives as a demand for justice rather than an alibi for oppression. This act of reframing constitutes the climax of the novel, with high-stakes causes and effects. As his family tries desperately to get to higher ground in the rising flood and buffeting storm, Skeetah suddenly finds that he must choose to save either Esch's life or China's. Esch's father finally realizes that she is pregnant and, in a sudden fit of anger, he shoves her off their precarious perch into the very swirling water that they are trying to escape. Skeetah can jump in and save Esch, but only if he releases China, whom he is carrying in a sling. Even inaction will constitute a choice, since without intervention Esch will drown and saving her will require abandoning China. Confronted with the extreme options produced by the storm, Skeetah's self-serving, superficial insistence on the value of every living creature becomes unsustainable. In effect, the storm enforces an experience of suffering agency that requires him to reckon with the choices that accompany the either/or quality of life as diagrammed by the novel. When push quite literally comes to shove, Skeetah faces up to the burden of suffering agency and opts to jump in after Esch.

There is no sense, however, that in choosing Esch over China, Skeetah has capitulated to the idea of a human's life as inherently more valuable than a dog's. That China retains a profound claim on his care is clear in the novel's final scene, which depicts Skeetah waiting in the woods with resolute conviction that China will return. Rather than attesting to any guiding principles, his choice merely demonstrates that Esch's life is marginally more important *to him*. What is revealed is not a new universal—humans over dogs, for example—but rather his necessarily particular commitment to the lives for which he cares. Suffering agency emerges here when Skeetah abandons his willful blindness regarding this apportioning of care to the various lives around him, which, as his earlier actions make clear, is a choice in its own right. Skeetah's narrative arc demonstrates that insisting on either the universal value of all life or the inevitable importance of some lives over others merely denies rather than erases one's own intransigent agency in relation to the fostering of lives. You can disavow the act of choosing or the damage done by your choice, but you will have chosen nonetheless. Once the impartial power of Katrina has ripped away both the veil of false universals and the alibi of inequality as a fact of nature, the experience of suffering agency emerges as the only just response to the distribution of thriving.

If there is something disturbing about this transformation of the torturous, enforced quality of suffering agency into an instrument of awakening, then I think we must read this transformation in light of the imperative that constitutes the novel's title, which asks that something of significance be retrieved from even the most seemingly sterile ground. By making use of the apparently unpromising elements to hand—from the negative association of African American men with dog fighting to the catastrophic destruction of Hurricane Katrina—the novel salvages from its characters' impoverished world a profound and urgent reassessment of supposedly universal norms in the wake of life-interest, much as the characters salvage parts and materials from the busted machines and collapsing outbuildings that fill the Pit. The textual existence of *Salvage the Bones* as a novel is the result of this same ingenious and hardscrabble repurposing. The destruction of Katrina provides the impetus of the text as an aesthetic object, in a fashion that makes art from the remains and salvaging into an art.[40] Yet to salvage here is not to transcend but instead to found one's efforts at resistance in the same evidence of damage that makes change necessary. Salvaging figures a particular and transformative relationship to the very intersection of becoming and lack that defines the subject of life-interest; to salvage is to confront the finitude of resources with an ingenuity capable of wresting becoming from lack itself. Rather than sanctifying its characters' deprivation, *Salvage the Bones* utterly revalues their responses to it. It turns the defining feature of their struggle to survive—the attempt to wrest from inadequate resources the means of flourishing—into an indispensable and revelatory figure for thinking the problem of justice in the present. In so doing, the novel salvages from salvaging itself a way to insist on the significance of its characters' lives.

Esch's pregnancy, finally acknowledged by all by the end of the novel, operates as a crux in this salvaging of significance. The highly politicized specter of African American teen pregnancy in the postwar era—since the

1980s often tied to the rhetoric of "welfare queens"—takes part in the centuries-long construction of African American women's sexuality and reproductive capacity in a way that underpins their designation as disposable lives.[41] As Hong notes, reproductive respectability has emerged since the 1960s as the means by which "value and vulnerability" are distributed within racialized communities, by holding out "the promise of protection from premature death" for some who achieve such respectability.[42] In other words, Esch's pregnancy, so clearly lacking the markers of respectability earned by those women who bear children as adults within heterosexual monogamous marriage, would in this paradigm consign her to the part of the racialized community that has no grounds to insist on thriving. Although the narrative trajectory surrounding her pregnancy moves from denial and secrecy to disclosure and acceptance, the novel clearly underscores the distance between this transformation and the achievement of reproductive respectability. The father of Esch's baby, Manny, refuses to acknowledge his paternity, so there is no hope of salvation through heterosexual commitment, and in the novel's final scenes it is implied that the role of father will be played by Esch's brothers and their friend Big Henry rather than a single biological paternal figure. Moreover, Esch ties her growing acceptance of her pregnancy not to a model of reproductive heterosexual coupledom but rather to China's status as a champion dog fighter: when she attacks Manny after his denial of her claim on him, for example, she describes the suddenness and ferocity of her attack by saying, "I was on him like China" (203). Esch and her community achieve a means of understanding and fostering her pregnancy by the narrative's conclusion, but there is no sense that doing so will increase Esch's association with the sort of monogamous heterosexual commitment that renders childbearing a means of incorporation into the ranks of those enabled to thrive.

In refusing to tie Esch's self-acceptance and achievement of support to reproductive respectability, the novel drives a wedge between its own politics of salvage and the promise of selective redemption that turns African American women's sexuality into a means of dividing those who will and will not be offered a chance to survive within racialized communities. Rather than depicting Esch as ready to join the ranks of those classed as respectable enough to thrive, the novel revalues the very ground on which her incorporation into those ranks is foreclosed: it depicts Esch's identification with China's tremendous power as emerging from her pregnancy and her location of a necessary, supportive community as emerging in part from the same social world that contained her casual sex partners. That the last words of the novel inscribe an ongoing connection among China, Esch, and maternity—"[China] will know that I am a mother"—places this intervention as a culmination of the salvaging that shapes the novel as a whole (260). When it shows Esch coming to terms with her pregnancy while underscoring her ongoing distance from reproductive respectability, *Salvage the Bones* figures a pointed refusal of the specific biopolitical framework through which some African American women are promised incorporation and a chance at escaping premature death. In so doing, the novel insists upon the distance between its own imagination of salvaging and the sort of highly partial selection for thriving that Hong describes.

The novel accomplishes this sustained reconfiguration of the microeconomic mode in part by representing the choice to foster some lives over others primarily among its African American characters rather than the white liberals who make such decisions in *What Is the What* and *Never Let Me Go*. Although the Pit is the result of structures through which powerful and privileged humans decide on the fate of humans who are neither, *Salvage the Bones* concentrates on the way in which exactly the same sort of decisions unfold within the Pit itself, in the choices that the Batistes make about the distribution of resources in Bois Sauvage. In so doing, it turns the very partiality of the microeconomic mode—its focus on white men of the sort who rarely face survival concerns in everyday life—inside out; it reveals the intrinsic partiality of this mode as a mask for the choices the privileged make every day regarding who will and will not thrive. This approach repurposes not only suffering agency but life-interest itself, in a fashion different from the first two novels I analyze here. If *What Is the What* argues that those with abundant resources can escape life-interest to retain the values of liberal individualism, then *Never Let Me Go* presents this same group as making inevitably interested choices regarding the designation of disposable lives. By tracing Skeetah's journey from willful blindness to suffering agency, *Salvage the Bones* deploys the parameters of the microeconomic mode instead to restore contingency to these choices: the novel indicates that, precisely because they are shaped by the vagaries of individual interest rather than the predetermined, survival-of-the-fittest logic that underpins Man2, there is nothing inevitable or irremediable about the decisions that determine which lives are disposable and which are enabled to thrive. In this framing, the novel insists that there is an opportunity to be seized—salvaged—from the proposition that we are all subjects of life-interest who cannot help but make choices regarding survival.

In order to make this argument, the novel illuminates and relies on aspects of the microeconomic mode that can be put in the service of radical critique of racial capitalism, particularly the emphasis on finite material resources, the flourishing of some at the expense of others, and the possibility of transforming this dynamic once we recognize it as a contingent product of human action rather than a fact of nature. However, it is crucial to recognize that the experiential landscape mapped by the microeconomic mode remains a stripped-down account of human existence skewed to emphasize individual agency, cost–benefit analysis, and agonized choices regarding survival at the expense of all other dynamics. The ingenious way that *Salvage the Bones* turns this model to its own purposes does not make the model any less selective, discrete, or self-reinforcing as a means of explaining the world. *Salvage the Bones* deploys this model in order to change its significance into something much closer to a radical critique of racial capital, but it does so in a fashion that highlights the dangers of the model rather than endorsing its claim to capture the entire world. In my next and final chapter, I illuminate the significance of this distinction by examining in more detail the either/or logic that presents life as always existing at the expense of other life. Although this logic may be used to figure the way in which some lives become disposable as a result of the material forces of global racial capital, I argue that it also operates in ways that cannot be aligned with radical critiques of capital. To describe and account for this divergence, I consider the relationship between classic narratives of primitive accumulation and the either/or approach to survival we find in the microeconomic mode.

Chapter Six

BINARY LIFE

By way of a conclusion, I want to consider a bit more explicitly the political flexibility and portability that the microeconomic mode possesses as an aesthetic technology. On the one hand, as this book has argued, this mode makes an implicit argument in insisting that humans are essentially subjects of life-interest who must wrestle with suffering agency. On the other hand, however, its increasing coherence as a cultural formation makes it possible to invoke this mode in contexts in which the meaning of this argument differs significantly. In what follows, I explore this ideological flexibility in relation to the life-for-a-life logic I identify in chapter 5. In that chapter, I examine partial fictions, or works that evaluate the challenges this logic presents to liberal and radical critiques of domination and dispossession. In effect, partial fictions present the relationship between life-interest and justice as a kind of riddle: when there is no choice but to foster some lives over others, these novels ask, what is to keep subjects of life-interest from simply preserving those lives about which they care most at the expense of those they don't? This is the conundrum skirted by Dave Eggers's *What Is the What: The Autobiography of Valentino Achak Deng: A Novel* (2006), posed at length in Kazuo Ishiguro's *Never Let Me Go* (2005), and answered by Jesmyn Ward's *Salvage the Bones* (2011), which insists that subjects of life-interest admit the violence of our choices and come to grips with the suffering agency required to make them as just as we can.

Yet this question begs another, which I have left deliberately to one side until now: why does the microeconomic mode insist that it is necessary to make a choice between lives in the first place? Texts in the microeconomic mode that I discuss in this volume give answers to this question that are as varied as their invocation of this either/or choice is consistent. Consider the almost complete absence of food in Cormac McCarthy's *The Road* (2006), which makes the decision whether or not to share a spoonful or two a matter of life and death. The kill-or-be-killed rules of the survival game. The existence of clones to be "donated" to sustain the nonclones in *Never Let Me Go*. The strange carnivorous island-organism in Yann Martel's *Life of Pi* (2001), which sustains itself by consuming human flesh. The natural world as modeled in *Salvage the Bones*, in which no life can grow without expense to other life. Even the acts of self-mutilation in *127 Hours* (2010) and *Saw* (2004) express a version of this logic: a chunk of living flesh forfeited to preserve the life of the whole. When the imposition of survival games, the global reduction of resources to starvation levels, and the advent of futuristic clone technology all lead to the same kind of choice between lives, there would appear to be something at issue that exceeds specific concerns about biotechnology or environmental crisis or peak oil. That is, the repetition of this either/or logic of life across such different contexts suggests that its prominence cannot be explained solely with reference to the particular threats used to conjure it.

In this chapter, I map out the particular features and import of this either/or dynamic, or what I call "binary life." I do so in part by considering the relationship between binary life and the division between disposable and valued lives instantiated by global racial capital. Particularly when the subject of life-interest makes choices regarding access to resources required for survival, the logic of binary life appears to resemble the dynamics of dispossession and necropolitical decision endemic to racial capitalism.[1] However, I will suggest that this resemblance dwindles if we follow this either/or logic of life through to its inevitable conclusion: a relentlessly subtractive approach to resources that ultimately reduces the represented world itself to nearly nil. This subtractive form, I argue, diverges at a basic level from the way in which racial capital divides and distributes access to thriving. In order to trace this difference, I explore the function of natural law theory in justifying forms of primitive accumulation and consider the relationship between such narratives of accumulation and the production of binary life in the microeconomic mode. By comparing the binary logic of life to the ur-narratives of primitive accumulation, I demonstrate that binary life functions differently from the distribution of necessary resources produced by capital because the narrative trajectory of binary life forecloses crucial results of accumulation itself. Instead, I argue, we can trace the origins and operations of binary life to a particular algorithmic understanding of what it means to be a choosing subject within the circuits of control.[2]

In John Locke's famous account, labor in the state of nature creates property: by mixing his labor with the soil, the industrious Man in the state of nature comes to possess that ground in much the same way that he possesses his individual person.[3] As has frequently been pointed out, this depiction erases the implicitly and explicitly violent acts of dispossession through which property in fact comes to be, from the enclosure of the commons to the projects of settler colonialism.[4] In their persuasive critique of the ontological turn in queer theory, Jordy Rosenberg argues that the resurgence of primitive accumulation in contemporary capital has reanimated the ancestral temporality attributed to the state of nature by Locke and other natural law theorists.[5] If we accept Rosenberg's argument that it is post-Fordist versions of primitive accumulation that render the property narratives of natural law theory resonant in the present, then we should expect this resonance to be reflected in the temporality that accompanies accumulation itself. Whether justified through the developmental temporality of labor or the anticipatory temporality of future use, accumulation refers to an increase over time.[6] Even primitive accumulation operates in this fashion: via disavowed acts of theft, one person or group dramatically increases the amount of property they possess; what they have after is more than they had before. Narrating the process of primitive accumulation requires combining the ancestral temporality of the state of nature with the incremental temporality of accumulation—the increase of property and goods over time.

This is the temporal signature, for example, of what is perhaps the most famous extended literary allegory of emergence from the state of nature: Daniel Defoe's *Robinson Crusoe* (1719).[7] After arriving on his island with barely the clothes on his back, Crusoe acquires and accrues tools and seeds

from his half-sunken ship, grows food, constructs an increasingly elaborate shelter, and adds to his store of provisions. Lists describing this process are everywhere in the novel and constitute one of its most distinctive
formal features. Enumeration is the way that *Robinson Crusoe* emphasizes
accumulation, in the form of work done and goods increased. Although
these lists bear a specific relationship to eighteenth-century mercantilism
and circulation of commodities, the additive process captured in Crusoe's
lists defines castaway stories of a certain type: narratives that provide readers with the pleasure of watching many of the familiar features of civilization regenerated in miniature, more or less from scratch.[8] In these
Robinsonades, castaways arrive in an environment that is devoid of the
effects of human culture, and they gradually and incrementally produce a
scaled-down version of the built world. In the process, the protagonists
demonstrate through their industry, ingenuity, and grit that they deserve
what results. The world they create repeats and rationalizes the original act
of accumulation that was the occupation of the island: the production of
something out of seemingly nothing serves to prove that there was nothing there—no recognized property claim—in the first place. The additive
temporality of accumulation is its own justification.

Of course, the effect of primitive accumulation is the reverse for Friday:
he has no choice but to labor on land that belongs to Crusoe. Not only does
his dispossession by Crusoe leave him with less, but also he is understood
to be in this state because he has done less and saved less, at least according to the origin stories provided by Locke and others. As Karl Marx puts
it in his sardonic summary of such stories, "long, long ago, there were two
sorts of people: one, the diligent, intelligent and above all frugal élite; the
other, lazy rascals, spending their substance, and more, in riotous living."[9]
In time, the story goes, "it came to pass that the former sort accumulated
wealth, and the later sort finally had nothing to sell except their own skins."[10]
In consuming rather than accumulating, the lazy rascals in effect dispos-
sess themselves. Whereas Crusoe and his ilk exist in a developmental temporality in which each day increases their goods and resources, the Fridays
of this world occupy a narrative of dwindling. The same linear chunk of
imagined prehistory that amplifies and adds to the property of the former
sees the shrinking and subtraction of the property of the latter. In both the
Marxist critique of primitive accumulation and the celebratory origin stories of political economy, the subtraction of the means to sustain life for

some people unfolds alongside the accumulation of those means for others.

The subtractive side of this account certainly resonates with live models, in which people frequently find themselves left with nothing except their own skins. It is hard to imagine a more thorough reversal of the accumulation process than what we find in *The Road*, for example.[11] What is striking, however, is how little evidence there is of the other half of the narrative, with its focus on additive temporality—on the construction of a world of increasing complexity through the application of labor over time. The father and son in *The Road* aren't starving because other people are feasting; even the bad guys who are living on human flesh will run out of people to eat eventually. Because food is decreasing dramatically and globally over time, any accumulation of it will necessarily be exceedingly temporary; eventually food will be scarce enough that even those with accumulated food will have to begin consuming rather than adding to their stores—unless they die first. (Of course, it is still possible to accumulate other goods in the novel, like the useless *kruggerands* the man finds stored in a basement survival cache or the sex slaves he sees marching behind one group of cannibals. But without sufficient food to maintain survival, even those with slaves will be dead or eaten or both in the end.) This subtractive logic is formalized in survival games, where its binary, iterative quality becomes particularly evident. Survival game contestants may initially divide themselves into two warring bands of allies, but the ascendant group will necessarily subdivide into a new grouping of allies and antagonists once the original enemy group is eliminated. Reality shows such as *Survivor* (2000 to the present) depend on just this logic to guarantee their inevitable dramas of allegiance and betrayal: warring groups reform as ever-smaller groups as the number of contestants dwindles, until the victor defeats his final antagonist and the world represented by the game is reduced to a single player.

What the survival game suggests, in other words, is that there is a kind of engine to this subtractive logic that propels the narrative to its own diminution and collapse. Once human beings understand themselves as units of life-interest, that understanding shapes both self-relation and the relation to others. For the subject of life-interest, one's own existence centers on a binary choice between life and death, and so does the existence of other human beings. And because both subjects encounter one another in this way, they appear to one another in the form of a mutually exclusive choice between their two lives: life or death, kill or be killed, him or me. However, with each confrontation between two lives, the benefit gained for the one who lives does not accumulate but rather repeats each time the switch flips between 1 and 0, between the one life that lives and the other that does not. Life preserved again and again creates a benefit for the life in question, but it does not produce an increase in life; rather, this choice continually and necessarily results in one less life. The recurring either/or logic exemplified in the survival game gives narrative form to this fusion of human interaction with serial binary decision—that is, binary life. With each iteration of the cycle, the total number of lives in question decreases. The result is a narrative structure that is essentially fractal: the either/or expression of binary life repeats over and over, each time on a smaller scale, up to the point at which there are no more lives to choose between.

Rather than arising from a particular act of primitive accumulation—including those that have been argued to characterize post-Fordist capital—this fractal logic thus interacts in a more complex way with the features associated with the control society. If, as I argue in chapters 3 and 4, the subject of life-interest arises at the intersection of the discretization of life, binary choice, and the human organism as a single unit of existence, then I think we can understand the permeation of binary life as one of the ongoing consequences of this redefinition, albeit one that has particular consequences for narratives regarding the use of some lives to foster others. That is, the subtractive logic of binary life models what happens when subjects of life-interest encounter each other, and what happens is a kind of inevitable, repetitive choice against one life and in favor of the other. When this subject chooses whether or not to save his own life at the expense of someone else's, the fusion of individual human life and agential choice is expressed in a reified form. In choosing who will live, the subject of life-interest expresses binary choice in the currency of life itself: life constitutes both the cost (one life paid) and the benefit (the other life retained). This subject chooses as a life, decides between lives, and pays in the coin of life for the option chosen. In both its doubling of the lives at issue in each choice and in its fractal, iterative structure, binary life emerges as a logical extension and intensification of life-interest itself.

In contrast, representations of accumulation and dispossession operate outside this subtractive logic, even when they resemble the microeconomic mode in the stark extremity in which they display the direct consumption of life. We can trace this distinction, for example, in the film *Mad Max: Fury Road* (2015).[12] In a postapocalyptic Australian wasteland, Mad Max roams a world defined by scarcity and the radical reduction of life, a status neatly indicated by his killing and eating a two-headed lizard in the film's opening scene. Soon after this opening, he is captured by a group of War Boys, soldiers suffering from radiation sickness, and taken to a cliff-top fortress in which a despot hoards water, soldiers, and slaves. Max is quickly identified and tattooed as a "universal donor" and becomes a living Blood Bag for one of the War Boys. Meanwhile, we see the ruler of the Citadel, Immortan Joe, order the release of a limited amount of water to the crowd below, who fight desperately over the inadequate supply. Joe warns the crowd not to become "addicted" to the water, as if they have a choice about needing it. After the escape of renegade Imperator Furiosa, we learn that she has fled with Joe's sex slaves, five young women whom he has been trying to impregnate; one is already visibly heavily pregnant. In the sere deprivation of the landscape, the fight over the supplies required for self-preservation, and the treatment of humans as living fuel and brood mares, we can recognize both the fixation on sheer survival and the collapse of personhood that also feature in the microeconomic mode.

What we do not see, however, is the suffering agency that constitutes another defining feature of the microeconomic mode. Actions undertaken both inside and in resistance to the Citadel do not appear almost as unwelcome and painful as their alternative; benefits do not carry costs that almost make them not worth choosing. Characters who are the focus of the narrative do not preserve themselves or others through sacrifices of lives or flesh that they can hardly bear to make. Instead, the subject who makes the most consequential decisions regarding the flourishing or the disposability of life, Immortan Joe, does so with glee rather than anguish. And, most crucially, there is no sense of the relentless subtraction that arises from binary life. Instead, the film suggests that there would be enough water to sustain all the life clustered around the Citadel were Joe not determined to hoard it. That is, the Citadel is defined by the violent accumulation of resources by the powerful, who are positioned to thrive indefinitely unless deposed, rather than the logic of binary life, in which even the formerly powerful eventually face death due to the dwindling, inadequate means of survival. There are seemingly enough resources in the Citadel to protect the powerful within it from anything like the iterative, binary choices that eventually reduce the world toward zero within the microeconomic mode.

Crucially, however, there is a moment at which this dynamic almost shifts and the narrative tilts toward the diminishing world of binary life. After Furiosa finds out from the Mothers, a roving matriarchal band, that the Green Place she sought is gone, she and the other women prepare to try to cross the salt flats—the dried-up ocean—in search of some more verdant land. They have enough water for only 160 days, after which they will have no chance of getting back, a hope that Max argues will not fix "what is broken." At the last moment, Max convinces them to turn back instead, to return to the Citadel and claim the green and the water there, instead of pursuing the vain hope represented by the salt flats. Had they instead set off across the desert expanse, however, they would have entered into the imaginative terrain defined by the microeconomic mode. With inadequate water for all of them to make it across the flats and no hope of any better conditions on the other side, they would eventually have found their supplies too low to sustain them all. Much like the starving bands in *The Road*, they would in the end have been forced to choose who would die of thirst first, then second, and so on. They would have become subject to the reductive logic of binary life in which the choice to preserve one life is necessarily also the choice for another life to end—and the choice would repeat until there would be no one left to do the choosing. By juxtaposing the threat of binary life with the hoarded plenty of the Citadel, *Fury Road* illuminates the distinction between the narrative mechanism of binary life, which always leads to ever fewer lives, and the dynamic of primitive accumulation, in which inadequate resources for some mean ample resources and a captive labor force for others. When scarcity is figured via binary life, any group initially able to thrive will inevitably reduce toward zero as the narrative progresses, whereas when scarcity is figured as the result of primitive accumulation, the possibility remains that resources might be distributed so that more lives will thrive in an ongoing fashion.

It is this latter possibility that Max raises when Furiosa and her band propose trying to cross the salt flats. To do so would be to attempt to survive according to the terms of the act of accumulation that made the Citadel powerful and those around it unable to thrive. As Furiosa puts it while considering Max's suggestion, "Joe owns the water, so he owns us." Much like the laborer robbed of the means of subsistence can either work or starve, life in the Citadel rests on the choice between submission and death.[13] But if Furiosa and her band set out across the flats, then they will be acquiescing to a short and torturous future defined by an either/or approach to life in its purest form. This is a future in which you never stop paying for life because there is never enough of what you need to live. What Max offers instead is an option beyond this binary: he asks Furiosa not *Which life shall exist at the expense of which other life?* but rather *What are you willing to do to create a world not defined by such binary choices?* His option offers the chance to redistribute resources outside the inexorably subtractive logic of binary life. Or, to put it from the opposite direction, we might say that binary life here stands in not for the act of primitive accumulation per se but rather for the danger of accepting the false scarcity of primitive accumulation as a true account of the world as it is—of acceding to a logic in which we can never do better than simply choosing between submission and death, between flourishing for some and disposability for others. In this way, the climax of the film turns on Furiosa's rejection of the very conflation that I am arguing against here: when she takes up Max's suggestion rather than entering the deathly landscape of the salt flats, she refuses to accept the reductive binary logic of life as an accurate reflection of the actual conditions of her world and the possibilities for material justice.

Understood as a narrative form, binary life thus possesses both a relentlessly reductive fractal structure and considerable elasticity as an aesthetic technology for rendering situations in which some lives exist at the expense of others. On the one hand, in its unremitting aesthetics of subtraction, binary life resonates with material histories of necropolitical decision and dispossession in which the capacity of some lives to thrive involves ensuring that others cannot. As *Salvage the Bones* makes clear, binary life can thus be deployed as an aesthetic technology for making visible the way in which certain lives flourish at the expense of other lives in the context of contemporary racial capital.[14] On the other hand, however, if subjects of life-interest primarily encounter one another via the subtractive unfolding of binary life, then it arguably becomes impossible to make the conceptual leap depicted in *Fury Road,* to imagine an approach to resource distribution or other negotiations of material justice that does not result in one group being at the least much worse off and more likely dead. In effect, social organizations premised on equal access to thriving are logically foreclosed from within the narrative structure of binary life: the switch can flip to 1 or 0, but it cannot flip to both equally. Within this structure, neither liberal ameliorative nor radical redistributive approaches to justice can be sustained, since any temporarily equitable distribution of resources will inevitably shift in due course toward the fostering of some at the expense of others. Even if characters pursue radical redistribution in favor of the historically dispossessed, the iterative, reductive structure of binary life will soon cleave this group into opposed subgroups of thriving and disposable lives. That there is no suggestion this continual division will happen after Furiosa and her band take the Citadel, for example, distinguishes the triumphant act of redistribution that ends *Fury Road* from the unfolding of binary life.

In sum, then, the same internal coherence and built-in propulsion that gives binary life its portability also conveys an implicit claim that necropolitical decision and human dwindling cannot be avoided or opposed. None of the works I examine in this book manage both to engage this logic and to disprove it. They capitulate to it as ecotragedy or hide from it in animal fables or don it as a form of tragic masculinity or turn it into a game to be won by the agent most capable of suffering, but they do not manage to show that this is not how the world works for subjects of life-interest. In its brilliant figuration of salvaging as suffering agency, *Salvage the Bones* offers the most visionary approach that I address in this volume, by making something politically powerful and formally remarkable from binary life; it does so, however, by resignifying rather than invalidating the logic of this mode. Once one accepts the governing parameters of the microeconomic mode—once one is a unit of life-interest—there seems to be no way out of the perception that human lives in the plural necessarily encounter the problem of binary life. Binary life can be leveraged to tell very different stories about the consumption of some lives in order to foster others, but in every case, its narrative logic necessarily reduces the world to an ever-diminishing circuit of humans who can perceive one another only as options or obstacles in a continual series of life-or-death choices. Although this mode appears particularly resonant when it comes to material histories of dispossession and disposable life, it is thus imperative to attend to the specific unfolding of binary life as a formulaic, repetitive reduction in human beings via a series of either/or choices that once begun seemingly cannot be avoided. The aesthetic harshness of the microeconomic mode is an index of the conceptual violence required to redefine humans according to such logic: to grant life-interest, sovereign capture and binary life the same unrelenting facticity we accord to our existence within living human flesh. A crucial element of this conceptual violence lies in the suggestion that there is only one approach to the problem of material and organic finitude, and that approach equals a necropolitical decision made over and over until there is no one left to do the choosing. To collapse the distinction between the linear, iterative logic of binary life and the radically asymmetrical relations to thriving propagated in racial capital would be to capitulate to comprehending and acting in relation to these asymmetries as subjects of life-interest.

NOTES

INTRODUCTION

1. I discuss the dissemination of this aesthetic and the range of my archive beyond the boundaries of the United States in what follows.
2. Lorna Bradbury, "The Bunker Diary: Why Wish This Book on a Child?" *Telegraph*, June 24, 2014, http://www.telegraph.co.uk/culture/books/10920101/The-Bunker -Diary-why-wish-this-book-on-a-child.html. For an overview of the controversy, see "Carnegie medal row over 'depressing' winner grows," *Guardian*, June 25, 2014, https://www.theguardian.com/books/2014/jun/25/carnegie-medal-row -depressing-winner-frank-cottrell-boyce.
3. See also Anna McCarthy, "Reality Television: A Neoliberal Theater of Suffering," *Social Text* 25, no. 4 93 (2007): 17–42. Although McCarthy focuses on works that foreground suffering and bodily injury, the dynamics she is tracing include features that are absent in the microeconomic mode such as randomness. I discuss the relationship between the microeconomic mode and neoliberalism in what follows. For a critical account of the turn to suffering as a politically enabling category, see Bonnie Honig, *Antigone, Interrupted* (Cambridge: Cambridge University Press, 2013). Honig mounts a variety of evidence against the view that mortal finitude "soften[s] us up for the call of the other" (17). As my analysis through this volume indicates, the microeconomic mode offers little proof of this softening toward the other in situations that foreground mortal finitude—rather, the reverse. For a critique of Honig's account, see Giunia Gatta, "Suffering and the Making of Politics: Perspectives from Jaspers and Camus," *Contemporary Political Theory* 14, no. 4 (2015): 335–54.
4. The dynamics I describe in relation to suffering agency have some resonance with Saidiya Hartman's description of the status of agency as assigned to African Americans after emancipation: as Hartman puts it, "the enduring legacy of slavery was readily discernible in the travestied liberation, castigated agency, and blameworthiness

of the free individual." Hartman, *Scenes of Subjection: Terror, Slavery, and Self-Making in Nineteenth-Century America, Race and American Culture* (New York: Oxford University Press, 1997), 6. Suffering agency differs from the castigated agency Hartman describes in several ways—most importantly, in that castigated agency served to reinforce categorical divisions among humans that emancipation threatened to undo. In contrast, a key element of suffering agency is its seeming power to erase such distinctions. Indeed, the threat that suffering agency poses to any celebratory conception of the white man as agential individual is one of the dangers consistently explored in the microeconomic mode. In general, this mode's insistence that every human being is equally suffering from a combination of choice and embodiment scrambles exactly the sort of punitive hierarchies of agency whose subtlety and violence Hartman illuminates, although it also depicts a nostalgia for these hierarchies that align the viewpoint of the microeconomic mode with that of the liberal individual. So, while suffering agency is not the castigated agency that Hartman describes, the microeconomic mode nevertheless returns us to, undermines, and often struggles to reinstitute conceptual divisions on which both chattel slavery and castigated agency depend, including slave/Man, flesh/agency, submission/sovereignty, and so on. For more on these dynamics, see the final section of chapter 1 and chapters 2, 5, and 6. Compare also Lauren Berlant's argument regarding "lateral agency" in "Slow Death (Sovereignty, Obesity, Lateral Agency)," *Critical Inquiry* 33, no. 4 (2007): 754–80. Berlant's focus is on making legible the kinds of actions that cannot be read as agential within a paradigm that "characterize[s] the subjects of appetites (for example, people) as always fully present to their motives, desires, feelings, and experiences, or as even desiring to be" (277n60). Whereas Berlant is interested in versions of agency that fall outside the "causality, subjectivity and life-making embedded in normative notions of agency," the microeconomic mode depicts a kind of hypostasized version of many of the normative features of agency as fused with a compulsive kind of embodiment (758).

5. Sylvia Wynter, "Unsettling the Coloniality of Being/Power/Truth/Freedom: Towards the Human, After Man, Its Overrepresentation—an Argument," *CR: The New Centennial Review* 3, no. 3 (2003): 316. I discuss the relationship between the liberal individual and the subject of life-interest in detail in chapter 2.

6. Lionel Robbins, *An Essay on the Nature and Significance of Economic Science* (London: MacMillan, 1932), 15.

7. Roger E. Backhouse and Steven G. Medema describe the gradual canonization of Robbins's definition as it relates to shifts in the topics and methods of postwar economics in "Retrospectives: On the Definition of Economics," *Journal of Economic Perspectives* 23, no. 1 (2009): 221–34.

8. Although I do not address this point in the brief overview to choice theories that I provide in this section, there is also a significant methodological range in the deployment of this model in terms of level of abstraction and engagement with empirical evidence, from Milton Friedman's infamous assertion that the question of realism is irrelevant for economic theory to the subfield of econometrics, which aims to provide an empirical and quantitative basis for economic analysis and prediction. See Milton Friedman, "The Methodology of Positive Economics," in *The Philosophy of Economics: An Anthology*, 3rd ed., ed. Daniel M. Hausman (New York:

Cambridge University Press, 2008); and G. S. Maddala and Kajal Lahiri, *Introduction to Econometrics* (New York: Wiley, 2009).

9. Approaches to rationality have also been challenged by the increasing body of scientific evidence regarding the process of human choice, evidence often addressed via behavioral economics. See, for example, Richard H. Thaler and Cass R. Sunstein, *Nudge: Improving Decisions About Health, Wealth, and Happiness* (New Haven, Conn: Yale University Press, 2008).

10. As Daniel M. Hausman and Michael S. McPherson put it, "A utility function is just an assignment of numbers to alternatives in a way that indicates preference. 'Maximizing utility' is simply doing what one most prefers. Utility is not itself an object of preference. It is not something sought or traded off against other things, because it is not a thing at all" (236). Hausman and McPherson critique the sleight of hand in contemporary mainstream economics that conflates utility with both material welfare and the satisfaction of self-defined preferences. See Hausman and McPherson, "The Philosophical Foundations of Mainstream Normative Economics," in *The Philosophy of Economics*, 3rd ed., ed. Daniel M. Hausman (New York: Cambridge University Press, 2008), particularly 238–39.

11. The classic account is Roy Radner, "Satisficing," *Journal of Mathematical Economics* 2 (1975): 253–62.

12. In general, the various components I have described here could be seen to combine in different areas of choice theory as follows: (1) game theory: strong rationality (i.e., assumption of the desire to gain the least bad consequences), specific definition of utility (narrow self-interest), individual/small-group focus; (2) macroeconomics: weak rationality (transitive preferences), specific definition of utility (maximization of consumer satisfaction or material welfare), aggregate focus (view of the massed phenomena created by individual decisions); and (3) microeconomics: weak rationality, specific definition of utility, individual focus (specific economic units including consumers, workers, firms, and markets). One of the key forms of choice theory, rational choice theory, combines many of these elements but eschews the focus on allocative choice that defines game theory and other macro- and microeconomic approaches. Its model involves weak rationality, a nonspecific definition of utility and an aggregate focus in the context of nonallocative choices. Because it is nonallocative, rational choice theory does not belong to the analytic rubric described by Robbins's definition. See my discussion of this distinction as it relates to economic imperialism in this section. The evolution and role of rational choice theory is explored in S. M. Amadae's excellent *Rationalizing Capitalist Democracy: The Cold War Origins of Rational Choice Liberalism* (Chicago: University of Chicago Press, 2003).

13. The axiomatic, foundational status of this view of individual choice can be glimpsed in its treatment by microeconomic textbooks, which customarily situate the discipline in relation to these features in their opening chapter before descending into disciplinary complexities. For example: "Economics is the study of how individuals and societies choose to use the scarce resources that nature and previous generations have provided. The key word in this definition is *choose*. Economics is a behavioral, or social, science. In large measure, it is the study of how people make choices. The choices that people make, when added up, translate into social choices." Karl E. Case, Ray C. Fair, and Sharon M. Oster, *Principles of Microeconomics*, 12th ed.

(Hoboken, N.J.: Pearson Higher Education, 2017), 35, emphasis in original. "*Every choice involves important elements of scarcity. Sometimes the most relevant scarcity will involve money, but not always. Coping with scarcity is the essence of the human condition.*" Robert H. Frank, *Microeconomics and Behavior*, 9th ed. (New York: McGraw-Hill Education, 2015), 3, emphasis in original. "Is economics about money: How people make it and spend it? Is it about business, government and jobs? Is it about why some people and some nations are rich and others poor? Economics is about all these things. But its core is the study of *choices* and their *consequences.*" Michael Parkin, *Microeconomics*, global ed. (Harlow, United Kingdom: Pearson, 2016), 1, emphasis in original. The remarkably ubiquitous recourse to italics in such passages indicates something of the authors' commitment to communicating the tremendous importance of these axiomatic features. The identification of microeconomics as a subfield in the second half of the twentieth century arises from and attests to the growing power of this view of the discipline. Although its topics and methods are usually traced to the marginalist revolution of the 1870s, microeconomics emerges after the 1960s as a named subdiscipline focused on the study of individual economic units—including consumers, workers, firms, and markets—as they interact to create dynamics such as demand, price, and so on. The use of the term "microeconomic" lags behind the emergence of the specialization itself. For example, Paul Samuelson's hugely influential textbook, *Economics: An Introductory Analysis*, is widely associated with the dissemination and growing influence of what became recognized as microeconomic topics and methods, but the term itself does not appear in the original 1948 edition. See Paul A. Samuelson, *Economics: An Introductory Analysis* (1948; repr. New York: McGraw-Hill, 1997). In his foreword to the 1997 edition, Samuelson notes that when he wrote the original text, "the word 'macroeconomics' had not yet come into the dictionary" (iii). For an overview of the twentieth-century history of microeconomic approaches in the decades before its identification as such, see Roger Backhouse, *A History of Modern Economic Analysis* (London: Blackwell, 1985), 284–94.

14. As Amadae demonstrates, the trajectory of rational choice theory in fact operates in the opposite direction: rather than moving from economics into political science, the key questions and original methods of rational choice theory developed in policy circles and only later came to be associated with economics as a discipline. See Amadae, *Rationalizing Capitalist Democracy*, 75–80. Although it continues to play a role in political science, rational choice theory no longer overshadows other approaches to the same extent that it once did. For early and wide-ranging critiques of its methods and predominance, see Jane J. Mansbridge, ed., *Beyond Self-Interest* (Chicago: University of Chicago Press, 1990); and Donald P. Green and Ian Shapiro, *Pathologies of Rational Choice Theory: A Critique of Applications in Political Science* (New Haven, Conn.: Yale University Press, 1996). In his celebratory account, Edward Lazear defines economic imperialism as "the extension of economics to topics that go beyond the classical scope of issues, which include consumer choice, theory of the firm, (explicit) markets, macroeconomic activity, and the fields spawned directly by these areas." See Lazear, "Economic Imperialism," *Quarterly Journal of Economics* 115, no. 1 (2000): 103.

15. For a thorough account of the distinctions between marginalist economic theory— usually considered the origin of microeconomics—and rational choice theory, see

Amadae, *Rationalizing Capitalist Democracy*, 220–48. On Kenneth Arrow's rejection of utility maximization in particular, see Backhouse and Medema, "Retrospectives," 228. As Amadae also notes, it is not uncommon to find rational choice methods conflated with utility maximization in overviews of the discipline despite these differences. See, for instance, Lazear, "Economic Imperialism," 136–37.

16. Gary Becker's 1992 Nobel Prize in Economics was "for having extended the domain of microeconomic analysis to a wide range of human behaviour and interaction, including nonmarket behaviour." "Gary S. Becker—Facts," *Nobelprize.org*, http://www.nobelprize.org/nobel_prizes/economic-sciences/laureates/1992/becker-facts.html. Lazear observes that "in modern decades Gary Becker is surely the economist who has done the most to expand the boundaries of economics into the other social sciences, particularly sociology. Sociology arose in the early part of this century as a reaction against individual rationalism. Over his career Becker has reasserted the ability of economics, with its assumption of rational, maximizing behavior, to explain social phenomena that were in the purview of sociology. In virtually every area of economic imperialism, Becker's work plays a prominent and often controversial role." Lazear, "Economic Imperialism," 105.

17. In similar if more sweeping terms, Michel Foucault argues that, for Becker, "economic analysis can perfectly well find its points of anchorage and effectiveness if an individual's conduct answers to the single clause that the conduct in question reacts to reality in a non-random way." See Michel Foucault, *The Birth of Biopolitics: Lectures at the Collège De France, 1978–79*, trans. Graham Burchell (Basingstoke, U.K.: Palgrave Macmillan, 2008), 269. I am indebted here to Foucault's analysis, but it proceeds from a level of generality that leaves aside the way Becker's approach evolves from specific microeconomic concepts such as utility maximization. Whereas Foucault stresses that Becker's position is not shared by the economic mainstream, my account suggests the way in which it nevertheless emerges from the foundational axioms of microeconomics as a field. I address Foucault's account in more detail in this section.

18. Gary S. Becker, *The Economic Approach to Human Behavior* (Chicago: University of Chicago Press, 1976), 167.

19. Becker, *The Economic Approach*, 7.

20. Becker describes his method as tautological but defends it on the grounds of its predictive power. Becker, *The Economic Approach*, 7.

21. Becker, *The Economic Approach*, 9–10.

22. For a far-reaching version of this argument, see Regenia Gagnier's *The Insatiability of Human Wants: Economics and Aesthetics in Market Society* (Chicago: University of Chicago Press, 2000), 19–60. The marginalists still relied on cardinal approaches to utility that allowed for quantitative comparisons, but their shift to a subjective theory of value provides the foundation for what became the ordinalist approach.

23. The impossibility of interpersonal utility comparisons is one of the points of significant conceptual and ideological overlap between microeconomics and rational choice theory. Many of the most famous interventions of the latter school concern the revelation of logical fallacies that haunt the attempt to define collective forms of utility (i.e., the public good) and the approach to public policy that should be adopted in the wake of these insights. See, for example, Kenneth J. Arrow, *Social Choice and Individual Values* (1951; repr. New Haven, Conn.: Yale University Press, 2012).

24. In making this connection between microeconomics as a discipline and interest as a political category, I am echoing Michel Foucault's widely cited account of Chicago School economics, which links the genealogy of what he calls "the subject of interest" with the views of Becker in particular. To find the prehistory of Becker's version of *homo economicus*, Foucault suggests, we must turn not to the development of economics per se but to the political theory of the English empiricists, who invented interest as an "irreducible and non-transferable" quality of individual subjectivity (272). See Foucault, *The Birth of Biopolitics*, 250–71. I discuss Foucault's description of the subject of interest in chapter 2. Although these passages from *The Birth of Biopolitics* have also been central to shaping much recent work focused on neoliberalism, the microeconomic imagination does not engage numerous features commonly associated with the neoliberal subject, including self-entrepreneurship, empowerment discourse, and the imperative for self-improvement. There is significant overlap between the version of the human we find in the microeconomic mode and the subject hailed by neoliberal modes of governance—see, for example, my argument in "Suffering Agency: Imagining Neoliberal Personhood in North America and Britain," *Social Text* 31, no. 2 115 (2013): 83–101—but my focus in this volume is on the specificities of the microeconomic mode. For a range of work on the relationship between neoliberalism and contemporary aesthetics, see Jane Elliott and Gillian Harkins, "Genres of Neoliberalism," special issue, *Social Text* 31, no. 2 115 (2013); Gillian Harkins, *Everybody's Family Romance: Reading Incest in Neoliberal America* (Minneapolis: University of Minnesota Press, 2009); Rachel Greenwald Smith, *Affect and American Literature in the Age of Neoliberalism* (New York: Cambridge University Press, 2015); Jeremy Gilbert, ed., "Neoliberal Culture," special issue, *New Formations* 80–81 (Winter 2013); Emily Johansen and Alissa G. Karl, *Neoliberalism and the Novel* (London: Routledge, 2016); and Mitchum Huehls, *After Critique: Twenty-First-Century Fiction in a Neoliberal Age* (Oxford: Oxford University Press, 2016). For related conversations see also Alison Shonkwiler and Leigh Claire La Berge, *Reading Capitalist Realism* (Iowa City: University of Iowa Press, 2014).

25. Stephen Engelmann's excellent analysis terms this dynamic "monistic interest," or the "reflexive relation that renders commensurable all other relations, thereby subordinating each of them, however construed, to its logic of economy" (4). See Engelmann, *Imagining Interest in Political Thought: Origins of Economic Rationality* (Durham, N.C.: Duke University Press, 2003), 1–47. My use of "interest" roughly correlates to Engelmann's monistic version.

26. Seb Franklin addresses this larger trajectory in *Control: Digitality as Cultural Logic* (Cambridge, Mass.: MIT Press, 2015). I read the microeconomic mode in relation to his argument in chapter 4.

27. See note 24.

28. See, for example, Michael Hardt and Antonio Negri, *Empire* (Cambridge, Mass.: Harvard University Press, 2000); Gilles Deleuze, "Postscript on the Societies of Control," *October* 59 (Winter 1992): 3–7; Maurizio Lazzarato, "From Capital-Labour to Capital-Life," *Ephemera: theory & politics in organization* 4, no. 3 (2004): 187–208; Maurizio Lazzarato, "Immaterial Labor," in *Radical Thought in Italy: A Potential Politics*, ed. Michael Hardt and Paolo Virno, trans. Maurizia Boscagli, Cesare Casarino, Paul Colilli, Ed Emory, Michael Hardt, and Michael Turits (Minneapolis: University of Minnesota Press, 2006), 133–48; Paolo Virno, *A Grammar of the*

Multitude: For an Analysis of Contemporary Forms of Life, trans. Isabella Berto-letti, James Cascaito, and Andrea Casson (Cambridge, Mass.: MIT Press, 2004).

29. See chapter 4 of this volume.

30. Giorgio Agamben, *Homo Sacer: Sovereign Power and Bare Life* (Stanford, Calif.: Stanford University Press, 1998).

31. Dawn Raffel, "The Most Addictive Books of the Last 25 Years: *Life of Pi*," March 3, 2015, http://www.oprah.com/book/books-that-defined-a-generation-life-of-pi?editors _pick_id=57175.f.

1. LIVE MODELS

1. Steven D. Levitt and Stephen J. Dubner, *SuperFreakonomics: Global Cooling, Patriotic Prostitutes, and Why Suicide Bombers Should Buy Life Insurance* (New York: HarperCollins, 2009), 26–81.

2. I do not address the film adaptations of either *The Road* or *Life of Pi* as both downplay and dilute many of the features that I argue are central to the way the novels themselves generate live models.

3. See the introduction for a discussion of this version of interest.

4. In some postapocalyptic tales, of course, the result is a chaotic unleashing of natural and social forces presented as too overwhelming to parse or contain. In the versions that concern me here, the postapocalyptic instead reflects the tendency to selection and distillation also found in survival and castaway tales. I define survival narratives as those that focus on threats to life caused by privation, the natural environment, or both—though other threats may accompany these, as in *The Road*—and in which protagonists are responsible for obtaining their own resources and maintaining their own safety, either as isolated individuals or within small groups that manage to combine aims and resources for a time.

5. To be clear: other genres such as science fiction and fantasy can also thematize modeling and reduction.

6. The close relationship between the modeling of political and social structures and the castaway and survival genres is evidenced by the countless Hobbesian and Lockean readings of Daniel Defoe's *Robinson Crusoe*. See, for example, Stuart Sim and David Walker, *The Discourse of Sovereignty, Hobbes to Fielding: The State of Nature and the Nature of the State* (Aldershot, U.K.: Ashgate, 2003). I address the role of the Hobbesian state of nature in relation to the microeconomic mode in more detail in chapter 2 and consider *Robinson Crusoe* in relation to live models in chapter 6.

7. Aron Ralston, *Between a Rock and a Hard Place* (New York: Atria, 2004); Danny Boyle, dir., *127 Hours* (Los Angeles: Twentieth Century Fox Film Corp., 2011).

8. From A. O. Scott's review in the *New York Times*: "How, more precisely, do you turn an experience of confinement and tedium—take a moment to consider the weight of that title—into a kinetic, suspenseful visual spectacle? How do you turn an immobilized protagonist into the hero of a motion picture, emphasis on motion?" Scott, "The Tale of a Shocking Fall and a Gritty Resolve," *New York Times*, November 4, 2010, C1.

9. Obviously, this doubled quality can also be found in science fiction that represents the everyday through a future world, and there is considerable overlap between the

two, as my discussion of *The Road* suggests. What makes modeling genres distinct is the quality of contraction and subtraction I have been describing.

10. For the classic account of the uncanny in relation to the figure of the doll, see Sigmund Freud, *The Uncanny*, trans. David McLintock (1899; repr. London: Penguin, 2003), 317–61.

11. Cormac McCarthy, *The Road* (London: Picador, 2006), 93. All further citations given in the text.

12. For a different account of the contemporary importance of endurance, see Elizabeth Povinelli, *Economies of Abandonment: Social Belonging and Endurance in Late Liberalism* (Durham, N.C.: Duke University Press, 2011).

13. On the background, involuntary unfolding of physical life as affect, see Brian Massumi, *Parables for the Virtual: Movement, Affect, Sensation* (Durham, N.C.: Duke University Press, 2002), 36. I discuss the relationship among affect, life, and the microeconomic mode in chapter 4.

14. The body of critical work on *The Road* is now substantial and approaches the novel from a number of perspectives. See, for example, Andrew Hoberek, "Cormac McCarthy and the Aesthetics of Exhaustion," *American Literary History* 23, no. 3 (2011): 483–99; Ashley Kunsa, "Maps of the World in Its Becoming: Post-Apocalyptic Naming in Cormac McCarthy's *The Road*," *Journal of Modern Literature* 33, no. 1 (2009): 57–74; Raymond Malewitz, "Regeneration Through Misuse: Rugged Consumerism in Contemporary American Culture," *PMLA: Publications of the Modern Language Association of America* 127, no. 3 (2012): 526; Susan Mizruchi, "Risk Theory and the Contemporary American Novel," *American Literary History* 22, no. 1 (2010): 109–35; Christopher Pizzino, "Utopia at Last: Cormac McCarthy's *The Road* as Science Fiction," *Extrapolation: A Journal of Science Fiction and Fantasy* 51, no. 3 (2011): 358–75; Arielle Zibrak, "Intolerance, a Survival Guide: Heteronormative Culture Formation in Cormac McCarthy's *The Road*," *Arizona Quarterly: A Journal of American Literature, Culture, and Theory* 68, no. 3 (2012): 103–28; and Mark Fisher, "The Lonely Road," *Film Quarterly* 63, no. 3 (2010): 14–17. On the relationship between my argument and Fisher's, see note 17, below.

15. I discuss the cannibal as a figure in the microeconomic mode in chapter 2. On the life-for-a-life logic that is manifested in the cannibal, see chapter 6.

16. There are no apostrophes used with most contractions in the novel.

17. Fisher makes a similar observation when he argues that, in *The Road*, "the strange implication is that only when nature has perished can human beings actually descend into the state of nature: only then can they emerge as what they 'really are.'" See Fisher, "The Lonely Road," 16. However, in Fisher's reading, the novel misses this irony and accepts and endorses this account of humanity. I'm arguing instead that the novel makes this irony central to its question regarding whether we should accept a world organized around interest simply because it appears natural. I address the relationship between the Hobbesian state of nature and the microeconomic mode in chapter 2.

18. I use the term "dialectical" here to refer simply to the logical structure by which two opposing positions are synthesized in a third, rather than in the more specific Marxist sense.

19. Relatively little critical attention has been paid to *Life of Pi*, but there has been some discussion of its relationship to postmodernism, its concerns with animals and

religion, and its status as a shipwreck/survivor narrative. See Cole Stewart, "Believing in Tigers: Anthropomorphism and Incredulity in Yann Martel's *Life of Pi*," *Studies in Canadian Literature/Etudes en Littérature Canadienne* 29, no. 2 (2004): 22–36; Rebecca Duncan, "*Life of Pi* as Postmodern Survivor Narrative," *Mosaic: A Journal for the Interdisciplinary Study of Literature* 41, no. 2 (2008): 167–83; June Dwyer, "Yann Martel's *Life of Pi* and the Evolution of the Shipwreck Narrative," *Modern Language Studies* 35, no. 2 (2005): 9–21; Gregory Stephens, "Feeding Tiger, Finding God: Science, Religion, and 'the Better Story' in *Life of Pi*," *Intertexts* 14, no. 1: 41–59; and Florence Stratton, "'Hollow at the Core': Deconstructing Yann Martel's *Life of Pi*," *Studies in Canadian Literature/Etudes en Littérature Canadienne* 29, no. 2 (2004): 5–21.

20. Yann Martel, *Life of Pi* (Edinburgh: Canongate, 2003), 215–16. All further citations given in the text.

21. Given its attachment to and attempt to rejuvenate these hierarchies, the novel's narrative prioritization of animal and plant life must be distinguished from the diverse range of arguments that critique or theorize across the binaries of living/ nonliving, human/nonhuman, and human species/other species. For influential contributions across a range of perspectives, see for example Jane Bennett, *Vibrant Matter: A Political Ecology of Things* (Durham, N.C.: Duke University Press, 2010); Rosi Braidotti, *The Posthuman* (New York: Polity, 2013); Mel Y. Chen, *Animacies: Biopolitics, Racial Mattering, and Queer Affect* (Durham, N.C.: Duke University Press, 2012); Anna Lowenhaupt Tsing, *The Mushroom at the End of the World: On the Possibility of Life in Capitalist Ruins* (Princeton, N.J.: Princeton University Press, 2015); Nicole Shukin, *Animal Capital: Rendering Life in Biopolitical Times, Posthumanities* (Minneapolis: University of Minnesota Press, 2009); and Cary Wolfe, *Before the Law: Humans and Other Animals in a Biopolitical Frame* (Chicago: University of Chicago Press, 2013).

22. On the relationship between the uncanny and agency, see my essay "Stepford U.S.A.: Second-Wave Feminism, Domestic Labor, and the Representation of National Time," *Cultural Critique* 70, no. 1 (2008): 41–43.

23. On animacy as it relates to the living/nonliving binary in particular, see Chen, *Animacies*. On animatedness as related to racialization in particular, see Sianne Ngai, *Ugly Feelings* (Cambridge, Mass.: Harvard University Press, 2005), 89–125.

24. For the classic account of this aspect of postmodernist narrative, see Linda Hutcheon, *A Poetics of Postmodernism: History, Theory, Fiction* (New York: Routledge, 1988).

25. On the division between those made to live and let die, see Michel Foucault, *"Society Must Be Defended": Lectures at the Collège De France, 1975–76*, trans. David Macey (New York: Picador, 2003), 239–59. For critiques of and correctives to the Eurocentric focus of the biopolitical theory of Foucault and Giorgio Agamben, see João Biehl, "Vita: Life in a Zone of Social Abandonment," *Social Text* 19, no. 3 68 (2001): 131–49; Grace Kyungwon Hong, *Death Beyond Disavowal: The Impossible Politics of Difference* (Minneapolis: University of Minnesota Press, 2015), 25–28; Achille Mbembe, "Necropolitics," trans. Libby Meintjes, *Public Culture* 15 (2003): 11–40; Scott Lauria Morgensen, "The Biopolitics of Settler Colonialism: Right Here, Right Now," *Settler Colonial Studies* 1, no. 1 (2011): 52–76; Alexander G. Weheliye, *Habeas Viscus: Racializing Assemblages, Biopolitics, and Black Feminist Theories of*

the Human (Durham, N.C.: Duke University Press, 2014); Ewa Plonowska Ziarek, "Bare Life on Strike: Notes on the Biopolitics of Race and Gender," *South Atlantic Quarterly* 107 (2008): 89–105. See also Neferti X. Tadiar's argument regarding the way in which "investor subjects" require "processes of dispossession to create and maintain a population of 'surplused' people as monetized aggregates of disposable life." Tadiar, "Life-Times of Disposability Within Global Neoliberalism," *Social Text* 31, no. 115 2 (2013): 27.

26. Martha Mitchell, dir., *House*, season 2, episode 23, "Who's Your Daddy?" aired May 16, 2006, on Fox.

27. Although his extended clash with a profit-obsessed boss in season 1 demonstrated that House's interest is in locating "the answer" rather than improving the bottom line, even this commitment to truth finds a reflection in the tendency of governmentality to boil every employment decision down to performance metrics: whenever House's shenanigans get him into trouble, he need only point to his high success rate in solving cases to stymie his critics. This plotline involved an African American millionaire who attempted to rationalize hospital operations in a way that would maximize profits and benefit his own pharmaceutical company, a process that led him to try to fire House. The casting of an African American in this role is in keeping with the series' association of the business of medicine with House's female boss; in both cases, minorities/women ventriloquize the elements of neoliberalism that serve corporate interests, a tendency that the series desires to disavow. Regarding House's commitment to truth over profit, see Leigh E. Rich, Jack Simmons, David Adams, Scott Thorp, and Michael Mink, "The Afterbirth of the Clinic: A Foucauldian Perspective On 'House M.D.' and American Medicine in the 21st Century," *Perspectives in Biology and Medicine* 51 (2008). On neoliberal governance through performance metrics, see Rose, *Powers of Freedom: Reframing Political Thought* (Cambridge: Cambridge University Press, 1999), 151–53.

28. I discuss the relationship between the microeconomic mode and the game form in chapters 3 and 4.

29. Foucault, *"Society Must Be Defended,"* 255. See also note 25, above.

2. LIFE-INTEREST

1. A brief word on terminology: I use "Man" throughout this book when I am engaged with natural law theory and its conception of the political subject. The distinction between "Man" and "savage," for example, cannot be equated with one between "human beings" and "savages," as Man is a specific definition of human being and the notion of the "savage" functions to solidify this definition in a specific way. I use "liberal individual" to refer to the yoking together of the "subject of interest" and the "subject of right" under liberalism as described by Michel Foucault; these subjects belong to distinct spheres but are both aspects of the liberal individual. See my discussion of these terms in this chapter. I refer to the "liberal subject" to describe the subject of liberal forms of rule such as those theorized by John Locke, which encounter their limit at the sphere of interest in which the liberal individual also operates.

2. One key exception is Roberto Esposito's *Bíos: Biopolitics and Philosophy*, which examines the fissures created by the "immunitary" role of self-preservation

in constituting the liberal subject. See Esposito, *Bíos: Biopolitics and Philosophy*, trans. Timothy Campbell (Minneapolis: University of Minnesota Press, 2008).

3. John Locke, *Two Treatises of Government* (Cambridge: Cambridge University Press, 1998), §6, 270–71. Italics in original.

4. Locke, *Two Treatises of Government*, §6, 271. Italics in original.

5. Locke, *Two Treatises of Government*, §17, 279. Italics in original.

6. C. B. Macpherson, *The Political Theory of Possessive Individualism: Hobbes to Locke* (Oxford: Oxford University Press, 2011), 248.

7. Locke, *Two Treatises of Government*, §27, 287. Italics in original.

8. Macpherson, *The Political Theory of Possessive Individualism*, 269.

9. Michel Foucault, *The Birth of Biopolitics: Lectures at the Collège De France, 1978–79*, trans. Graham Burchell (Basingstoke, U.K.: Palgrave Macmillan, 2008), 274, 272.

10. Foucault, *The Birth of Biopolitics*, 274.

11. Foucault, *The Birth of Biopolitics*, 275.

12. Foucault, *The Birth of Biopolitics*, 275.

13. Foucault, *The Birth of Biopolitics*, 276.

14. Foucault, *The Birth of Biopolitics*, 282.

15. Hannah Arendt, *The Human Condition*, Charles R. Walgreen Foundation Lectures (Chicago: University of Chicago Press, 1958), 284–85.

16. Arendt, *The Human Condition*, 284–85.

17. Hannah Arendt, *Between Past and Future: Six Exercises in Political Thought* (1954; repr. Cleveland, Ohio: Meridian, 1963), 155.

18. Arendt, *Between Past and Future*, 155.

19. Michel Foucault, *"Society Must Be Defended": Lectures at the Collège De France, 1975–76*, trans. David Macey (New York: Picador, 2003), 243.

20. See Sylvia Wynter's theorization "of the West's *Man*, in its now biohumanist, *homo oeconomicus* prototype . . . [and] its systemic overrepresentation as being isomorphic with the being of being human." Wynter, "Human Being as Noun? Or Being Human as Praxis—Towards the Autopoetic Turn/Overturn: A Manifesto," August 25, 2007, https://www.scribd.com/doc/237809437/Sylvia-Wynter-The-Autopoetic -Turn, 68. On the relationship between Wynter's conception of "bio-economic man" and the subject of life-interest, see chapter 5.

21. On the relationship between Benthamite utilitarianism and monistic interest, see Stephen G. Engelmann, *Imagining Interest in Political Thought: Origins of Economic Rationality* (Durham, N.C.: Duke University Press, 2003), 48–76.

22. Foucault, *The Birth of Biopolitics*, 243.

23. Foucault, *The Birth of Biopolitics*, 240.

24. Michael Hardt and Antonio Negri, *Empire* (Cambridge, Mass.: Harvard University Press, 2000), 386.

25. See the introduction to this volume, where I define the microeconomic imagination in more detail and distinguish it from the microeconomic mode.

26. Important readings of Hobbes in relation to game theory and rational choice theory include Jean Hampton, *Hobbes and the Social Contract Tradition* (New York: Cambridge University Press, 1986); Gregory S. Kavka, *Hobbesian Moral and Political Theory* (Princeton, N.J.: Princeton University Press, 1986); and David Gauthier, "Hobbes's Social Contract," *Noûs* 22, no. 1 (1988): 71–82.

27. Thomas Hobbes, *Leviathan: A Critical Edition*, vol. 2 (London: Continuum, 2005), 104.

28. Thomas Hobbes, *On the Citizen*, trans. Richard Tuck (Cambridge: Cambridge University Press, 1998), 3.

29. Hobbes, *Leviathan*, 104.

30. Hobbes, *Leviathan*, 137. Whether this outcome in fact logically follows from Hobbes's central propositions remains a matter of debate. For example, Macpherson argues that Hobbes "moved from his original physiological postulates to the conclusion that all men necessarily seek ever more power over others, by introducing assumptions which are valid only for possessive market societies." Macpherson, *The Political Theory of Possessive Individualism*, 68.

31. Hampton, *Hobbes and the Social Contract Tradition*, 16. Among those who read Hobbes as centrally concerned with interest, there is little agreement regarding how he understood the concept. See Dean Mathiowetz, *Appeals to Interest: Language, Contestation, and the Shaping of Political Agency* (University Park: Pennsylvania State University Press, 2011), 108n5. Here my point is not that Hobbes uses the term "interest" or takes this concept as a central category in *Leviathan* but rather that some aspects of his description of choice in the state of nature resemble interest as I am using the term. In his account of the development of economic interest as a counter to the passions, Albert O. Hirschman argues that Hobbes subscribes to an earlier strategy of "countervailing passions" but nevertheless provides a foundation for this use of interest as a counter to the passions. Hirschman, *The Passions and the Interests: Political Arguments for Capitalism Before Its Triumph* (Princeton, N.J.: Princeton University Press, 1977), 31–32.

32. Hobbes, *Leviathan*, 103.

33. Locke, *Two Treatises of Government*, 279, §16; italics in original.

34. Locke, *Two Treatises of Government*, 279, §16. Yaseen Noorani argues persuasively that liberal approaches to the war on terror rely on much the same logic by assuming that threats to self-preservation necessarily generate a nonnormative zone of action. Noorani, "The Rhetoric of Security," *CR: The New Centennial Review* 5 (2005): 13–41.

35. For one account of these debates, see David Gauthier, "Review: Taming Leviathan," *Philosophy and Public Affairs* 16, no. 3 (1987): 280–98.

36. Kavka argues against the utility of defining all self-generated actions as inherently egoistic, which he refers to as "tautological egoism," in readings of Hobbes and in general. See Kavka, *Hobbesian Moral and Political Theory*, 35. C. A. J. Coady, following Kavka, admits that "perhaps Hobbes occasionally succumbs to" tautological egoism. See Coady, "Hobbes and 'the Beautiful Axiom.'" *Philosophy: The Journal of the Royal Institute of Philosophy* 65, no. 251 (1990): 7.

37. Engelmann offers a persuasive account of Hobbes's approach to interest focused on this distinction. See Engelmann, *Imagining Interest*, 22–26. Both Engelmann and Mathiowetz argue against including Hobbes in the intellectual history of interest as a form of calculating rationality for this reason. See Mathiowetz, *Appeals to Interest*, 106–39.

38. Both Hampton (*Hobbes and the Social Contract Tradition*) and Kavka (*Hobbesian Moral and Political Theory*) read Hobbes's state of nature as a version of the prisoner's dilemma, the most widely known game-theory problem, although they

arrive at different conclusions. On the social and intellectual history of the prisoner's dilemma, see William Poundstone, *Prisoner's Dilemma* (1992; repr. New York: Knopf, 2011). Carol Kay describes the importance of opaque interiority for Hobbes's view of human nature in *Political Constructions: Defoe, Richardson, and Sterne in Relation to Hobbes, Hume, and Burke* (Ithaca, N.Y.: Cornell University Press, 1988), 26–30. I discuss the way in which the microeconomic mode engages the sort of choices explored by the prisoner's dilemma—that is, choices made difficult because of the opacity of others' interests—in chapter 3.

39. For an account of the difference self-preservation should but does not make in rational choice readings of Hobbes, see Patrick Neal, "Hobbes and Rational Choice Theory," *Western Political Quarterly* 41, no. 4 (1988): 635–52.

40. Alexander Weheliye, *Habeas Viscus: Racializing Assemblages, Biopolitics, and Black Feminist Theories of the Human* (Durham, N.C.: Duke University Press, 2014), 27. According to Weheliye, this framework "in turn, authorizes the conflation of racialization with mere biological life, which, on the one hand, enables white subjects to 'see' themselves as transcending racialization due to their full embodiment of this particular genre of the human while responding antipathetically to nonwhite subjects as bearers of ontological cum biological lack, and, on the other hand, in those subjects on the other side of the color line, it creates sociogenically instituted physiological reactions against their own existence and reality." Weheliye, *Habeas Viscus*, 27. As I will suggest in this section, the status of white male protagonists as subjects of life-interest is frequently envisioned as a breakdown of this framework, one that places these men at a new disadvantage with regard to the torments and dangers of embodiment. Yet this very perception makes clear the importance of distinguishing between what Weheliye (after Hortense Spillers) calls "flesh" and the tormented embodiment of the subject of life-interest; this narrative of emerging disadvantage, often presented in such a way that presumes audience sympathy for these white men, attests to the microeconomic mode's attachment to the same racializing assemblages that distinguished the genre of Man from flesh (Weheliye, *Habeas Viscous*, 39). Or, to put it another way, I do not think that flesh as Weheliye defines it can come to be occupied by those humans formerly equated with the liberal individual without changing the category of flesh itself.

41. Locke, *Two Treatises of Government*, §49, 301; and Hobbes, *Leviathan*, 102–3. Italics in original.

42. For a foundational account of this temporalization process in anthropology as a discipline, see Johannes Fabian's *Time and the Other: How Anthropology Makes Its Object* (New York: Columbia University Press, 2002).

43. Orlando Patterson traces the role of slavery in creating the ideal of freedom in Western culture from antiquity through the Middle Ages in *Freedom: Slavery in the Making of Western Culture* (New York: Basic Books, 1991).

44. In Patterson's words, "freedom began its career as a social value in the desperate yearning of the slave to negate what, for him or her, and for nonslaves, was a peculiarly inhuman condition"; the "idea of freedom has never been divorced form this, its primordial, servile source." Patterson, *Freedom*, 9.

45. Mary Nyquist, *Arbitrary Rule: Slavery, Tyranny, and the Power of Life and Death* (Chicago: University of Chicago Press, 2013), 7. Nyquist argues that war slavery doctrine plays a crucial if uneven role in the design of both arguments regarding

"political slavery," which presented life under a tyrannical ruler as a form of slavery, and arguments that evolved simultaneously to exonerate chattel slavery. For her general definition of war slavery doctrine, see pp. 5–11 in particular.

46. See Orlando Patterson, *Slavery and Social Death: A Comparative Study* (Cambridge, Mass.: Harvard University Press, 1982), 35–76.

47. Locke, *Two Treatises of Government*, §23, 284.

48. Locke, *Two Treatises of Government*, §24. Debate regarding the extent to which Locke's writings on slavery—as opposed to his financial transactions—justify or aimed to justify chattel slavery in the Americas as it was being practiced contemporaneously are vociferous and ongoing. For an overview of the major positions taken, see Nyquist, *Arbitrary Rule*, 326–29. My attention here is specifically to the role that self-preservation plays in the opposed positions of the liberal individual and the enslaved person.

49. In her analysis of his engagement with the Haitian revolution, Susan Buck-Morss describes Hegel's approach to slavery in similar terms: "Those who once acquiesced to slavery demonstrate their humanity when they are willing to risk death rather than remain subjugated. The law . . . that acknowledges them merely as 'a thing' can no longer be considered binding, although according to Hegel, it was the slave himself who was responsible for his lack of freedom by initially choosing life over liberty, mere self-preservation." Buck-Morss, "Hegel and Haiti," *Critical Inquiry* 26, no. 4 (2000): 848–49. Although Hegel preserves the inverse relationship between liberty and self-preservation that is characteristic of slavery, the slave's overthrowing of this relationship is central to his account in a way that it is not in the natural law version of the argument. Achille Mbembe reads this concatenation of subjectivity and self-preservation from the opposite direction and argues that, for Hegel, "becoming subject therefore supposes upholding the work of death. To uphold the work of death is precisely how Hegel defines the life of the Spirit. The life of the Spirit, he says, is not that life which is frightened of death, and spares itself destruction, but that life which assumes death and lives with it." One might also compare Frantz Fanon's reading of Hegel in *Black Skin, White Masks*: "He who is reluctant to recognize me is against me. In a fierce struggle I am willing to feel the shudder of death, the irreversible extinction, but also the possibility of impossibility." See Fanon, *Black Skin, White Masks*, trans. Richard Philcox (New York: Grove Press, 2008), 193. In a footnote to this sentence, Fanon adds, "When we began this work we wanted to devote a section to a study of the black man's attitude toward death. We considered it essential because people kept saying that the black man does not commit suicide. Monsieur Achille, in a lecture of his, is adamant about it, and Richard Wright, in one of his short stories, has a white character say: 'If I were a Negro I'd commit suicide,' meaning that only a black man can accept such treatment without feeling drawn to suicide" (Fanon, *Black Skin*, 193n8). That Fanon provides statistics to demonstrate that black suicide is not at all rare suggests the implicit persistence of war slavery doctrine and the link it forges between self-preservation and submission: if the sheer fact of continued existence functions as an unmistakable sign that one has submitted to one's fate, then the truth that black suicide is indeed frequent provides the counterargument. For an account of this nexus focused instead on the preservation of the state, see also Denise Ferreira da Silva's argument regarding the relationship between racial violence and sovereign

self-preservation in "No-Bodies: Law, Raciality and Violence," *Griffith Law Review* 18, no. 2 (2009): 214–36.

50. Hobbes, *Leviathan*, 161.

51. Foucault makes a similar point in arguing that Hobbes does not understand his mode of sovereignty as domination because it is willed out of self-preservation: "Once the defeated have shown a preference for life and obedience, they make their victors their representatives and restore a sovereign to replace the one who was killed in the war. It is therefore not the defeat that leads to the brutal and illegal establishment of a society based upon domination, slavery, and servitude; it is what happens during the defeat, or even after the battle, even after the defeat, and in a way, independently of it. It is fear, the renunciation of fear, and the renunciation of the risk of death. It is this that introduces us into the order of sovereignty and into a juridical regime: that of absolute power. The will to prefer life to death: that is what founds sovereignty, and it is as juridical and legitimate as the sovereignty that was established through the mode of institution and mutual agreement." Foucault, *"Society Must Be Defended,"* 95.

52. See Stephen Kershnar, "A Liberal Argument for Slavery," *Journal of Social Philosophy*, 34 (2003): 510–36. On why such arguments must be considered libertarian rather than liberal, see Samuel Freeman, "Illiberal Libertarians: Why Libertarianism Is Not a Liberal View," *Philosophy & Public Affairs* 30 (2001): 105–51. I discuss the trope of voluntary enslavement in relation to *The Bourne Ultimatum* in chapter 4.

53. Wynter, "Human Being as Noun?," 26. See also note 20.

54. Cătălin Avramescu, *An Intellectual History of Cannibalism*, trans. Alistair Ian Blyth (Princeton, N.J.: Princeton University Press, 2009), 9.

55. On cannibal, colonialism, and conquest, see Daniel Cottom, *Cannibals and Philosophers: Bodies of Enlightenment* (Baltimore: Johns Hopkins University Press, 2001); and Rebecca Weaver-Hightower, *Empire Islands: Castaways, Cannibals, and Fantasies of Conquest* (Minneapolis: University of Minnesota Press, 2007). Over the last thirty years, a series of debates has unfolded in response to the view propagated in William Arens's controversial *The Man-Eating Myth: Anthropology and Anthropophagy* (New York: Oxford University Press, 1979), which argues that accounts of cannibalism were largely exaggerated or fabricated in order to grant imperialism a moral force. See Shirley Lindenbaum, "Thinking About Cannibalism," *Annual Review of Anthropology* 33, no. 1 (2004): 475–98. Avramescu traces the convergence of as well as the distinctions between the savage as a figure in natural law theory and the savage as described after encounters with indigenous peoples in the Americas. In particular, the savage in natural law theory was essentially fearful while the savage encountered in the Americas was frequently depicted as displaying "uncanny courage in the face of death and pain." Avramescu, *An Intellectual History of Cannibalism*, 73.

56. Avramescu, *An Intellectual History of Cannibalism*, 2.

57. Avramescu, *An Intellectual History of Cannibalism*, 25.

58. Avramescu, *An Intellectual History of Cannibalism*, 25–31.

59. This approach is not to be confused with the use of cannibalism as a metaphor for human behavior within the commonwealth and the arena constituted by positive law. Compare Maggie Kilgour's seminal analysis in *From Communion to Cannibalism: An Anatomy of Metaphors of Incorporation* (Princeton, N.J.: Princeton University Press, 1990) as well as Jennifer Brown, *Cannibalism in Literature and*

Film (London: Palgrave Macmillan, 2012), and essays in Kristen Guest, ed., *Eating Their Words: Cannibalism and the Boundaries of Cultural Identity* (Syracuse: State University of New York Press, 2014). On the importance of the cannibal metaphor to the development of capital in particular, see Crystal Bartolovich, "Consumerism, or the Cultural Logic of Late Capital," in *Cannibalism and the Colonial World*, ed. Francis Barker, Peter Hulme, and Margaret Iversen (Cambridge: Cambridge University Press, 1998), 204–37.

60. In Yann Martel's words,

> The reason Richard Parker—or, more accurately, "the case of the *Mignonette*"—has gone down in history, at least in knowledgeable legal circles, is that upon their return to England, the survivors (they were rescued shortly after killing R. P. by a Swedish ship) were tried for murder, a first. Up till then, murder committed under duress, because of severe necessity, was informally accepted as justifiable. But with the *Mignonette*, the powers-that-be decided to examine the question more closely. The case went all the way to the Lords and set a legal precedent. The captain was found guilty of murder. To this day, the only excuse for murder remains self-defense, and any British legal team that tries to argue otherwise will get a lecture from the judge about the *Mignonette*. Murder committed in extreme circumstances for the sake of sustaining life remains illegal (though those who commit it usually get light sentences). That's one Richard Parker.

Martel also lists three other instances in which the name "Richard Parker" is invoked in a story of shipwreck and cannibalism. Martel, "How Richard Parker Got His Name," https://www.amazon.com/gp/feature.html?ie=UTF8&docId=309590. I discuss *Life of Pi* in more detail in chapter 1.

61. Cormac McCarthy, *The Road* (London: Picador, 2007), 148. I discuss *The Road* in greater detail in chapter 1. Mark Fisher considers *The Road* in relation to the Hobbesian state of nature in his essay on the film adaptation. Fisher, "The Lonely Road," *Film Quarterly* 63, no. 3 (2012): 14–17.

62. McCarthy, *The Road*, 33, 95, 195. On cannibalism, organicism, and savagery in *The Road* as a response to post-9/11 America, compare Heather Hicks, *The Post-Apocalyptic Novel in the Twenty-First Century: Modernity Beyond Salvage* (New York: Palgrave Macmillan, 2016), 82–88.

63. See also Jordy Rosenberg's description of the "primitive/brink" temporality that they argue is endemic to the ontological turn. Rosenberg traces this temporality and the ontological turn in general to "neoliberal forms of settler colonialism and financialized capital accumulation." Rosenberg, "The Molecularization of Sexuality: On Some Primitivisms of the Present," *Theory & Event* 17 (2014). I discuss the difference between the temporality of accumulation and the narrative structure of what I call "binary life" in chapter 6.

3. SURVIVAL GAMES

1. Originally released in 1997, *Funny Games* was remade for a U.S. audience in 2007. *Left 4 Dead* has a sequel (*Left 4 Dead 2*, released in 2009) as well as several

downloadable add-ons, the most recent appearing in 2012. I do not discuss survival horror video games in this volume, but many clearly possess numerous features that I associate with the microeconomic mode. Any reading in this vein would need to consider carefully the particular significance of the player's own choices in the gaming medium and what this feature enables or forecloses in terms of the dynamics of life-interest I trace across this book.

2. On the distinction between gaming and gamification, see Ian Bogost, "Gamification Is Bullshit," *Atlantic*, August 9, 2011. http://www.theatlantic.com/technology /archive/2011/08/gamification-is-bullshit/243338/.

3. For arguments describing this shift, see Gilles Deleuze, "Postscript on the Societies of Control," *October* 59 (1992): 3–7; Michael Hardt and Antonio Negri, *Empire* (Cambridge, Mass.: Harvard University Press, 2000); Maurizio Lazzarato, "Immaterial Labor," trans. Maurizia Boscagli, Cesare Casarino, Paul Colilli, Ed Emory, Michael Hardt, and Michael Turits, in *Radical Thought in Italy: A Potential Politics*, ed. Paolo Virno and Michael Hardt (Minneapolis: University of Minnesota Press, 2006), 133–48; and Paolo Virno, *A Grammar of the Multitude: For an Analysis of Contemporary Forms of Life*, trans. Isabella Bertoletti, James Cascaito, and Andrea Casson (Cambridge, Mass.: MIT Press, 2004). Although there are significant disagreements among these theorists in terms of the way they describe the form, reach, and global dispersion of this shift in contemporary capital, I focus on their general areas of overlap in order to illuminate the particular overarching distinction that concerns me here: that between the subject of immaterial labor and the subject of life-interest. As has frequently been noted, the perceived shift to immaterial labor implies a perspective trained on the global North; post-Fordist capital does not erase but rather displaces the processes and consequences of industrial labor to the global South. On the complexity of these interactions, see Neferti X. M. Tadiar, "Life-Times of Disposability Within Global Neoliberalism," *Social Text* 31 (2013): 19–48. I use the term "immaterial labor," but many others circulate to describe similar or related dynamics, including "cognitive capitalism," "affective labor," and so on.

4. Classic examples include the "holodeck" episodes of *Star Trek: The Next Generation*, such as Joseph L. Scanlon's "The Big Goodbye" (January 11, 1988).

5. See Jean Baudrillard, *Simulacra and Simulation*, trans. Sheila Glaser (Ann Arbor: University of Michigan Press, 1994); Marshall McLuhan, *Understanding Media: The Extensions of Man* (New York: McGraw-Hill, 1964); and Fredric Jameson, *Postmodernism, or, the Cultural Logic of Late Capitalism* (London: Verso, 1991), respectively. In the twenty-first century, some game narratives continue the postmodern engagement with questions of virtuality while also incorporating some elements of the survival game paradigm. For one such recent hybrid, see Mark Neveldine, dir., *Gamer* (Santa Monica, Calif.: Lionsgate, 2009).

6. Compare also Mark Seltzer's "Parlor Games: The Apriorization of the Media," *Critical Inquiry* 36 (2009): 100–33. The dynamics that Seltzer traces move in more or less the opposite direction from those I analyze here: he is concerned with the epistemological complexity that games and models introduce via their "doubling of reality" and the relationship between this doubling and "the self-reference system of modern society [that], like the self-reference system of modern literature, gives itself priority over all external reference." Seltzer, "Parlor Games," 103, 107. That Seltzer engages many of the discourses that I suggest contributed to the evolution

of the microeconomic imagination, including cybernetics and game theory, may suggest something of the hold that the microeconomic imagination now possesses on what is considered real: whereas he traces the participation of these discourses in the apriorization of media, I argue here that survival games in the microeconomic mode operate in part through a transgressive immediacy.

7. Alexander R. Galloway, *Gaming: Essays on Algorithmic Culture* (Minneapolis: University of Minnesota Press, 2006), 19.

8. Roger Caillois, *Man, Play, and Games*, trans. Meyer Barash (Urbana: University of Illinois Press, 2001), 43.

9. Caillois, *Man, Play, and Games*, 6.

10. Even when competitors in survival games do choose to play, they do so because there is something else that they fear more than death; they do not have the freedom simply to walk away without thereby encountering consequences they find prohibitively dire. In *The Hunger Games* series, for example, heroine Katniss first volunteers for the games rather than letting her younger, more vulnerable sister do so. I discuss *The Hunger Games* trilogy in more detail later in this chapter.

11. See, for example, Jane McGonigal, *Reality Is Broken: Why Games Make Us Better and How They Can Change the World* (New York: Penguin, 2011). She and her fellow gamification gurus in effect rehearse a long-standing Left argument about the homology between game structures and neoliberalism but from a celebratory rather than a critical perspective. Compare versions of this argument in its critical guise in McKenzie Wark, *Gamer Theory* (Boston: Harvard University Press, 2007); and Andrew Baerg, "Governmentality, Neoliberalism, and the Digital Game," *symploke* 17, no. 1 (2009): 115–27.

12. Kinji Fukasaku, *Battle Royale* (2000; U.S. theatrical 3-D, distributed by Anchor Bay Films, 2011). I refer here to the film rather than the novel by Koushun Takami on which the film is based. See Koushun Takami, *Battle Royale*, trans. Yuji Oniki (San Francisco: Haikasoru, 2009).

13. Gary S. Becker, Kevin M. Murphy, and Jörg L. Spenkuch, "The Manipulation of Children's Preferences, Old-Age Support, and Investment in Children's Human Capital," *Journal of Labor Economics* 34, no. 2, part 2 (April 2016): S3–S30.

14. Gillian Flynn, *Gone Girl* (London: Weidenfeld and Nicolson, 2012). Kindle edition, 224. All further citations given in the text itself.

15. For a different reading of the role of contemporary capital in *Gone Girl*, compare Emily Johansen, "The Neoliberal Gothic: *Gone Girl, Broken Harbor*, and the Terror of Everyday Life," *Contemporary Literature* 57, no. 1 (2016): 30–55.

16. On noir and the effect of twenty-first-century capital on the imagination of the white working-class community, see Gillian Harkins's "Virtual Predators: Neoliberal Loss and Human Futures in the Cinema of Pedophilia," *Social Text* 31, no. 2 115 (2013): 123–44.

17. Ellen Fein and Sherrie Schneider, *The Rules: Time-Tested Secrets for Capturing the Heart of Mr. Right* (New York: Warner Books, 1995). Compare Elizabeth A. Povinelli's argument regarding the idealized contingency of falling in love in a regime of self-responsibilization in *The Empire of Love: Toward a Theory of Intimacy, Genealogy, and Carnality* (Durham, N.C.: Duke University Press, 2008).

18. A typical example from *Elle*: Kayleen Schaefer, "Game, Set, and Cyber-Match: How to Seal the Deal Instead of Staying on the Hook for Monthly Fees: Three New Guides

to Online Dating, Five Tactical Tips for All Womankind," *Elle*, January 15, 2013, http://
www.elle.com/life-love/sex-relationships/online-dating-tips-women-guide.
Although it configures the rules and goal quite differently, a similar form of gamification can be observed in pickup artist culture, which asserts that any man who is
sufficiently motivated can adopt behaviors that will enable him to achieve the prize
of bedding the woman he chooses. See Seb Franklin, *Control: Digitality as Cultural
Logic* (Cambridge, Mass.: MIT Press, 2015), 139–40. The circulation of economic
rhetoric and logics in online dating is critiqued in Eva Illouz, *Cold Intimacies: The
Making of Emotional Capitalism* (Cambridge, U.K.: Polity Press, 2007); and Alain
Badiou, *In Praise of Love*, trans. Nicolas Truong (New York: New Press, 2012).
19. Examples include Bim Adewunmi, "I Used to Scorn 'Cool Girls,' but Now See They
Don't Really Exist," *Guardian*, September 17, 2012, https://www.theguardian.com
/commentisfree/2012/sep/17/cool-girl-gone-girl; and Anne Helen Peterson, "Jennifer
Lawrence and the History of Cool Girls," *Buzzfeed*, February 28, 2014, https://www
.buzzfeed.com/annehelenpetersen/jennifer-lawrence-and-the-history-of-cool
-girls?utm_term=.rxVZRVRLDm#.bcDX1B1jNz.
20. I concentrate here on the original 2004 film (James Wan, dir., *Saw* [London: Entertainment Film Distributors, 2004]), which provides the template for the six sequels.
Although there are some interesting variations, the sequels for the most part elaborate on the dynamics I identify in the first film, primarily through an escalation
of ever more outlandish and grisly traps and ever less believable means of continuing Jigsaw's influence after his death in the second film. One important difference
is that in *Saw II* (Darren Lynn Bousman, dir., *Saw II* [Santa Monica, Calif.: Lionsgate, 2005]) and *Saw III* (Bousman, *Saw III* [Santa Monica, Calif.: Lionsgate, 2006]),
Amanda does not allow any of her victims a real chance of escape as she no longer
believes that the victim learns anything through the process.
21. Bousman, *Saw II*.
22. For example, other choices include those between killing someone else and dying
oneself, killing someone else and letting one's own loved ones die, and so on. Also
referred to as games or tests, the traps are subdivided by the series' fans into "competition traps," "tests," "trials," "final trials," and so on. See "Traps," in *Sawpedia*,
http://sawfilms.wikia.com/wiki/Traps.
23. To the extent that the viewer's own efforts to unravel the mystery mirror the protagonists' attempts to escape their traps, the twist might be understood to operate as
a parallel invocation of sovereignty, via what Alexander Galloway calls "disingenu-
ous informatics." As he puts it, "the knowledge-reversal film aims at doling out data
to the audience, but only to show at the last minute how everything was otherwise."
Galloway, *Gaming*, 94. In the terms of my argument, this last-minute reversal reveals
the power of the film over the viewer: our capacity to win through to the correct
answer is shown to be subject to the caprice of the film diegesis itself, much as the
protagonists in the film can only act within the arbitrary parameters of the traps in
which they have been placed. Matt Hills makes a similar argument regarding the
way in which the "final twist" renders the "films' ludic nature . . . diegetic and extra-
diegetic." See Matt Hills, "Cutting into Concepts of 'Reflectionist' Cinema? The
Saw Franchise and Puzzles of Post-9/11 Horror," in *Horror After 9/11: World of Fear,
Cinema of Terror*, ed. Aviva Briefel and Sam J. Miller (Austin: University of Texas
Press), 119. See also Seb Franklin's argument regarding the relationship between

programmability, the "switching moment," and the "epistemological reversal plot." Seb Franklin, *Control*, 156–57. I discuss the relationship between the microeconomic mode and Franklin's approach to programmability in chapter 4.

24. For other readings of the importance of individual choice and gaming in the films, compare Christopher Sharrett, "The Problem of *Saw*: 'Torture Porn' and the Conservatism of Contemporary Horror Films," *Cineaste: America's Leading Magazine on the Art and Politics of the Cinema* 35, no. 1 (2009): 32–37; Hills, "Cutting into Concepts," 107–23; Dean Lockwood, "All Stripped Down: The Spectacle of 'Torture Porn,' " *Popular Communication* 7, no. 1 (2009): 40–48; Evangelos Tziallas, "Torture Porn and Surveillance Culture," *Jump Cut: A Review of Contemporary Media* 52 (Summer 2010); and James Aston and John Walliss, eds., *To See the Saw Movies: Essays on Torture Porn and Post-9/11 Horror* (Jefferson, N.C.: McFarland, 2013).

25. Michel Foucault, *Discipline and Punish: The Birth of the Prison*, trans. Alan Sheridan (New York: Vintage, 1995), 3–6. The United States' war on terror has prompted renewed discussion of the relationship between torture and sovereignty in the context of contemporary and historic geopolitics. See, for example, Paul W. Kahn, *Sacred Violence: Torture, Terror, and Sovereignty* (Ann Arbor: University of Michigan Press, 2008); Bonnie Mann, *Sovereign Masculinity: Gender Lessons from the War on Terror* (New York: Oxford University Press, 2014); and Jason Ralph, *America's War on Terror: The State of the 9/11 Exception from Bush to Obama* (Oxford: Oxford University Press, 2013). On the *Saw* franchise and the war on terror, see Aston and Walliss, eds., *To See the Saw Movies*. I discuss the ticking-time-bomb torture scenario in the final section of this chapter.

26. I am indebted here to Elaine Scarry's foundational work in *The Body in Pain: The Making and Unmaking of the World* (New York: Oxford University Press, 1985), particularly her argument regarding the importance of the supremely individual and self-contained nature of pain in the symbolic operations of torture. However, the results produced in the survival game require and illuminate agency on the part of the victim in a fashion that is expressly and brutally foreclosed in the classic scenario she describes, in which the point of torture is to amplify the agency of the torturer by eradicating it for the victim. Mitchell Dean and John T. Parry both note that torture can always be argued to carry a choice on the part of the victim since the subject supposedly always has the option to stop the pain simply by deciding to talk. See Dean, *Governmentality: Power and Rule in Modern Society* (London: Sage Publications, 1999), 12; and Parry, "Escalation and Necessity: Defining Torture at Home and Abroad," in *Torture: A Collection*, ed. Sanford Levinson (Oxford: Oxford University Press), 153. See also Darius Rejali's argument regarding the pastoral aims of torture in *Torture & Modernity: Self, Society, and State in Modern Iran* (Boulder, Colo.: Westview Press, 1994), 76. There is also a resemblance between the dynamics of suffering agency I trace in the *Saw* torture scenarios and what Jeremy Wisnewski and R. D. Emerick tellingly refer to as the "economic model" of torture, which "understands torture as an exchange of pain and information, question and answer, costs and benefits." Wisnewski and Emerick, *The Ethics of Torture* (London: Continuum, 2009), 8. What for all of these thinkers is an erroneous attribution of agency to the victim becomes in the *Saw* franchise the true focus and result of the torture process.

27. For arguments describing transformed relationships between biology and economics in post-Fordist capital, see Melinda Cooper, *Life as Surplus: Biotechnology and Capitalism in the Neoliberal Era* (Seattle: University of Washington Press, 2011); Melinda Cooper and Cathy Waldby, *Clinical Labor: Tissue Donors and Research Subjects in the Global Bioeconomy* (Durham, N.C.: Duke University Press, 2014); Kalindi Vora, *Life Support: Biocapital and the New History of Outsourced Labor* (Minneapolis: University of Minnesota Press, 2015); and Sarah Franklin and Margaret Lock, "Animation and Cessation: The Remaking of Life and Death," in *Remaking Life and Death: Toward an Anthropology of the Biosciences*, ed. Sarah Franklin and Margaret Lock (Santa Fe, N.M.: School of American Research Press, 2003), 3–22.

28. I do not address the film adaptations of *The Hunger Games* trilogy here. For brevity's sake, I follow much contemporaneous media coverage in using *"Game of Thrones"* as an umbrella term when I am discussing features common to both the novels and their adaptation, although only the first novel in the series bears this title. However, my analysis here focuses primarily on the novels, which I refer to by name or as *A Song of Ice and Fire*, the title of the novel series as a whole.

29. For a canonical example of this argument, see Tania Modleski, *Loving with a Vengeance: Mass-Produced Fantasies for Women*, 2nd ed. (New York: Routledge, 2008).

30. George R. R. Martin, *A Game of Thrones* (London: HarperVoyager, 2011), 492. This statement also served as a tagline for season 1 of the television adaptation.

31. For an account of this problem elaborated in a more familiar philosophical guise, see William Rasch, *Sovereignty and Its Discontents: On the Primacy of Conflict and the Structure of the Political* (London: Birkbeck Law Press, 2004), esp. 89–91.

32. Farah Mendlesohn coins the term "portal-quest fantasy" and analyzes several such tales in *Rhetorics of Fantasy* (Middletown, Conn.: Wesleyan University Press, 2008).

33. George R. R. Martin, *A Storm of Swords, Part 1* (London: HarperVoyager, 2011), 192.

34. Martin, *A Storm of Swords*; italics in original.

35. George R. R. Martin, *A Clash of Kings* (London: HarperVoyager, 2011), 534.

36. Martin, *A Clash of Kings*, 104, 119, 52, 210.

37. I discuss the relationship between game theory and the microeconomic imagination in the introduction to the volume. For an account of the history and development of game theory, see William Poundstone, *Prisoner's Dilemma* (1992; repr. New York: Knopf, 2011).

38. On the relationship between the Hobbesian state of nature and the microeconomic mode in general, see chapter 2.

39. Taken together, the *A Song of Ice and Fire* novels contain over a thousand named characters. One of the most significant differences between the novels and the HBO series is that the series reduces the number of characters and subplots found in the novels, frequently by fusing several characters into one. Even having done so, however, *Game of Thrones* still had the largest cast of all the television shows on air during its third season. James Hibberd, "'Game of Thrones' Scoop: Season 3 Character List Revealed," *Entertainment Weekly*, May 29, 2012, http://www.ew.com/article/2012/05/29/game-of-throne-season-3-cast.

40. As Jessica Benjamin puts it, "both in theory and in practice our culture knows only one form of individuality: the male stance of over-differentiation, of splitting off

and denying the tendencies toward sameness, merging, and reciprocal responsiveness." Benjamin, "The Bonds of Love: Rational Violence and Erotic Domination," *Feminist Studies* 6, no. 1 (1980): 150.

41. Scarry argues, "To have pain is to have *certainty*; to hear about pain is to have *doubt*" because "pain enters into our midst as at once something that cannot be denied and something that cannot be confirmed (thus it comes to be cited in philosophical discourse as an example of conviction, or alternatively as an example of skepticism)." Scarry, *The Body in Pain*, 13, italics in original. Compare also Arjun Appadurai's argument regarding "the body as a site of violent closure in situations of categorical uncertainty." Appadurai, "Dead Certainty: Ethnic Violence in the Era of Globalization," *Public Culture* 10, no. 2 (1998): 234. Appadurai ties "vivisectionist" forms of ethnic violence to the abstractions that circulate in contemporary global capital; he posits that these "abstractions inspire grotesque forms of bodily violence because such violence "offer[s] temporary ways to render these abstractions graspable" (240). My argument here is that sadism substitutes an overwhelming interest in escaping pain for whatever other interest the victim may have possessed. That is, in the microeconomic mode, vivisectionist violence doesn't find the answer to an epistemological riddle so much as render the riddle moot.

42. Martin, *A Game of Thrones*, 157. Italics in original.

43. Compare arguments regarding the limitations of Scarry's approach for understanding the forms of torture adopted in the war on terror in Stephanie Athey, "The Torture Device: Debate and Archetype," *Torture*, ed. Zalloua Zahi and Shampa Biswas (Seattle: University of Washington Press, 2011); and Michael P. Vicaro, "A Liberal Use of 'Torture': Pain, Personhood, and Precedent in the U.S. Federal Definition of Torture," *Rhetoric & Public Affairs* 14, no. 3: 401–26. I focus here on this archetype as it appears in *Unthinkable*, as I am interested in tracing the way it is both preserved and remade via the logic of life-interest.

44. As Jeremy Wisnewski and R. D. Emerick put it,

> the Ticking Time-Bomb Argument . . . depends precisely on economic considerations: we are asked to imagine a scenario in which only torture will enable us to track down a bomb that is set to detonate in a densely populated urban area. The case is meant to draw on our more utilitarian intuitions—on our desire to save the many at the cost of merely one. If there is a seemingly compelling argument in favor of limited permissibility (which is . . . the most commonly defended view for the permissibility of torture), the ticking-bomb argument is it. Likewise, it is the strongest of "economic" arguments for torture, as it makes the benefits of the hypothetical torture quite high, and the costs (seemingly) low (Wisnewski and Emerick, *The Ethics of Torture*, 16)

45. Wisnewski and Emerick, *The Ethics of Torture*, 16.

46. Gregor Jordan, dir., *Unthinkable* (Houston, Texas: Lleju Productions, 2010). The television series *24* is particularly well known as a vehicle for this scenario. I have chosen to focus on *Unthinkable* because its attempts to be evenhanded make it more revealing than the overtly jingoistic *24*.

47. On the ubiquity of and political and ethical problems with the ticking-time-bomb scenario, see, for example, David Luban, "Liberalism, Torture, and the Ticking Bomb," *Virginia Law Review* 91, no. 6 (2005): 1425–61. I'm grateful to audience

members at the ASAP/5 conference in October 2013 for questions regarding the relationship between the ticking-time-bomb trope and the microeconomic mode. At the time, I was unconvinced of the connection, but the discussion encouraged me to consider the issue further.

48. In the extended version of the film, Yusuf's agency persists even past the end of his battle with H, as the last shot of the film is of a still-concealed fourth bomb. H has suspected that Yusuf planted this secret fourth bomb in case he revealed the locations of the first three under torture, but, while H is arguing with his gullible superiors about continuing the torture, Yusuf manages to shoot himself, leaving no one left to question.

49. Tellingly, the torturer's suffering agency has also been explored in another context in which the moral authority of the goal at hand is seemingly unquestionable: that of parents attempting to either rescue or avenge the death of their child. As their ambiguous titles indicate, the films *Prisoners* (2013) and *The Tortured* (2010) turn on the question of whether the torturer-parents are any less trapped and tormented than their seeming victims. Denis Villeneuve, dir., *Prisoners* (Burbank, Calif.: Warner Bros., 2013); and Robert Lieberman, dir., *The Tortured* (New York: IFC Films, 2010).

4. SOVEREIGN CAPTURE

1. "We no longer find ourselves dealing with the mass/individual pair. Individuals have become '*dividuals*,' and masses, samples, data, markets, or '*banks*.'" Gilles Deleuze, "Postscript on the Societies of Control," *October* 59 (1992): 5, italics in original. For related arguments focused on immaterial labor in particular, see also Michael Hardt and Antonio Negri, *Empire* (Cambridge, Mass.: Harvard University Press, 2000); Maurizio Lazzarato, "Immaterial Labor," trans. Maurizia Boscagli, Cesare Casarino, Paul Colilli, Ed Emory, Michael Hardt, and Michael Turits, in *Radical Thought in Italy: A Potential Politics*, ed. Paolo Virno and Michael Hardt (Minneapolis: University of Minnesota Press, 2006), 133–48; and Paolo Virno, *A Grammar of the Multitude: For an Analysis of Contemporary Forms of Life*, trans. Isabella Bertoletti, James Cascaito, and Andrea Casson (Cambridge, Mass.: MIT Press, 2004).

2. Michel Foucault, *"Society Must Be Defended": Lectures at the Collège De France, 1975–76*, trans. David Macey (New York: Picador, 2003), 241.

3. In his foundational definition of sovereignty, Jean Bodin states that "it is the distinguishing mark of the sovereign that he cannot in any way be subject to the commands of another, for it is he who makes law for the subject, abrogates law already made, and amends obsolete law. No one who is subject either to the law or to some other person can do this. That is why it is laid down in the civil law that the prince is above the law, for the word law in Latin implies the command of him who is invested with sovereign power." Jean Bodin, *Six Books of the Commonwealth*, abr. and trans. J. M. Tooley (Oxford: Blackwell, 2009), 68. William Rasch describes sovereignty and decision in relation to determinate judgment in *Sovereignty and Its Discontents: On the Primacy of Conflict and the Structure of the Political* (London: Birkbeck Law Press, 2004), 28–29.

4. Michel Foucault, *Discipline and Punish: The Birth of the Prison*, trans. Alan Sheridan (New York: Vintage, 1995), 55.

5. As Foucault puts it in his description of penal torture in seventeenth-century France, "the practice of torture was not an economy of example, in the sense in which it was to be understood at the time of the *ideologues* (that the representation of the penalty should be greater than the interest of the crime), but a policy of terror: to make everyone aware, through the body of the criminal, of the unrestrained presence of the sovereign." Foucault, *Discipline and Punish*, 49. On the historical relationship between juridical torture and truth in particular, see Page DuBois, *Torture and Truth* (New York: Routledge, 1991); and Lisa Silverman, *Tortured Subjects: Pain, Truth, and the Body in Early Modern France* (Chicago: University of Chicago Press, 2001).

6. Foucault, *"Society Must Be Defended,"* 240.

7. Seb Franklin, *Control: Digitality as Cultural Logic* (Cambridge, Mass.: MIT Press, 2015), 19.

8. Franklin, *Control*, 14.

9. Franklin, *Control*, 94.

10. Franklin, *Control*, 163.

11. Franklin, *Control*, 160.

12. Franklin, *Control*, 160.

13. Paul Greengrass, dir. *The Bourne Ultimatum* (Universal City, Calif.; Universal Pictures, 2007).

14. This distinction is similarly temporalized in Joss Whedon's *Dollhouse*, a series focused on a group of humans who have contracted to serve as programmed "dolls" in different scenarios as paid for by various customers.

15. Gilles Deleuze and Felix Guattari, *A Thousand Plateaus: Capitalism and Schizophrenia*, trans. Brian Massumi (London: Bloomsbury, 2013), 157.

16. Jasbir K. Puar, "Bodies with New Organs: Becoming Trans, Becoming Disabled," *Social Text* 33, no. 3 124 (2015): 58.

17. Puar, "Bodies with New Organs," 63.

18. Puar, "Bodies with New Organs," 63.

19. Puar, "Bodies with New Organs," 67.

20. Ann Pellegrini and Jasbir Puar, "Affect," *Social Text* 27, no. 3 100 (2009): 37.

21. Jasbir K. Puar, "Coda: The Cost of Getting Better: Suicide, Sensation, Switchpoints," *GLQ: A Journal of Lesbian and Gay Studies* 18, no. 1 (2012): 155.

22. Brian Massumi, *Parables for the Virtual: Movement, Affect, Sensation* (Durham, N.C.: Duke University Press, 2002), 36.

23. Massumi, *Parables for the Virtual*, 36. Italics in original.

24. Massumi, *Parables for the Virtual*, 31–32. Italics in original.

25. Massumi, *Parables for the Virtual*, 36.

26. Examples of this definition of horror include Barbara Creed, "Horror and the Monstrous-Feminine: An Imaginary Abjection," in *Horror, the Film Reader*, ed. Mark Jancovich (New York: Routledge, 2002), 69; Anna Powell, *Deleuze and Horror Film* (Edinburgh: Edinburgh University Press, 2005), 9; and Bridget Cherry, *Horror* (New York: Routledge, 2009), 55, 63.

27. Horror cinema is increasingly defined by the work it performs on viewers in specifically affective terms. See, for example, Steven Shaviro, "Body Horror and Post-Socialist Cinema: György Pálfi's *Taxidermia*," *Film Philosophy* 15, no. 2 (2011). For

an overview of such approaches, including those that define affect more broadly, see Cherry, *Horror*, 52–93.

28. Linda Williams, "Film Bodies: Gender, Genre, and Excess," *Film Quarterly* 44, no. 4 (1991): 4.

29. Brigitte Peucker, *The Material Image: Art and the Real in Film* (Stanford, Calif.: Stanford University Press, 2007), 163.

30. Xavier Aldana Reyes describes the relationship between the startle effect, horror, and what she calls "somatic empathy" in *Horror Film and Affect: Towards a Corporeal Model of Viewership* (New York: Routledge, 2016), 151–56.

31. Massumi, *Parables of the Virtual*, 36.

32. Discussions of the role of horror in *Leviathan* include Elisabeth Anker, "The Liberalism of Horror," *Social Research: An International Quarterly* 81, no. 4 (2014): 795–823; and Thomas Fahy, "Hobbes, Human Nature, and the Culture of American Violence in Truman Capote's *In Cold Blood*," in *The Philosophy of Horror*, ed. Thomas Fahy (Lexington: University Press of Kentucky, 2010), 57–71.

5. PARTIAL FICTIONS

1. J. A. Bayona, dir., *The Impossible* (Burbank, Calif.: Warner Bros. Pictures, 2012).

2. Sylvia Wynter, "Unsettling the Coloniality of Being/Power/Truth/Freedom: Towards the Human, after Man, Its Overrepresentation—an Argument," *CR: The New Centennial Review* 3, no. 3 (2003): 288.

3. For foundational theorizations of racial capital, see Cedric J. Robinson, *Black Marxism: The Making of the Black Radical Tradition* (Chapel Hill: University of North Carolina Press, 2000); W. E. B. Du Bois, *Black Reconstruction in America: An Essay toward a History of the Part Which Black Folk Played in the Attempt to Reconstruct Democracy in America, 1860–1880* (1896; repr. New York: Oxford University Press, 2007); and C. L. R. James, *The Black Jacobins; Toussaint L'Ouverture and the San Domingo Revolution*, 2nd ed. (1938; repr. New York: Vintage, 1963).

4. For accounts of this division, see, for example, Alexander G. Weheliye, *Habeas Viscus: Racializing Assemblages, Biopolitics, and Black Feminist Theories of the Human* (Durham, N.C.: Duke University Press, 2014); Lisa Lowe, *The Intimacies of Four Continents* (Durham, N.C.: Duke University Press, 2015); Saidiya V. Hartman, *Scenes of Subjection: Terror, Slavery, and Self-Making in Nineteenth-Century America, Race and American Culture* (New York: Oxford University Press, 1997); and Grace Kyungwon Hong, *The Ruptures of American Capital: Women of Color Feminism and the Culture of Immigrant Labor* (Minneapolis: University of Minnesota Press, 2006).

5. Universal Declaration of Human Rights, *Yearbook of the United Nations, 1948–49* (New York: United Nations Publications, 1950), 535. As Pheng Cheah puts it, "Whether self-consciously or by historical osmosis, the philosophical justification of human rights found in the Declaration is indebted to Kant's definition of the dignity of man in his second formulation of the categorical imperative." Cheah, *Inhuman Conditions: On Cosmopolitanism and Human Rights* (Cambridge, Mass.: Harvard University Press, 2009), 154. Samuel Moyn points out that the historiography of human

rights has identified several different historical moments, including that of Immanuel Kant, as constituting the "singular cosmopolitan breakthrough." Moyn, "The Universal Declaration of Human Rights of 1948 in the History of Cosmopolitanism," *Critical Inquiry* 40, no. 4 (2014): 366.

6. Universal Declaration of Human Rights, *Yearbook of the United Nations*, 535.

7. Although legal persons are assumed to possess the dignity associated with personhood as a universal human attribute, the conviction that all humans are dignified persons simultaneously circulates as the ground on which claims for the extension of legal personality may be staked. For an introductory account of legal personhood in the United States, see "What We Talk About When We Talk About Persons: The Language of a Legal Fiction," *Harvard Law Review* 114 (2001): 1745–68. This overview both differentiates between the commonplace understanding of personhood and legal personality and argues that "courts have not been able to distinguish cleanly between these two points of view, alternately treating the issue of personhood as a commonsense determination of what is human or as a formal legal fiction unrelated to biological conceptions of humanity" (1745). For an account of the denial of personhood in the contemporary United States via criminalization in particular, see Lisa Cacho's argument that "permanently criminalized people" in the United States constitute a group "*ineligible for personhood.*" Cacho, *Social Death: Racialized Rightlessness and the Criminalization of the Unprotected* (New York: New York University Press, 2012), 6; italics in the original. In Cacho's definition, "to be ineligible for personhood is a form of social death; it not only defines who does not matter, it also makes mattering meaningful" (6). For an evocative account of the constitution and exclusions of personality in American legal history, see, for example, Colin Dayan, *The Law Is a White Dog: How Legal Rituals Make and Unmake Persons* (Princeton, N.J.: Princeton University Press, 2011). On the tautology of human rights discourse as registered in narrative form, see, for example, Joseph R. Slaughter, *Human Rights, Inc.: The World Novel, Narrative Form, and International Law* (New York: Fordham University Press, 2007).

8. As Lisa Lowe puts it, "liberal philosophy, culture, economics, and government have been commensurate with, and deeply implicated in, colonialism, slavery, capitalism and empire." Lowe, *The Intimacies of Four Continents*, 2. Important critical accounts of this relationship also include Paul Gilroy, *The Black Atlantic: Modernity and Double Consciousness* (Cambridge, Mass.: Harvard University Press, 1993); Hartman, *Scenes of Subjection*; Wynter, "Unsettling the Coloniality of Being/Power/Truth/Freedom"; Dipesh Chakrabarty, *Provincializing Europe: Postcolonial Thought and Historical Difference*, *Princeton Studies in Culture/Power/History* (Princeton, N.J.: Princeton University Press, 2000); Achille Mbembe, "Necropolitics," *Public Culture* 15, no. 1 (2003): 11–40; and Weheliye, *Habeas Viscus*. I discuss the relationship between the figuration of slavery in natural law theory, the liberal individual, and life-interest in particular in chapter 2. For critiques of human rights as a category from a range of perspectives, see Hannah Arendt, *The Origins of Totalitarianism*, 2nd ed. (New York: Meridian Books, 1958), 290–302; Giorgio Agamben, *Homo Sacer: Sovereign Power and Bare Life* (Stanford, Calif.: Stanford University Press, 1998); Wendy Brown, "The Most We Can Hope For: Human Rights and the Politics of Fatalism," *South Atlantic Quarterly* 103, no. 2/3 (2004): 451–63; Cheah, *Inhuman Conditions*; Randall Williams, *The Divided World: Human*

Rights and Its Violence (Minneapolis: University of Minnesota Press, 2010); and Samuel Moyn, *The Last Utopia* (Cambridge, Mass.: Harvard University Press, 2012).

9. Although the Western imperialist impetus for and effects of the UDHR have been a frequent site of critique, Lydia Liu also traces the competing versions of universalism that contributed to drafts of the UDHR and argues—contra Moyn, in particular—that "many of the principles within those norms [of universal human rights] were elaborated and fought out with the participation of Third World thinkers and diplomats." Liu, "Shadows of Universalism: The Untold Story of Human Rights around 1948," *Critical Inquiry* 40, no. 4 (2014): 394. In other words, the critique of occlusion has produced its own forms of occlusion in some quarters.

10. Conflict over questions of resource access and distribution famously shaped the debates regarding the final format of the UDHR's Article 25, which states "Everyone has the right to a standard of living adequate for the health and well-being of himself and of his family, including food, clothing, housing and medical care and necessary social services, and the right to security in the event of unemployment, sickness, disability, widowhood, old age or other lack of livelihood in circumstances beyond his control." Universal Declaration of Human Rights, *Yearbook of the United Nations,* 536. For a record of the debate, see the Commission on Human Rights, Third Session, Summary Record of the Seventy-First Meeting, June 28, 1948 [held June 14, 1948], UDHR E/CN.4/SR.71.

11. Hong, *The Ruptures of American Capital,* 8.

12. For a range of such critiques, see, for example, Neferti X. M. Tadiar, "Life-Times of Disposability Within Global Neoliberalism," *Social Text* 31, no. 2 115 (2013): 19–48; Kalindi Vora, *Life Support: Biocapital and the New History of Outsourced Labor* (Minneapolis: University of Minnesota Press, 2015); Jin Haritaworn, Adi Kuntsman, and Silvia Posocco, *Queer Necropolitics* (Abingdon, Oxon: Routledge, 2014); Ruth Wilson Gilmore, *Golden Gulag: Prisons, Surplus, Crisis, and Opposition in Globalizing California,* American Crossroads, no. 21 (Berkeley: University of California Press, 2007); and Lorenzo Veracini, "Facing the Settler Colonial Present," in *The Limits of Settler Colonial Reconciliation: Non-Indigenous People and the Responsibility to Engage,* ed. Sarah Maddison, Tom Clark, and Ravi de Costa (Singapore: Springer Singapore, 2016), 35–48.

13. See Wynter, "Unsettling the Coloniality of Being/Power/Truth/Freedom," 318–21.

14. I use "Deng" to refer to the real-world, historical person of Valentino Achak Deng and "Achak" to refer to the character based upon him in *What Is the What.*

15. Slaughter argues that the developmental narrative of the bildungsroman is foundational both to the rhetoric of human rights and to the human rights novel. Slaughter, *Human Rights, Inc.,* 86–139. Readings of *What Is the What* in relation to human rights include Sean Bex and Stef Craps, "Humanitarianism, Testimony, and the White Savior Industrial Complex: *What Is the What* Versus *Kony 2012,*" *Cultural Critique* 92, no. 1 (2016): 32–56; Robert Eaglestone, "'You Would Not Add to My Suffering If You Knew What I Have Seen': Holocaust Testimony and Contemporary African Trauma Literature," *Studies in the Novel* 40, no. 1/2 (2008): 72–85; Mitchum Huehls, "Referring to the Human in Contemporary Human Rights Literature," *MFS Modern Fiction Studies* 58, no. 1 (2012): 1–21; and Michelle Peek, "Humanitarian Narrative and Posthumanist Critique: Dave Eggers's *What Is the What,*" *Biography* 35, no. 1 (2012): 115–36.

16. Dave Eggers, *What Is the What: The Autobiography of Valentino Achak Deng: A Novel* (New York: Penguin, 2008). Kindle edition, 213. All further citations given in the text.
17. These quotations appear only in the preface as printed in the first edition of the novel, rather than in the edition from which I have drawn my quotations. Dave Eggers, *What Is the What: The Autobiography of Valentino Achak Deng: A Novel* (San Francisco: McSweeney's, 2006), 5.
18. Eggers, *What Is the What*, 2006, 5.
19. Slaughter, *Human Rights, Inc.*, 205–26.
20. Mitchum Huehls also reads the parable in relation to its "catachrestic" nature but draws different conclusions about this quality. Compare Huehls, "Referring to the Human," 13–15.
21. Consider, for example, Lynn Hunt's account of the emergence of this dynamic (*Inventing Human Rights* [New York: Norton, 2007]) as well as the more qualified assessments offered in James Dawes, *That the World May Know: Bearing Witness to Atrocity* (Cambridge, Mass.: Harvard University Press, 2007); and Kay Schaffer and Sidonie Smith, *Human Rights and Narrated Lives: The Ethics of Recognition* (New York: Palgrave Macmillan, 2004).
22. Jodi Melamed, "The Spirit of Neoliberalism: From Racial Liberalism to Neoliberal Multiculturalism," *Social Text* 24, no. 4 89 (2006): 14.
23. Melamed, "The Spirit of Neoliberalism," 17.
24. Melamed, "The Spirit of Neoliberalism," 17–18.
25. Kazuo Ishiguro, *Never Let Me Go* (New York: Vintage International, 2006), 255. All further citations given in the text.
26. Readings that concern the relationship between humanism, biotechnology, and ethics in the novel include Matthew Eatough, "The Time That Remains: Organ Donation, Temporal Duration, and Bildung in Kazuo Ishiguro's *Never Let Me Go*," *Literature and Medicine* 29, no. 1 (2011): 132–60; Gabriele Griffin, "Science and the Cultural Imaginary: The Case of Kazuo Ishiguro's *Never Let Me Go*," *Textual Practice* 23, no. 4 (2009): 645–63; Mark Jerng, "Giving Form to Life: Cloning and Narrative Expectations of the Human," *Partial Answers: Journal of Literature and the History of Ideas* 6, no. 2 (2008): 369–93; Myra J. Seaman, "Becoming More (Than) Human: Affective Posthumanisms, Past and Future," *Journal of Narrative Theory* 37, no. 2 (2007): 246–75; and Anne Whitehead, "Writing with Care: Kazuo Ishiguro's *Never Let Me Go*," *Contemporary Literature* 52, no. 1 (2011): 54–83.
27. As Joan Copjec points out, the uncanny double can be traced to the creation of the Enlightenment subject and its split between the empirical self, which can act in the material world but can also be acted upon, and the transcendental self, which is wholly free but lacks the capacity to cause effects in the material world. The double customarily represents a scrambling of these relations into various nightmare forms—for example, the subject who finds his place taken by the nefarious, all-powerful double, or wakes to the horror that he himself is the automatized imposter. Copjec, "Vampires, Breast-Feeding, and Anxiety," *October* 58 (1991): 25–43. For an argument regarding the uncanny double as a figure for threats to agency in particular, see Jane Elliott, "Stepford U.S.A: Second-Wave Feminism, Domestic Labor, and the Representation of National Time," *Cultural Critique* 70, no. 1 (2008): 32–62.

28. Although the leeway granted to Hailsham is revoked in part because of a scandal that stoked public fears regarding genetic experimentation, Miss Emily explains to Ruth and Tommy that the scandal involved a researcher who was attempting to create a new generation of children that would be "demonstrably superior" to the rest of humanity (259). That is, the threat arises not from threatening sameness but from threatening difference, in the form of exceptionality.

29. The potential for parents to replace dead children is a particularly frequent touchstone in these debates. For examples of this thought experiment marshaled in support of a variety of arguments, see George J. Annas, "Why We Should Ban Human Cloning," *New England Journal of Medicine* 339, no. 2 (1998): 122–25; Dan W. Brock, "Cloning Human Beings: An Assessment of the Ethical Issues Pro and Con," in *Clones and Clones: Facts and Fantasies About Human Cloning*, ed. Martha Craven Nussbaum and Cass R. Sunstein, 141–64 (New York: Norton, 1998); Jean Bethke Elshtain, "To Clone or Not to Clone," in Nussbaum and Sunstein, eds., *Clones and Clones*, 181–89; and Kerry Lynn Macintosh, *Human Cloning: Four Fallacies and Their Legal Consequences, Cambridge Bioethics and Law* (Cambridge, Mass.: Cambridge University Press, 2013), 29–30.

30. In the terms of the UDHR, for example, "the free and full development of personality" is protected through rights to freedom of opinion, freedom of information, education, and participation in the arts. Universal Declaration of Human Rights, *Yearbook of the United Nations,* 536–57.

31. Charles Taylor, *Sources of the Self: The Making of the Modern Identity* (Cambridge, Mass.: Harvard University Press, 1989), 376. Taylor also notes the inherent contradictions between the Kantian and Romantic models of human value. My point here is that they circulate together in the human rights rhetoric that the guardians mirror.

32. Taylor, *Sources of the Self,* 390.

33. I am indebted here to Mark Currie's reading of Kathy's longing for captivity as conveyed in this scene, although I identify the origin of that longing differently. Currie, "Controlling Time: *Never Let Me Go,*" in *Kazuo Ishiguro: Contemporary Critical Perspectives*, ed. Sean Matthews and Sebastian Groes, 91–103 (London: Continuum, 2009).

34. Wynter, "Unsettling the Coloniality of Being/Power/Truth/Freedom," 318. There are also significant differences between Man2 as described by Wynter and the subject of life-interest, most crucially in the centrality of evolution and the color line in defining the boundaries of Man2. As I suggest at the start of this chapter, the microeconomic mode forecloses the large temporal sweeps and population focus required to make either evolution or racial categorization function in exactly the way that Wynter describes in relation to Man2. Although these distinctions are important, I am interested here in the aspects of Man2 that seem in danger of being rejuvenated in a new form via the microeconomic mode: the naturalization of competition for resources (the economic as natural) and an economic view of the environment as defined by scarcity (the environment as economy), which together are presented as justifying the thriving of some lives at the expense of others. This is the danger, I suggest, against which *Salvage the Bones* organizes its narrative.

35. Wynter, "Unsettling the Coloniality of Being/Power/Truth/Freedom," 320–21.

36. As this reference to monism and assemblage suggests, the fictional landscape of *Salvage the Bones* might be seen to evoke a quasi-Deleuzian view of the human as part of the vital, self-organizing assemblage of matter. Yet the rejection of lack and negativity associated with Deleuzian materialism is conspicuously absent from the becoming of life in Bois Sauvage. Instead, the assemblages that constitute the novel's represented world register as indications of inherent limitation and material finitude rather than generative profusion. See Gilles Deleuze and Félix Guattari, *Anti-Oedipus: Capitalism and Schizophrenia*, trans. Mark Seem, Helen R. Lane, and Robert Hurley (Minneapolis: University of Minnesota Press, 1983).

37. As Donald Worster puts it, "the 'New Ecology' that . . . emerged by the middle decades of the twentieth century saw nature through . . . the forms, processes, and values of the modern economic order as shaped by technology." Worster, *Nature's Economy: A History of Ecological Ideas*, 2nd ed. (New York: Cambridge University Press, 1994), 306. The relationship between this model of the environment and the microeconomic imagination can be traced in a number of overlapping features, including the contribution of cybernetics to both the microeconomic imagination and the new ecology. On cybernetics and ecology, see Gregory Bateson, *Mind and Nature: A Necessary Unity, Advances in Systems Theory, Complexity, and the Human Sciences* (Cresskill, N.J.: Hampton Press, 2002). For an account of the way Bateson's thought contributed to the development of the "ecological" as a category, see Peter Harries-Jones, *A Recursive Vision: Ecological Understanding and Gregory Bateson* (Toronto: University of Toronto Press, 1995).

38. As I suggest in my analysis of the treatment of animals in *Life of Pi* in chapter 1, the reconfiguration of the boundaries of the human associated with life-interest cannot be equated with posthumanist or other arguments that challenge the human species/ nonhuman species binary. In *Salvage the Bones*, the flattening of the hierarchical relationship between humans and animals does not arise from a critique of humanism that seeks to expand the universal value of life—the sort of critique with which Skeetah's comment would be associated—but rather emerges because of the combination of the physical qualities of life-interest, which emphasize the needs that humans share with other animals, and the prioritization of individual choice, which means that subjective preference rather than universal recognition hold sway. Rather than challenging structures of domination, the leveling that emerges from this combination enables both Skeetah's dismissal of Esch's needs in favor of his preferences and his instrumentalization of China's life for his own purposes over and against her own thriving—for example, when he has her fight soon after she gives birth. As my reading in the remainder of this chapter indicates, *Salvage the Bones* suggests that positive political possibilities might be wrested from this leveling but cannot be assumed to be its cause or necessary effect. For a range of work that reconsiders the animal as a category, see Jacques Derrida, "The Animal That Therefore I Am (More to Follow)," trans. David Wills, *Critical Inquiry* 28, no. 2 (2002): 369–418; Nicole Shukin, *Animal Capital: Rendering Life in Biopolitical Times*, Posthumanities Series (Minneapolis: University of Minnesota Press, 2009); Cary Wolfe, *Animal Rites: American Culture, the Discourse of Species, and Posthumanist Theory* (Chicago: University of Chicago Press, 2003) and *Before the Law: Humans and Other Animals in a Biopolitical Frame* (Chicago: University of

Chicago Press, 2013); and the essays collected in Cary Wolfe, ed., *Zoontologies: The Question of the Animal* (Minneapolis: University of Minnesota Press, 2003).

39. For an account of structural violence as a concept, see Paul Farmer, *Pathologies of Power: Health, Human Rights, and the New War on the Poor*, California Series in Public Anthropology (Berkeley: University of California Press, 2003), 29–50. Compare also Rob Nixon, "Neoliberalism, Slow Violence, and the Environmental Picaresque," *Modern Fiction Studies* 55 (2009): 443–67; and the account of "slow death" in Jin Haritaworn, Adi Kuntsman, and Silvia Posocco, "Introduction," *Queer Necropolitics*, ed. Jin Haritaworn, Adi Kuntsman, and Silvia Posocco (Abingdon, Oxon: Routledge, 2014), 7–10. Haritaworn, Kuntsman, and Posocco revise the term as proposed in Lauren Berlant, "Slow Death (Sovereignty, Obesity, Lateral Agency)," *Critical Inquiry* 33, no. 4 (2007): 754–80.

40. Salvaging in these terms should be distinguished from neoliberal resilience discourse as defined by Robin James. James argues that "instead of expending resources to *avoid* damage, resilience discourse *recycles damage into more resources*. Resilience discourse thus follows a very specific logic: first, damage is incited and made manifest; second, that damage is spectacularly overcome, and that overcoming is broadcast and/or shared, so that: third, the person who has overcome is rewarded with increased human capital, status, and other forms of recognition and recompense, because: finally, and most importantly, this individual's own resilience boosts society's resilience." James, *Resilience & Melancholy: Pop Music, Feminism, Neoliberalism* (Winchester, UK: Zero Books, 2015), 7, italics in the original. Salvaging here does not achieve the spectacular overcoming that James positions as central to resilience, because salvaging foregrounds the persistent damaged state of inadequate resources. Likewise, because of the way in which *Salvage the Bones* repurposes the either/or, cost-benefit logic of the microeconomic mode, it operates directly against the benefits-for-all promise resilience discourse offers when it ties individual resilience to society's resilience. I discuss the novel's critique of such promise in the conclusion to this chapter. For a different approach to salvaging in relation to personhood in African American and Caribbean literature, see Angela Naimou, *Salvage Work: U.S. and Caribbean Literatures Amid the Debris of Legal Personhood* (New York: Fordham University Press, 2015). Compare also Anna Lowenhaupt Tsing's account of "salvage accumulation" as "the process through which lead firms amass capital without controlling the conditions under which commodities are produced." Tsing, *The Mushroom at the End of the World: On the Possibility of Life in Capitalist Ruins* (Princeton, N.J.: Princeton University Press, 2015), 63.

41. On the "welfare queen" in relation to the historical construction of African American women's sexuality, see Patricia Hill Collins, *Black Feminist Thought: Knowledge, Consciousness, and the Politics of Empowerment*, 2nd ed. (New York: Routledge, 2000), 78–81; Wahneema Lubiano, "Black Ladies, Welfare Queens, and State Minstrels: Ideological War by Narrative Means," in *Race-ing Justice, En-Gendering Power*, ed. Toni Morrison (New York: Pantheon, 1992), 323–63; and Cathy J. Cohen, "Punks, Bulldaggers, and Welfare Queens: The Radical Potential of Queer Politics?" *glq: A Journal of Lesbian and Gay Studies* 3, no. 4 (1997): 437–65. For central theorizations of African American women's sexuality in general, see Hazel V. Carby, *Reconstructing Womanhood: The Emergence of the Afro-American Woman Novelist*

(New York: Oxford University Press, 1987), Collins, *Black Feminist Thought*; Darlene Clark Hine, "Rape and the Inner Lives of Black Women in the Middle West," *Signs* 14, no. 4 (1989): 912–20; Angela Y. Davis, *Blues Legacies and Black Feminism: Gertrude "Ma" Rainey, Bessie Smith, and Billie Holiday* (New York: Pantheon, 1998); Claudia Tate, *Domestic Allegories of Political Desire: The Black Heroine's Text at the Turn of the Century* (New York: Oxford University Press, 1992); and Hortense Spillers, "Mama's Baby, Papa's Maybe: An American Grammar Book," *Diacritics* 17, no. 2 (1987): 64–81. On the framing of African American women's sexuality in *Salvage the Bones* in particular, see Erica R. Edwards, "Sex after the Black Normal," *differences* 26, no. 1 (2015): 141–67. Edwards's rich essay also argues that "Sex is, throughout *Bones*, disarticulated from the family romance, as is reproduction," but her reading moves in opposite directions to mine, particularly in suggesting that Skeetah's devotion to China is presented as an unequivocal good and model for "radical collectivity." Edwards, "Sex after the Black Normal," 158.

42. Hong, *Death Beyond Disavowal*, 21, 30. Hong cites the Moynihan report (published in 1965) as enabling a shift from an approach that condemned racialized communities on the grounds of reproductive respectability to an approach that uses reproductive respectability as the grounds for selecting a portion of racialized communities for incorporation and the promise of protected life. See Hong, *Death Beyond Disavowal*, 21–23.

6. BINARY LIFE

1. Achille Mbembe, "Necropolitics," *Public Culture* 15 (2003): 11–40.
2. On the relationship between control and the subject of life-interest, see chapter 4.
3. John Locke, *Two Treatises of Government* (Cambridge: Cambridge University Press, 1998), §28, 288.
4. As Lorenzo Veracini and others have argued, primitive accumulation in settler colonialism differs from forms that result in a captive labor population. Rather than forcing the dispossessed into wage labor, settler-colonial capitalism works to eliminate the dispossessed entirely. Veracini, *The Settler Colonial Present* (New York: Palgrave Macmillan, 2015), 91–94.
5. Jordy Rosenberg, "The Molecularization of Sexuality: On Some Primitivisms of the Present," *Theory & Event* 17, no. 2 (2014). For other accounts of the relationship between primitive accumulation and the global dynamics of post-Fordist capital, compare, for example, David Harvey, *The New Imperialism* (Oxford: Oxford University Press, 2003); Silvia Federici, "On Primitive Accumulation, Globalization and Reproduction," *Friktion* (September 9, 2017), https://friktionmagasin.dk/on -primitive-accumulation-globalization-and-reproduction-c299e08c3693; Claudia von Werlhof, "'Globalization' and the 'Permanent' Process of 'Primitive Accumulation': The Example of the MAI, the Multilateral Agreement on Investment," *Journal of World-Systems Research*, 7, no. 3 (2000): 728–47. For an analysis of Marx's account of primitive accumulation in relation to recent work in the historiography of American chattel slavery, see Nikhil Pal Singh, "On Race, Violence, and So-Called Primitive Accumulation," *Social Text* 34, no. 3 128 (2016): 27–50.

6. As Rosenberg notes, Brenna Bhandar argues that contemporary capital relies more on Jeremy Bentham's expectation-of-use justification for primitive accumulation than on Locke's labor theory. In both cases, however, the accumulation of the capital itself requires temporal duration. See Bhandar, "Property, Law, and Race: Modes of Abstraction," *U.C. Irvine Law Review* 4, no. 1 (2014): 209; and Rosenberg, "The Molecularization of Sexuality."

7. The canonical reading of economics in *Robinson Crusoe* remains Maximillian E. Novak, *Economics and the Fiction of Daniel Defoe* (New York: Russell & Russell, 1976). As has been frequently noted, Crusoe has access to many tools of civilization, which makes his situation rather more advanced than that encountered in the state of nature as envisioned by Locke. For a lucid explanation of the interplay between Hobbesian and Lockean states of nature on Crusoe's island, see Stuart Sim and David Walker, *The Discourse of Sovereignty, Hobbes to Fielding: The State of Nature and the Nature of the State* (Aldershot, U.K.: Ashgate, 2003), 135–50.

8. On this history and its relationship to Defoe's "listing rhetoric," see Wolfram Schmidgen, "Robinson Crusoe, Enumeration, and the Mercantile Fetish," *Eighteenth-Century Studies* 35, no. 1 (2001): 19–39. On the distinction between the version of the castaway tale focused on miniaturization and what I call live models, see chapter 1.

9. Karl Marx, *Capital: A Critique of Political Economy*, vol. 1 (New York: Penguin, 1981), 873.

10. Marx, *Capital.*

11. For a discussion of live models and *The Road,* see chapter 1.

12. George Miller, dir., *Mad Max: Fury Road* (Burbank, Calif.: Warner Bros., 2015).

13. I am indebted to Seb Franklin for discussions regarding the resemblance between suffering agency and the laborer's unwelcome choices in the wake of primitive accumulation.

14. For my discussion of this novel, see chapter 5.

BIBLIOGRAPHY

Adewunmi, Bim. "I Used to Scorn 'Cool Girls,' but Now See They Don't Really Exist." *Guardian*, September 17, 2012, https://www.theguardian.com/commentisfree/2012 /sep/17/cool-girl-gone-girl.

Agamben, Giorgio. *Homo Sacer: Sovereign Power and Bare Life*. Stanford, Calif.: Stanford University Press, 1998.

Aldana Reyes, Xavier. *Horror Film and Affect: Towards a Corporeal Model of Viewership*. New York: Routledge, 2016.

Amadae, S. M. *Rationalizing Capitalist Democracy: The Cold War Origins of Rational Choice Liberalism*. Chicago: University of Chicago Press, 2003.

Anker, Elisabeth. "The Liberalism of Horror." *Social Research: An International Quarterly* 81, no. 4 (2014): 795–823.

Annas, George J. "Why We Should Ban Human Cloning." *New England Journal of Medicine* 339, no. 2 (1998): 122–25.

Appadurai, Arjun. "Dead Certainty: Ethnic Violence in the Era of Globalization." *Public Culture* 10, no. 2 (1998): 225–47.

Arendt, Hannah. *Between Past and Future: Six Exercises in Political Thought*. 1954; repr. Cleveland, Ohio: Meridian, 1963.

——. *The Human Condition*. Charles R. Walgreen Foundation Lectures. Chicago: University of Chicago Press, 1958.

——. *The Origins of Totalitarianism*. 2nd ed. New York: Meridian Books, 1958.

Arens, William. *The Man-Eating Myth: Anthropology & Anthropophagy*. New York: Oxford University Press, 1979.

Arrow, Kenneth J. *Social Choice and Individual Values*. 1951; repr. New Haven, Conn.: Yale University Press, 2012.

Aston, James, and John Walliss. *To See the Saw Movies: Essays on Torture Porn and Post-9/11 Horror*. Jefferson, N.C.: McFarland, 2013.

Athey, Stephanie. "The Torture Device: Debate and Archetype." In *Torture*, ed. Zalloua Zahi and Shampa Biswas, 129–57. Seattle: University of Washington Press, 2011.

Avramescu, Cătălin. *An Intellectual History of Cannibalism*. Trans. Alistair Ian Blyth. Princeton, N.J.: Princeton University Press, 2009.

Backhouse, Roger. *A History of Modern Economic Analysis*. London: B. Blackwell, 1985.

Backhouse, Roger E., and Steven G. Medema. "Retrospectives: On the Definition of Economics." *Journal of Economic Perspectives* 23, no. 1 (2009): 221–34.

Badiou, Alain. *In Praise of Love*. Trans. Nicolas Truong. New York: New Press, 2012.

Baerg, Andrew. "Governmentality, Neoliberalism, and the Digital Game." *symploke* 17, no. 1 (2009): 115–27.

Bartolovich, Crystal. "Consumerism, or the Cultural Logic of Late Capital." In *Cannibalism and the Colonial World*, ed. Francis Barker, Peter Hulme, and Margaret Iversen, 204–37. Cambridge: Cambridge University Press, 1998.

Bateson, Gregory. *Mind and Nature: A Necessary Unity, Advances in Systems Theory, Complexity, and the Human Sciences*. Cresskill, N.J.: Hampton Press, 2002.

Baudrillard, Jean. *Simulacra and Simulation*. Trans. Sheila Glaser. Ann Arbor: University of Michigan Press, 1994.

Bayona, J. A., dir. *The Impossible*. Burbank, Calif.: Warner Bros. Pictures, 2012.

Becker, Gary S. *The Economic Approach to Human Behavior*. Chicago: University of Chicago Press, 1976.

Becker, Gary S., Kevin M. Murphy, and Jörg L. Spenkuch. "The Manipulation of Children's Preferences, Old-Age Support, and Investment in Children's Human Capital." *Journal of Labor Economics* 34, no. 2, pt. 2 (April 2016): S3–S30.

Benjamin, Jessica. "The Bonds of Love: Rational Violence and Erotic Domination." *Feminist Studies* 6, no. 1 (1980): 144–74.

Bennett, Jane. *Vibrant Matter: A Political Ecology of Things*. Durham, N.C.: Duke University Press, 2010.

Berlant, Lauren. "Slow Death (Sovereignty, Obesity, Lateral Agency)." *Critical Inquiry* 33, no. 4 (2007): 754–80.

Bex, Sean, and Stef Craps. "Humanitarianism, Testimony, and the White Savior Industrial Complex: What Is the What Versus Kony 2012." *Cultural Critique* 92, no. 1 (2016): 32–56.

Bhandar, Brenna. "Property, Law, and Race: Modes of Abstraction." *UC Irvine Law Review* 4, no. 1 (2014): 203–18.

Biehl, João. "Vita: Life in a Zone of Social Abandonment." *Social Text* 19, no. 3 68 (2001): 131–49.

Bodin, Jean. *Six Books of the Commonwealth*. Abr. and Trans. M. J. Tooley. 1955; repr. Oxford: Blackwell, 2009.

Bogost, Ian. "Gamification Is Bullshit," *Atlantic*, August 9, 2011, http://www.theatlantic .com/technology/archive/2011/08/gamification-is-bullshit/243338/.

Bousman, Darren Lynn, dir. *Saw II*. Santa Monica, Calif.: Lionsgate, 2005.

——. *Saw III*. Santa Monica, Calif.: Lionsgate, 2006.

Boyle, Danny, dir. *127 Hours*. Los Angeles: Twentieth Century Fox Film Corp., 2010.

Bradbury, Lorna. "The Bunker Diary: Why Wish This Book on a Child?" *Telegraph,* June 24, 2014, http://www.telegraph.co.uk/culture/books/10920101/The-Bunker-Diary-why -wish-this-book-on-a-child.html.

Braidotti, Rosi. *The Posthuman*. New York: Polity, 2013.
Brock, Dan W. "Cloning Human Beings: An Assessment of the Ethical Issues Pro and Con." In *Clones and Clones: Facts and Fantasies About Human Cloning*, ed. Martha Craven Nussbaum and Cass R. Sunstein, 141–64. New York: Norton, 1998.
Brown, Jennifer. *Cannibalism in Literature and Film*. London: Palgrave Macmillan, 2012.
Brown, Wendy. "The Most We Can Hope For: Human Rights and the Politics of Fatalism." *South Atlantic Quarterly* 103, no. 2/3 (2004): 451–63.
Buck-Morss, Susan. "Hegel and Haiti." *Critical Inquiry* 26, no. 4 (2000): 848–49.
Cacho, Lisa Marie. *Social Death: Racialized Rightlessness and the Criminalization of the Unprotected*. New York: New York University Press, 2012.
Caillois, Roger. *Man, Play, and Games*. Trans. Meyer Barash. Urbana: University of Illinois Press, 2001.
Carby, Hazel V. *Reconstructing Womanhood: The Emergence of the Afro-American Woman Novelist*. New York: Oxford University Press, 1987.
"Carnegie medal row over 'depressing' winner grows." *Guardian*, June 25, 2014, https://www.theguardian.com/books/2014/jun/25/carnegie-medal-row-depressing-winner-frank-cottrell-boyce.
Case, Karl E., Ray C. Fair, and Sharon M. Oster. *Principles of Microeconomics*. 12th ed. Hoboken, N.J.: Pearson Higher Education, 2017.
Cheah, Pheng. *Inhuman Conditions: On Cosmopolitanism and Human Rights*. Cambridge, Mass.: Harvard University Press, 2009.
Chen, Mel Y. *Animacies: Biopolitics, Racial Mattering, and Queer Affect*. Durham, N.C.: Duke University Press, 2012.
Cherry, Bridget. *Horror*. New York: Routledge, 2009.
Coady, C. A. J. "Hobbes and 'the Beautiful Axiom'." *Philosophy: The Journal of the Royal Institute of Philosophy* 65, no. 251 (1990): 4.
Cohen, Cathy J. "Punks, Bulldaggers, and Welfare Queens: The Radical Potential of Queer Politics?" *glq: A Journal of Lesbian and Gay Studies* 3, no. 4 (1997): 437–65.
Cole, Stewart. "Believing in Tigers: Anthropomorphism and Incredulity in Yann Martel's *Life of Pi*." *Studies in Canadian Literature/Etudes en Littérature Canadienne* 29, no. 2 (2004): 22–36.
Collins, Patricia Hill. *Black Feminist Thought: Knowledge, Consciousness, and the Politics of Empowerment*. 2nd ed. New York: Routledge, 2000.
Comaroff, Jean. "Beyond Bare Life: AIDS, (Bio)Politics, and the Neoliberal Order." *Public Culture* 19, no. 1 (2007): 197–219.
Commission on Human Rights. *Third Session, Summary Record of the Seventy-First Meeting*. June 28, 1948 [held June 14, 1948]. UDHR E/CN.4/SR.71.
Cooper, Melinda. *Life as Surplus: Biotechnology and Capitalism in the Neoliberal Era*. Seattle: University of Washington Press, 2011.
Cooper, Melinda, and Cathy Waldby. *Clinical Labor: Tissue Donors and Research Subjects in the Global Bioeconomy*. Durham, N.C.: Duke University Press, 2014.
Copjec, Joan. "Vampires, Breast-Feeding, and Anxiety." *October* 58 (1991): 25–43.
Cottom, Daniel. *Cannibals and Philosophers: Bodies of Enlightenment*. Baltimore: Johns Hopkins University Press, 2001.
Creed, Barbara. "Horror and the Monstrous-Feminine: An Imaginary Abjection." In *Horror, the Film Reader*, ed. Mark Jancovich, 67–76. London: Routledge, 2002.

Currie, Mark. "Controlling Time: *Never Let Me Go.*" In *Kazuo Ishiguro: Contemporary Critical Perspectives*, ed. Sean Matthews and Sebastian Groes, 91–103. London: Continuum, 2009.

Davis, Angela Y. *Blues Legacies and Black Feminism: Gertrude "Ma" Rainey, Bessie Smith, and Billie Holiday*. New York: Pantheon, 1998.

Dawes, James. *That the World May Know: Bearing Witness to Atrocity*. Cambridge, Mass.: Harvard University Press, 2007.

Dayan, Colin. *The Law Is a White Dog: How Legal Rituals Make and Unmake Persons*. Princeton, N.J.: Princeton University Press, 2011.

Dean, Mitchell. *Governmentality: Power and Rule in Modern Society*. London: Sage, 1999.

Deleuze, Gilles. "Postscript on the Societies of Control." *October* 59 (1992): 3–7.

Deleuze, Gilles, and Félix Guattari. *Anti-Oedipus: Capitalism and Schizophrenia*. Trans. Mark Seem, Helen R. Lane, and Robert Hurley. Minneapolis: University of Minnesota Press, 1983.

Derrida, Jacques. "The Animal That Therefore I Am (More to Follow)." Trans. David Wills. *Critical Inquiry* 28, no. 2 (2002): 369–418.

——. *A Thousand Plateaus: Capitalism and Schizophrenia*. Trans. Brian Massumi. London: Bloomsbury, 2013.

DuBois, Page. *Torture and Truth*. New York: Routledge, 1991.

Du Bois, W. E. B. *Black Reconstruction in America: An Essay toward a History of the Part Which Black Folk Played in the Attempt to Reconstruct Democracy in America, 1860–1880*. 1896; repr. New York: Oxford University Press, 2007.

Duncan, Rebecca. "*Life of Pi* as Postmodern Survivor Narrative." *Mosaic: A Journal for the Interdisciplinary Study of Literature* 41, no. 2 (2008): 167–83.

Dwyer, June. "Yann Martel's *Life of Pi* and the Evolution of the Shipwreck Narrative." *Modern Language Studies* 35, no. 2 (2005): 9–21.

Eaglestone, Robert. "'You Would Not Add to My Suffering If You Knew What I Have Seen': Holocaust Testimony and Contemporary African Trauma Literature." *Studies in the Novel* 40, no. 1/2 (2008): 72–85.

Eatough, Matthew. "The Time That Remains: Organ Donation, Temporal Duration, and Bildung in Kazuo Ishiguro's *Never Let Me Go.*" *Literature and Medicine* 29, no. 1 (2011): 132–60.

Edwards, Erica R. "Sex after the Black Normal." *differences* 26, no. 1 (2015): 141–67.

Eggers, Dave. *What Is the What: The Autobiography of Valentino Achak Deng: A Novel*. San Francisco: McSweeney's, 2006.

——. *What Is the What: The Autobiography of Valentino Achak Deng: A Novel*. New York: Penguin, 2008. Kindle edition.

Elliott, Jane. "Stepford U.S.A.: Second-Wave Feminism, Domestic Labor, and the Representation of National Time." *Cultural Critique* 70, no. 1 (2008): 41–43.

——. "Suffering Agency: Imagining Neoliberal Personhood in North America and Britain." *Social Text* 31, no. 2 115 (2013): 83–101.

Elliott, Jane, and Gillian Harkins. "Genres of Neoliberalism." Special issue, *Social Text* 31, no. 2 115 (2013).

Elshtain, Jean Bethke. "To Clone or Not to Clone." In *Clones and Clones: Facts and Fantasies About Human Cloning*, ed. Martha Craven Nussbaum and Cass R. Sunstein, 181–89. New York: Norton, 1998.

Engelmann, Stephen G. *Imagining Interest in Political Thought: Origins of Economic Rationality.* Durham, N.C.: Duke University Press, 2003.

Esposito, Roberto. *Bíos: Biopolitics and Philosophy.* Trans. Timothy Campbell. Posthumanities Series. Minneapolis: University of Minnesota Press, 2008.

Fabian, Johannes. *Time and the Other: How Anthropology Makes Its Object.* New York: Columbia University Press, 2002.

Fahy, Thomas. "Hobbes, Human Nature, and the Culture of American Violence in Truman Capote's *In Cold Blood.*" In *The Philosophy of Horror,* ed. Thomas Fahy, 57–71. Lexington: University Press of Kentucky, 2010.

Fanon, Frantz. *Black Skin, White Masks.* Trans. Richard Philcox. New York: Grove Press, 2008.

Farmer, Paul. *Pathologies of Power: Health, Human Rights, and the New War on the Poor.* California Series in Public Anthropology. Berkeley: University of California Press, 2003.

Federici, Silvia. "On Primitive Accumulation, Globalization and Reproduction." *Friktion,* September 9, 2017, https://friktionmagasin.dk/on-primitive-accumulation-globalization-and-reproduction-c299e08c3693.

Fein, Ellen, and Sherrie Schneider. *The Rules: Time-Tested Secrets for Capturing the Heart of Mr. Right.* New York: Warner Books, 1995.

Ferreira da Silva, Denise. "No-Bodies: Law, Raciality and Violence." *Griffith Law Review* 18, no. 2 (2009): 214–36.

Fisher, Mark. "The Lonely Road." *Film Quarterly* 63, no. 3: 14–17.

Flynn, Gillian. *Gone Girl: A Novel.* London:Weidenfeld and Nicolson, 2012. Kindle edition.

Foucault, Michel. *The Birth of Biopolitics: Lectures at the Collège De France, 1978–79.* Trans. Graham Burchell. Basingstoke, U.K.: Palgrave Macmillan, 2008.

——. *Discipline and Punish: The Birth of the Prison.* Trans. Alan Sheridan. New York: Vintage, 1995.

——. *"Society Must Be Defended": Lectures at the Collège De France, 1975–76.* Trans. David Macey. New York: Picador, 2003.

Frank, Robert H. *Microeconomics and Behavior.* 9th ed. New York: McGraw-Hill Education, 2015.

Franklin, Sarah, and Margaret Lock. "Animation and Cessation: The Remaking of Life and Death." In *Remaking Life and Death: Toward an Anthropology of the Biosciences,* ed. Sarah Franklin and Margaret Lock, 3–22. Santa Fe, N.M.: School of American Research Press, 2003.

Franklin, Seb. *Control: Digitality as Cultural Logic.* Cambridge, Mass.: MIT Press, 2015.

Freeman, Samuel. "Illiberal Libertarians: Why Libertarianism Is Not a Liberal View." *Philosophy & Public Affairs* 30 (2001): 105–51.

Freud, Sigmund. *The Uncanny.* Trans. David McLintock. 1899; repr. London: Penguin, 2003.

Friedman, Milton. "The Methodology of Positive Economics." In *The Philosophy of Economics: An Anthology,* 3rd ed., ed. Daniel M. Hausman, 145–78. New York: Cambridge University Press, 2008.

Fukasaku, Kinji, dir. *Battle Royale.* 2000; U.S. theatrical 3-D, distributed by Anchor Bay Films.

Gagnier, Regenia. *The Insatiability of Human Wants: Economics and Aesthetics in Market Society*. Chicago: University of Chicago Press, 2000.

Galloway, Alexander R. *Gaming: Essays on Algorithmic Culture*. Minneapolis: University of Minnesota Press, 2006.

Gatta, Giunia. "Suffering and the Making of Politics: Perspectives from Jaspers and Camus." *Contemporary Political Theory* 14, no. 4 (2015): 335–54.

Gauthier, David. "Hobbes's Social Contract." *Noûs* 22, no. 1 (1988): 71–82.

——. "Review: Taming Leviathan." *Philosophy and Public Affairs* 16, no. 3 (1987): 280–98.

Gilbert, Jeremy, ed. "Neoliberal Culture." Special issue, *New Formations* 80–81 (Winter 2013).

Gilmore, Ruth Wilson. "Fatal Couplings of Power and Difference: Notes on Racism and Geography." *The Professional Geographer* 54, no. 1 (2002): 15–24.

——. *Golden Gulag: Prisons, Surplus, Crisis, and Opposition in Globalizing California*. Berkeley: University of California Press, 2007.

Gilroy, Paul. *The Black Atlantic: Modernity and Double Consciousness*. Cambridge, Mass.: Harvard University Press, 1993.

Giorgi, Gabriel. "Improper Selves: Cultures of Precarity." *Social Text* 31, no. 2 115 (2013): 69–81.

Giorgi, Gabriel, and Karen Pinkus. "Zones of Exception: Biopolitical Territories in the Neoliberal Era." *Diacritics* 36, no. 2 (2006): 99–108.

Green, Donald P., and Ian Shapiro. *Pathologies of Rational Choice Theory: A Critique of Applications in Political Science*. New Haven, Conn.: Yale University Press, 1996.

Greengrass, Paul, dir. *The Bourne Ultimatum*. Universal City, Calif.: Universal Pictures, 2007.

Griffin, Gabriele. "Science and the Cultural Imaginary: The Case of Kazuo Ishiguro's *Never Let Me Go*." *Textual Practice* 23, no. 4 (2009): 645–63.

Guest, Kristen, ed. *Eating Their Words: Cannibalism and the Boundaries of Cultural Identity*. Syracuse: State University of New York Press, 2014.

Hampton, Jean. *Hobbes and the Social Contract Tradition*. New York: Cambridge University Press, 1986.

Hardt, Michael, and Antonio Negri. *Empire*. Cambridge, Mass.: Harvard University Press, 2000.

Haritaworn, Jin, Adi Kuntsman, and Silvia Posocco. *Queer Necropolitics*. Abingdon, Oxon: Routledge, 2014.

Harkins, Gillian. *Everybody's Family Romance: Reading Incest in Neoliberal America*. Minneapolis: University of Minnesota Press, 2009.

——. "Virtual Predators: Neoliberal Loss and Human Futures in the Cinema of Pedophilia." *Social Text* 31, no. 2 115 (2013): 123–44.

Harries-Jones, Peter. *A Recursive Vision: Ecological Understanding and Gregory Bateson*. Toronto: University of Toronto Press, 1995.

Hartman, Saidiya V. *Scenes of Subjection: Terror, Slavery, and Self-Making in Nineteenth-Century America*. New York: Oxford University Press, 1997.

Hausman, Daniel M., and Michael S. McPherson. "The Philosophical Foundations of Mainstream Normative Economics." In *The Philosophy of Economics: An Anthology*, 3rd ed., ed. Daniel M. Hausman. New York: Cambridge University Press, 2008.

Hibberd, James. "'Game of Thrones' Scoop: Season 3 Character List Revealed." *Entertainment Weekly*, May 29, 2012, http://www.ew.com/article/2012/05/29/game-of -throne-season-3-cast.

Hicks, Heather. *The Post-Apocalyptic Novel in the Twenty-First Century: Modernity Beyond Salvage*. New York: Palgrave Macmillan, 2016.

Hills, Matt. "Cutting into Concepts of 'Reflectionist' Cinema? The Saw Franchise and Puzzles of Post-9/11 Horror." In *Horror After 9/11: World of Fear, Cinema of Terror*, ed. Aviva Briefel and Sam J. Miller, 107–23. Austin: University of Texas Press.

Hine, Darlene Clark. "Rape and the Inner Lives of Black Women in the Middle West." *Signs* 14, no. 4 (1989): 912–20.

Hirschman, Albert O. *The Passions and the Interests: Political Arguments for Capitalism Before Its Triumph*. Princeton, N.J.: Princeton University Press, 1977.

Hobbes, Thomas. *Leviathan: A Critical Edition*. Vol. 2. London: Continuum, 2005.

——. *On the Citizen*. Trans. Richard Tuck. Cambridge: Cambridge University Press, 1998.

Hoberek, Andrew. "Cormac McCarthy and the Aesthetics of Exhaustion." *American Literary History* 23, no. 3: 483–99.

Hong, Grace Kyungwon. *Death Beyond Disavowal: The Impossible Politics of Difference*. Minneapolis: University of Minnesota Press, 2015.

——. *The Ruptures of American Capital: Women of Color Feminism and the Culture of Immigrant Labor*. Minneapolis: University of Minnesota Press, 2006.

Honig, Bonnie. *Antigone, Interrupted*. Cambridge: Cambridge University Press, 2013.

Huehls, Mitchum. *After Critique: Twenty-First-Century Fiction in a Neoliberal Age*. Oxford: Oxford University Press, 2016.

——. "Referring to the Human in Contemporary Human Rights Literature." *MFS: Modern Fiction Studies* 58, no. 1 (2012): 1–21.

Hunt, Lynn. *Inventing Human Rights*. New York: Norton, 2007.

Hutcheon, Linda. *A Poetics of Postmodernism: History, Theory, Fiction*. New York: Routledge, 1988.

Illouz, Eva. *Cold Intimacies: The Making of Emotional Capitalism*. Cambridge, U.K.: Polity Press, 2007.

Ingersoll, Earl G. "Taking Off into the Realm of Metaphor: Kazuo Ishiguro's *Never Let Me Go*." *Studies in the Humanities* 34, no. 1 (2007): 40–59.

Ishiguro, Kazuo. *Never Let Me Go*. New York: Vintage International, 2006.

James, C. L. R. *The Black Jacobins: Toussaint L'Ouverture and the San Domingo Revolution*. 2nd ed. 1938; repr. New York: Vintage, 1963.

James, Robin. *Resilience & Melancholy: Pop Music, Feminism, Neoliberalism*. Winchester, U.K.: Zero Books, 2015.

Jameson, Fredric. *Postmodernism, or, the Cultural Logic of Late Capitalism*. London: Verso, 1991.

Jerng, Mark. "Giving Form to Life: Cloning and Narrative Expectations of the Human." *Partial Answers: Journal of Literature and the History of Ideas* 6, no. 2 (2008): 369–93.

Johansen, Emily. "The Neoliberal Gothic: *Gone Girl*, *Broken Harbor*, and the Terror of Everyday Life." *Contemporary Literature* 57, no. 1 (2016): 30–55.

Johansen, Emily, and Alissa G. Karl, eds. *Neoliberalism and the Novel*. London: Routledge, 2016.

Jordan, Gregor, dir. *Unthinkable*. U.S.A.: Lleju Productions, 2010.

Kahn, Paul W. *Sacred Violence: Torture, Terror, and Sovereignty*. Ann Arbor: University of Michigan Press, 2008.

Kavka, Gregory S. *Hobbesian Moral and Political Theory*. Princeton, N.J.: Princeton University Press, 1986.

Kay, Carol. *Political Constructions: Defoe, Richardson, and Sterne in Relation to Hobbes*. Ithaca, N.Y.: Cornell University Press, 1991.

Kershnar, Stephen. "A Liberal Argument for Slavery." *Journal of Social Philosophy* 34, no. 4 (2003): 510–36.

Kilgour, Maggie. *From Communion to Cannibalism: An Anatomy of Metaphors of Incorporation*. Princeton, N.J.: Princeton University Press, 1990.

Kunsa, Ashley. "Maps of the World in Its Becoming: Post-Apocalyptic Naming in Cormac McCarthy's *The Road*." *Journal of Modern Literature* 33, no. 1 (2009): 57–74.

Lazear, Edward P. "Economic Imperialism." *Quarterly Journal of Economics* 115, no. 1 (2000): 99–146.

Lazzarato, Maurizio. "From Capital-Labour to Capital-Life." *Ephemera: theory & politics in organization* 4, no. 3 (2004): 187–208.

——. "Immaterial Labor." In *Radical Thought in Italy: A Potential Politics*, ed. Paolo Virno and Michael Hardt; trans. Paul Colilli, Ed Emory, Maurizia Boscagli, Cesare Casarino, and Michael Turits, 133–48. Minneapolis: University of Minnesota Press, 1996.

Levitt, Steven D., and Stephen J. Dubner, *SuperFreakonomics: Global Cooling, Patriotic Prostitutes, and Why Suicide Bombers Should Buy Life Insurance*. New York: Harper Collins, 2009.

Lieberman, Robert, dir. *The Tortured*. New York: IFC Films, 2010.

Lindenbaum, Shirley. "Thinking About Cannibalism." *Annual Review of Anthropology* 33, no. 1 (2004): 475–98.

Liu, Lydia H. "Shadows of Universalism: The Untold Story of Human Rights around 1948." *Critical Inquiry* 40, no. 4 (2014): 385–417.

Locke, John. *Two Treatises of Government*. Cambridge: Cambridge University Press, 1998.

Lockwood, Dean. "All Stripped Down: The Spectacle of 'Torture Porn'." *Popular Communication* 7, no. 1 (2009): 40–48.

Lowe, Lisa. *The Intimacies of Four Continents*. Durham, N.C.: Duke University Press, 2015.

Luban, David. "Liberalism, Torture, and the Ticking Bomb." *Virginia Law Review* 91, no. 6 (2005): 1425–61.

Lubiano, Wahneema. "Black Ladies, Welfare Queens, and State Minstrels: Ideological War by Narrative Means." In *Race-ing Justice, En-Gendering Power*, ed. Toni Morrison, 323–63. New York: Pantheon, 1992.

Macintosh, Kerry Lynn. *Human Cloning: Four Fallacies and Their Legal Consequences*. Cambridge Bioethics and Law. Cambridge, Mass.: Cambridge University Press, 2013.

Macpherson, C. B. *The Political Theory of Possessive Individualism: Hobbes to Locke*. Oxford: Oxford University Press, 2011.

Maddala, G. S., and Kajal Lahiri. *Introduction to Econometrics*. New York: Wiley, 2009.

Malewitz, Raymond. "Regeneration Through Misuse: Rugged Consumerism in Contemporary American Culture." *PMLA: Publications of the Modern Language Association of America* 127, no. 3: 526.

Mann, Bonnie. *Sovereign Masculinity: Gender Lessons from the War on Terror.* New York: Oxford University Press, 2014.

Mansbridge, Jane J., ed. *Beyond Self-Interest.* Chicago: University of Chicago Press, 1990.

Martel, Yann. "How Richard Parker Came to Get His Name." Amazon, n.d. Accessed August 22, 2016. https://www.amazon.com/exec/obidos/tg/feature/-/309590/104 -4043985-5498364.

———. *Life of Pi.* Edinburgh: Canongate, 2003.

Martin, George R. R. *A Clash of Kings.* London: Voyager, 2011.

———. *A Game of Thrones.* London: Voyager, 2011.

———. *A Storm of Swords.* New York: Bantam, 2000.

Marx, Karl. *Capital: A Critique of Political Economy,* Vol. 1. New York: Penguin, 1981.

Massumi, Brian. *Parables for the Virtual: Movement, Affect, Sensation.* Durham, N.C.: Duke University Press, 2002.

Mathiowetz, Dean. *Appeals to Interest: Language, Contestation, and the Shaping of Political Agency.* University Park: Pennsylvania State University Press, 2011.

Mbembe, Achille. "Necropolitics." Trans. Libby Meintjes. *Public Culture* 15, no. 1 (2003): 11–40.

McCarthy, Anna. "Reality Television: A Neoliberal Theater of Suffering." *Social Text* 25, no. 4 93 (2007): 17–42.

McCarthy, Cormac. *The Road.* London: Picador, 2006.

McGonigal, Jane. *Reality Is Broken: Why Games Make Us Better and How They Can Change the World.* New York: Penguin, 2011.

McLuhan, Marshall. *Understanding Media: The Extensions of Man.* New York: McGraw-Hill, 1964.

Melamed, Jodi. "The Spirit of Neoliberalism: From Racial Liberalism to Neoliberal Multiculturalism." *Social Text* 24, no. 4 89 (2006): 1–24.

Mendlesohn, Farah. *Rhetorics of Fantasy.* Middletown, Conn.: Wesleyan University Press, 2008.

Miller, George, dir. *Mad Max: Fury Road.* Burbank, Calif.: Warner Bros., 2015.

Mitchell, Martha, dir. *House.* Season 2, episode 23, "Who's Your Daddy?" Aired May 16, 2006, on FOX.

Mizruchi, Susan. "Risk Theory and the Contemporary American Novel." *American Literary History* 22, no. 1 (2010): 109–35.

Modleski, Tania. *Loving with a Vengeance: Mass-Produced Fantasies for Women.* 2nd ed. New York: Routledge, 2008.

Morgensen, Scott Lauria. "The Biopolitics of Settler Colonialism: Right Here, Right Now." *Settler Colonial Studies* 1, no. 1 (2011): 52–76.

Moyn, Samuel. *The Last Utopia.* Cambridge, Mass.: Harvard University Press, 2012.

———. "The Universal Declaration of Human Rights of 1948 in the History of Cosmopolitanism." *Critical Inquiry* 40, no. 4 (2014): 365–84.

Naimou, Angela. *Salvage Work: U.S. And Caribbean Literatures Amid the Debris of Legal Personhood.* New York: Fordham University Press, 2015.

Neal, Patrick. "Hobbes and Rational Choice Theory." *Western Political Quarterly* 41, no. 4 (1988): 635–52.

Neveldine, Mark, dir. *Gamer.* Santa Monica, Calif.: Lionsgate, 2009.

Ngai, Sianne. *Ugly Feelings.* Cambridge, Mass.: Harvard University Press, 2005.

Noorani, Yaseen. "The Rhetoric of Security." *CR: The New Centennial Review* 5, no. 1 (2005): 13–41.

Novak, Maximillian Erwin. *Economics and the Fiction of Daniel Defoe*. New York: Russell & Russell, 1976.

Nyquist, Mary. *Arbitrary Rule: Slavery, Tyranny, and the Power of Life and Death*. Chicago: University of Chicago Press, 2013.

Parkin, Michael. *Microeconomics*. Global ed. Harlow, U.K.: Pearson, 2016.

Parry, John T. "Escalation and Necessity: Defining Torture at Home and Abroad." In *Torture: A Collection*, ed. Sanford Levinson, 145–64. Oxford: Oxford University Press, 2004.

Patterson, Orlando. *Freedom: Slavery in the Making of Western Culture*. New York: Basic Books, 1991.

——. *Slavery and Social Death: A Comparative Study*. Cambridge, Mass.: Harvard University Press, 1982.

Peek, Michelle. "Humanitarian Narrative and Posthumanist Critique: Dave Eggers's 'What Is the What'." *Biography* 35, no. 1 (2012): 115–36.

Pellegrini, Ann, and Jasbir Puar. "Affect." *Social Text* 27, no. 3 100 (2009): 35–38.

Petersen, Anne Helen. "Jennifer Lawrence and the History of Cool Girls." *Buzzfeed*, February 28, 2014, https://www.buzzfeed.com/annehelenpetersen/jennifer-lawrence-and-the-history-of-cool-girls?utm_term=.rxVZRVRLDm#.bcDX1B1jNz.

Peucker, Brigitte. *The Material Image: Art and the Real in Film*. Stanford, Calif.: Stanford University Press, 2007.

Pizzino, Christopher. "Utopia at Last: Cormac McCarthy's the Road as Science Fiction." *Extrapolation: A Journal of Science Fiction and Fantasy* 51, no. 3 (2011): 358–75.

Poundstone, William. *Prisoner's Dilemma*. 1992; repr. New York: Knopf, 2011.

Povinelli, Elizabeth A. *Economies of Abandonment: Social Belonging and Endurance in Late Liberalism*. Durham, N.C.: Duke University Press, 2011.

——. *The Empire of Love: Toward a Theory of Intimacy, Genealogy, and Carnality*. Durham, N.C.: Duke University Press, 2008.

Powell, Anna. *Deleuze and Horror Film*. Edinburgh: Edinburgh University Press, 2005.

Puar, Jasbir K. "Bodies with New Organs: Becoming Trans, Becoming Disabled." *Social Text* 33, no. 3 124 (2015): 45–73.

——. "Coda: The Cost of Getting Better: Suicide, Sensation, Switchpoints." *GLQ: A Journal of Lesbian and Gay Studies* 18, no. 1 (2012): 149–58.

Radner, Roy. "Satisficing." *Journal of Mathematical Economics* 2 (1975): 253–62.

Raffel, Dawn. "The Most Addictive Books of the Last 25 Years: *Life of Pi*." March 3, 2015, http://www.oprah.com/book/books-that-defined-a-generation-life-of-pi?editors_pick_id=57175.f.

Ralph, Jason. *America's War on Terror: The State of the 9/11 Exception from Bush to Obama*. Oxford: Oxford University Press, 2013.

Ralston, Aron. *Between a Rock and a Hard Place*. New York: Atria, 2004.

Rasch, William. *Sovereignty and Its Discontents: On the Primacy of Conflict and the Structure of the Political*. London: Birkbeck Law Press, 2004.

Rejali, Darius. *Torture & Modernity: Self, Society, and State in Modern Iran*. Boulder, Colo.: Westview Press, 1994.

Rich, Leigh E., Jack Simmons, David Adams, Scott Thorp, and Michael Mink. "The Afterbirth of the Clinic: A Foucauldian Perspective on 'House M.D.' and American Medicine in the 21st Century." *Perspectives in Biology and Medicine* 51, no. 2 (2008): 220–37.

Robbins, Lionel. *An Essay on the Nature and Significance of Economic Science.* London: MacMillan, 1932.

Robinson, Cedric J. *Black Marxism: The Making of the Black Radical Tradition.* Chapel Hill: University of North Carolina Press, 2000.

Rose, Nikolas S. *Powers of Freedom: Reframing Political Thought.* Cambridge: Cambridge University Press, 1999.

Rosenberg, Jordy. "The Molecularization of Sexuality: On Some Primitivisms of the Present." *Theory & Event* 17, no. 2 (2014).

Samuelson, Paul A. *Economics: An Introductory Analysis.* 1948; repr. New York: McGraw-Hill, 1997.

Scarry, Elaine. *The Body in Pain: The Making and Unmaking of the World.* New York: Oxford University Press, 1985.

Schaefer, Kayleen. "Game, Set, and Cyber-Match: How to Seal the Deal Instead of Staying on the Hook for Monthly Fees: Three New Guides to Online Dating, Five Tactical Tips for All Womankind." *Elle*, January 15, 2013, http://www.elle.com/life-love/sex -relationships/online-dating-tips-women-guide.

Schaffer, Kay, and Sidonie Smith. *Human Rights and Narrated Lives: The Ethics of Recognition.* New York: Palgrave Macmillan, 2004.

Schmidgen, Wolfram. "Robinson Crusoe, Enumeration, and the Mercantile Fetish." *Eighteenth-Century Studies* 35, no. 1 (2001): 19–39.

Scott, A. O. "The Tale of a Shocking Fall and a Gritty Resolve." *New York Times*, November 4, 2010, C1.

Seaman, Myra J. "Becoming More (Than) Human: Affective Posthumanisms, Past and Future." *Journal of Narrative Theory* 37, no. 2 (2007): 246–75.

Sharrett, Christopher. "The Problem of *Saw*: 'Torture Porn' and the Conservatism of Contemporary Horror Films." *Cineaste: America's Leading Magazine on the Art and Politics of the Cinema* 35, no. 1 (2009): 32–37.

Shaviro, Steven. "Body Horror and Post-Socialist Cinema: György Pálfi's Taxidermia." *Film Philosophy* 15, no. 2 (2011).

Shonkwiler, Alison, and Leigh Claire La Berge. *Reading Capitalist Realism.* Iowa City: University of Iowa Press, 2014.

Shukin, Nicole. *Animal Capital: Rendering Life in Biopolitical Times.* Minneapolis: University of Minnesota Press, 2009.

Silverman, Lisa. *Tortured Subjects: Pain, Truth, and the Body in Early Modern France.* Chicago: University of Chicago Press, 2001.

Sim, Stuart, and David Walker. *The Discourse of Sovereignty, Hobbes to Fielding: The State of Nature and the Nature of the State.* Studies in Early Modern English Literature. Aldershot, U.K.: Ashgate, 2003.

Singh, Nikhil Pal. "On Race, Violence, and So-Called Primitive Accumulation." *Social Text* 34, no. 3 128 (2016): 27–50.

Slaughter, Joseph R. *Human Rights, Inc.: The World Novel, Narrative Form, and International Law.* New York: Fordham University Press, 2007.

Smith, Rachel Greenwald. *Affect and American Literature in the Age of Neoliberalism.* New York: Cambridge University Press, 2015.

Spillers, Hortense. "Mama's Baby, Papa's Maybe: An American Grammar Book." *Diacritics* 17, no. 2 (1987): 64–81.

Stephens, Gregory. "Feeding Tiger, Finding God: Science, Religion, and 'the Better Story' in *Life of Pi.*" *Intertexts* 14, no. 1: 41–59.

Stratton, Florence. " 'Hollow at the Core': Deconstructing Yann Martel's *Life of Pi.*" *Studies in Canadian Literature/Etudes en Littérature Canadienne* 29, no. 2 (2004): 5–21.

Tadiar, Neferti X. M. "Life-Times of Disposability Within Global Neoliberalism." *Social Text* 31, no. 2 115 (2013): 19–48.

Takami, Koushun. *Battle Royale.* Trans. Yuji Oniki. San Francisco: Haikasoru, 2009.

Tate, Claudia. *Domestic Allegories of Political Desire: The Black Heroine's Text at the Turn of the Century.* New York: Oxford University Press, 1992.

Taylor, Charles. *Sources of the Self: The Making of the Modern Identity.* Cambridge, Mass.: Harvard University Press, 1989.

Thaler, Richard H., and Cass R. Sunstein. *Nudge: Improving Decisions About Health, Wealth, and Happiness.* New Haven, Conn.: Yale University Press, 2008.

Tsing, Anna Lowenhaupt. *The Mushroom at the End of the World: On the Possibility of Life in Capitalist Ruins.* Princeton, N.J.: Princeton University Press, 2015.

Tziallas, Evangelos. "Torture Porn and Surveillance Culture." *Jump Cut: A Review of Contemporary Media* 52 (Summer 2010).

Universal Declaration of Human Rights. *Yearbook of the United Nations, 1948–49.* New York: United Nations Publications, 1950.

von Werlhof, Claudia. " 'Globalization' and the 'Permanent' Process of 'Primitive Accumulation': The Example of the MAI, the Multilateral Agreement on Investment." *Journal of World-Systems Research* 7, no. 3 (2000): 728–47.

Veracini, Lorenzo. "Facing the Settler Colonial Present." In *The Limits of Settler Colonial Reconciliation: Non-Indigenous People and the Responsibility to Engage,* ed. Sarah Maddison, Tom Clark, and Ravi de Costa, 35–48. Singapore: Springer Singapore, 2016.

——. *The Settler Colonial Present.* New York: Palgrave Macmillan, 2015.

Vicaro, Michael P. "A Liberal Use of 'Torture': Pain, Personhood, and Precedent in the U.S. Federal Definition of Torture." *Rhetoric & Public Affairs* 14, no. 3: 401–26.

Villeneuve, Denis, dir. *Prisoners.* Burbank, Calif.: Warner Bros., 2013.

Virno, Paolo. *A Grammar of the Multitude: For an Analysis of Contemporary Forms of Life.* Trans. Isabella Bertoletti, James Cascaito, and Andrea Casson. Cambridge, Mass.: MIT Press, 2004.

Vora, Kalindi. *Life Support: Biocapital and the New History of Outsourced Labor.* Minneapolis: University of Minnesota Press, 2015.

Wan, James, dir. *Saw.* London: Entertainment Film Distributors, 2004.

Wark, McKenzie. *Gamer Theory.* Boston: Harvard University Press, 2007.

Weaver-Hightower, Rebecca. *Empire Islands: Castaways, Cannibals, and Fantasies of Conquest.* Minneapolis: University of Minnesota Press, 2007.

Weheliye, Alexander G. *Habeas Viscus: Racializing Assemblages, Biopolitics, and Black Feminist Theories of the Human.* Durham, N.C.: Duke University Press, 2014.

"What We Talk About When We Talk About Persons: The Language of a Legal Fiction." *Harvard Law Review* 114, no. 6 (2001): 1745–68.

Whitehead, Anne. "Writing with Care: Kazuo Ishiguro's *Never Let Me Go.*" *Contemporary Literature* 52, no. 1 (2011): 54–83.

Williams, Linda. "Film Bodies: Gender, Genre, and Excess." *Film Quarterly* 44, no. 4 (1991): 2–13.

Williams, Randall. *The Divided World: Human Rights and Its Violence.* Minneapolis: University of Minnesota Press, 2010.

Wisnewski, Jeremy, and R. D. Emerick. *The Ethics of Torture.* London: Continuum, 2009.

Wolfe, Cary. *Animal Rites: American Culture, the Discourse of Species, and Posthumanist Theory.* Chicago: University of Chicago Press, 2003.

——. *Before the Law: Humans and Other Animals in a Biopolitical Frame.* Chicago: University of Chicago Press, 2013.

Wolfe, Cary, ed. *Zoontologies: The Question of the Animal.* Minneapolis: University of Minnesota Press, 2003.

Worster, Donald. *Nature's Economy: A History of Ecological Ideas.* 2nd ed. New York: Cambridge University Press, 1994.

Wynter, Sylvia. "Human Being as Noun? Or Being Human as Praxis—Towards the Autopoetic Turn/Overturn: A Manifesto," August 25, 2007, https://www.scribd.com/doc/237809437/Sylvia-Wynter-The-Autopoetic-Turn.

——. "Unsettling the Coloniality of Being/Power/Truth/Freedom: Towards the Human, After Man, Its Overrepresentation—an Argument." *CR: The New Centennial Review* 3, no. 3 (2003): 257–337.

Ziarek, Ewa Plonowska. "Bare Life on Strike: Notes on the Biopolitics of Race and Gender." *South Atlantic Quarterly* 107, no. 1 (2008): 89–105.

Zibrak, Arielle. "Intolerance, a Survival Guide: Heteronormative Culture Formation in Cormac McCarthy's *The Road.*" *Arizona Quarterly: A Journal of American Literature, Culture, and Theory* 68, no. 3: 103–28.

INDEX